AMERICA'S WAR ON GOD

Lorne F. Dey

ISBN: 1514279606
ISBN-13: 978-1514279601
5

*Woe to those who call evil good and good evil,
who put darkness for light and light for darkness,
who put bitter for sweet and sweet for bitter.
Woe to those who are wise in their own eyes
and clever in their own sight.*
Isaiah 5:20-21 (NIV)

Dedicated with love to my beautiful wife Maryann who has stuck by me through thick and thin.

Table of Contents

Preface

I recently read a comment by a man who had seen the 2014 movie, *God's Not Dead*. This man appeared to be deeply and genuinely disappointed that the movie did not answer many of the pressing questions he had concerning the existence of God and evidence for faith in Jesus Christ.

This is what *America's War on God* intends to satisfy, or at least provide a starting point for the uninformed individual who genuinely wants to know more about not only the evidences for God and Christianity, but why some assert that America was founded as a Christian nation and is now turning its back on its heritage.

Much of the information provided in this book is based upon my beliefs that have been formed over years of study and examining the various views of the combatants that are involved in this war against God in America. It is my hope that the content of these pages will lead to the transformation of the heart and mind of the reader and incline him or her to the one true God and only possible Savior of mankind and America.

Terms and usages

The various ways of how the Bible is referred to in this book are: The Bible, Scripture, Holy Bible, Holy Scripture, God's Word, Old Testament, and New Testament.

I also quote primarily from the New International Version of the Bible (NIV) and the New King James Version (NKJV) of the Bible. These are my favorite translations and to me, best convey Biblical themes and truths by combining accuracy and understandability. They also contain the best meanings from the oldest manuscripts and contribute to the best comprehension of verses and passages of the Bible. This is in contrast to paraphrased Bibles that may be easy to understand but are not as accurate in getting the true meaning from the best source manuscripts available.

If I state "From" a particular verse from the Bible it means that I am not showing the entire verse or maybe even all of parts of it as noted in many Bible versions, merely a portion of it.

I also decided, for ease and the sake of continuity, to put all the footnotes for each chapter at the end of the book under the "Notes" section.

When I capitalize the word "Church," I am referring to the entire Church of Jesus Christ in America including all the various denominations and not only a specific, singular church.

Lastly, I encourage the reader to have a Bible in hand as many Scripture verses are merely referenced and not written out for brevity sake.

Lorne Dey

Introduction

What has happened to America?

Any astute and honest person living in today's America who is old enough or has been paying close enough attention must admit that America has gone through radical change, just in the last few years. Issues that were once guarded because of the negative social stigmas associated with them such as homosexuality, same-sex marriage, transgender, are not only now "out of the closet," but the push is on by those who reject the God of the Bible to make them generally accepted by everyone. And those who don't go along are labeled homophobic, bigoted, racist, or worse under the claim that they are trying to hold back some kind of social progress.

Character issues like honesty, once held in high esteem, don't appear to matter much anymore either. American politicians who habitually lie to the public over and over can get elected or re-elected to the highest public office of the land, even after they've been exposed. Although these practices have been met with some support or indifference by a few in the past, they are now much more generally accepted by the masses, even by some who still consider them to be immoral but are too afraid to stand up against them.

Indeed, in very recent years there has been an almost exponential increase in the American public's acceptance of these once considered unsavory taboos. America's founding generation, for instance, considered homosexuality, then referred to in the slang as "buggery" to be so repugnant that decent people were loathe to talk or write about it even when necessary because the practice was deemed so unnatural and against nature and nature's God.

But this book is not merely an admonition to those who participate in sexual deviance or immorality; it is a warning to anyone whose habits and lifestyles embrace anything that is contrary to God's word the Bible, such as lying, cheating, stealing, etc. All these issues are spoken of in the Bible in very strong terms along with sobering warnings. However, in today's America, most are barely considered wrong anymore. Television and movies have so desensitized Americans toward adultery and fornication in particular that most think extramarital affairs and sex before marriage or living together out of wedlock, is really no big deal.

In less than two hundred and fifty years America has fallen from being founded upon Biblical precepts and Christian ideals— to many today openly waging war against the Bible, its God, and Christianity in particular by openly defying those precepts and those that still honor them.

America, the "city upon a hill,"[1] envisioned in 1630 by Puritan believer, John Winthrop, the first governor of the Massachusetts Bay Colony, and realized by two centuries of more believers in the Christian God—is fast deteriorating into the equivalent of a third-world oligarchy based upon Godless, Marxist principles.

When the French writer of law, Alexis de Tocqueville, visited America in 1831 he observed that the American colonists had brought to the New World a form of Christianity that had so infused public affairs as to create a religious form of government.[2] Now our leaders, using the often quoted but widely misunderstood phrase, "separation of church and state," deceptively tell the gullible masses that America's founding fathers never meant for any religion, including Christianity, to have any place in the halls of American government. Although it is an out-and-out lie, most Americans are either too corrupted by the world in which they live or unashamedly ignorant to question it.

With all this, it's not hard to see that there truly is an out-and-out total war against the Bible and the Bible's God.

To be sure, people in America now live in a country where its Christian heritage and the Biblical principles it was founded upon are rapidly being covered up by socialist politicians and left-leaning, activist judges spurred on by an ever-growing dumbed-down and wicked populace. Even school textbooks are being dishonestly rewritten in order to deceive new generations by eradicating the truth about the Godly principles upon which the American Constitution is based. And the Constitution itself is being labeled as "OUTDATED" by those who lust for more power and work tirelessly to abolish the inalienable rights provided in it.

The replacement? Amoral and relativistic, secular humanism based upon expediency and hedonistic human depravity that teaches that man is the center of the universe and not God its Creator.

Even America's Christian churches have lost their impact or "saltiness" as the Bible teaches because although America is filled with thousands of churches of various denominations, our nation is still slipping at an ever-increasing rate into moral and spiritual decay. Indeed, America appears to be in the time that the Apostle John prophesied about in the Book of Revelation. The church of Laodicea, written about by the apostle in Revelation Chapter 3 verses 14 to 17, is the lukewarm church that Christ said He would spew out of His mouth because it was neither hot nor cold. It is an apt description of the Christian Church in America today. Yes, it appears that America's opiate of prosperity and relative safety have put all too many Christians to sleep where they don't even recognize the time of moral decay in which they are living. Popular evangelists and teachers claiming to be followers of Jesus Christ don't preach on sin or hell because, as some of them claim, it's negative talk that tears down rather than builds up the hearer. Some even say that Christians and Muslims worship the same god even though the one bears no resemblance to the other, with one being a God of love, mercy and justice, and the other being a god of death, destruction, and vindictiveness.

The reasons for how all this has happened in America and why there is a war being waged against the Bible, the Bible's God, and Christianity is the subject of this book. My hope is that God will use it to call people "of understanding"—as the Jewish prophet Daniel prophetically calls those to whom God has given a realization about the wicked age in which we live—to greater service for the Gospel of Jesus Christ. It is also my hope that God will use this book to instilled such an "understanding" into those not already so endowed but who are seekers of truth and that they will find it within these pages.

Chapter 1
America's War on God

America's main problem today is not the government deficit, or burgeoning debt, or manufactured inflation. Nor is it illegal immigrants including Islamic extremists, members of Mexican drug cartels or other hostiles flooding across the border and into the country. It is also not America's homegrown multitude of corrupt politicians. Neither is it rampant substance use, legal or illegal, or pornography. It also isn't our vulnerability to a catastrophic Electro-Magnetic Pulse (EMP), natural or manmade. It isn't even the susceptibility of our nation's computerized infrastructure to a cyber attack. America's main problem is of a spiritual nature caused by rejecting, on a large scale, the Bible and the Bible's God. Belief in that God and the Bible are the two primary reasons that America has been the greatest nation that has ever existed on the planet. And now we are witnessing the abandonment of that same God and the Bible and how it is leading to America's rapid undoing.

When word began to circulate that I was working on a project called, *America's War On God*, some scoffed at the idea claiming that there is no such war going on and that the notion itself is ridiculous. Of course, a survey of people's definitions of what or who God even is would produce varying and widespread differences. But I assume at least some of the scoffers were alluding to the God of the Bible. I say "the God of the Bible" because there are so many differing ideas about God or a "Higher Being" that one has to differentiate. The God I will be talking about in this book is the Creator-God represented in the Judeo-Christian Bible who created all the visible and invisible elements of the known universe we live in.

To deny that there is a war against this God and the Bible, the instruction manual by which God has chosen to reveal Himself, is a denial of the America that exists today. The following is but a small sampling of headlines taken mostly from 2014 media sources that attest to the fact that there is indeed a war being waged of the kind I have described:

Obama Mocks and Attacks Jesus Christ and the Bible

Texas Pro-Abortion Protesters Chant 'Hail Satan!'

Ten commandments ordered away from Dixie County Court House

Football Team Forced to Remove Crosses From Helmets

Jerusalem and God Vote Gets Booed at Democratic Convention

Supreme Court Declares that Prayer in Public School is Unconstitutional

Supreme Court Rejects Ten Commandments

Federal judge rules Ten Commandments monument in front of City Hall violates First Amendment

Women Ordered to Stop Praying Inside Mall

Court Rules Against Same-Sex Marriage Bans in Wisconsin, Indiana

Kentucky Schools Remove 10 Commandments

Homosexuals Mock Christianity

Christian Beliefs Put Student in Danger of Expulsion

Pastor says that Christians and Muslims worship the same god

Mega-Pastor does not preach on sin or hell because it's negative talk

Atheists Bully Town to Eject Christ from Christmas Parade

City Council Meeting Opens with Invocation to Satan & Allah

Christian chaplain punished for sharing his faith in suicide prevention class

8th Grader Arrested by Police for Wearing Rosary to School Football Game

Atlanta mayor fires fire chief because of his Christian views

North Carolina city removes sculpture of soldier kneeling before cross

If these headlines don't prove that a war is being waged against God, the Bible, and Christianity in America, I don't know what else would or what other entity, writings, or group these headlines refer to.

Although there are many religions in America besides Christianity, there is almost never much said against any of them in the mainstream press with the exception of Scientology. On the contrary, religions such as Islam are almost never talked about in negative terms even when one or more of its adherents blow something up or people are killed as a result of them acting out what is promoted in the Qur'an (or Koran). Indeed, when atrocities are committed by followers of the Islamic faith, typically great pains are taken by big media to avoid the mention of any forms of the words Muslim or Islam for fear of putting that religion in a bad light. But if barbarities such as those continually perpetrated by followers of Islam were done by professing Christians you can bet that these same media entities would shout it from the rooftops and in the strongest and most condemning terms.

This is often true too of Judaism, also based upon the Bible and the Bible's God. Judaism came from the Hebrew people who now occupy the modern nation of Israel. To big media, Israel is made up of Jews and Jew is a reference to Judaism that, like Christianity, gets much of its instruction from the Bible's Old Testament. Of course not all Israelis follow the religion of Judaism just as all Americans don't identify with Christianity, but that doesn't matter to people working in the major news organizations in America, the associations to the Bible are enough to make both groups fair game to be maligned and misrepresented and typically with few if any negative repercussions.

It is interesting to note that in the 2014 clashes between the Islamic terrorist group, Hamas, operating in the Gaza strip and Israel's military, the IDF (Israeli Defense Forces), America's mainstream media constantly portrayed the IDF to look like it was the primary aggressor in the fighting even though it was the Hamas organization that began hostilities by firing rockets and missiles into Israel. Israel was simply trying to protect its citizenry by responding in kind. It was also Hamas that continually violated truces brokered between the two groups. But none of that was emphasized in the American mainstream media where a double standard was exercised by always showing members of the IDF engaged in military actions and maneuvers while seldom if ever showing members of Hamas doing the same if they showed them at all. What *was* typically televised was the destructive results of Israeli bombs and missiles in the inhabited areas of the Gaza strip and the resulting fallout and desperate conditions of the area's non-combatants.

As to why there are two sets of rules in today's America, one set for believers in the Bible and another for unbelievers, will become apparent in subsequent chapters. But for now I want to emphasize that there is mostly zero tolerance for Christian values and the Bible in America from those wielding any sort of authority or power in and out of government. Even though these self-proclaimed "progressives" of so-called civilized, human advancement claim to be open-minded and tolerant of everything, there is absolutely no tolerance for anything Christian or Bible related.

To illustrate this point, in 2014 the Mayor of Houston Texas, an admitted lesbian named Annise Parker, made headlines when she subpoenaed several Christian pastor's sermons who led churches in her city to find out if they contained any anti-homosexual rhetoric. Her bigoted, anti-Christian bias was exposed however because Mayor Parker didn't subpoena sermons from other area churches or places of worship from other religions such as Mormonism, the Jehovah's Witnesses' Watch Tower Bible and Tract Society, or Islam whose writings in the Qur'an also teach against sodomy and homosexuality.

Double standards like this are all too common in America today.

But why this vindictive and aggressive stance against Christianity when every other religion or man-made ideology is welcomed or even celebrated by those who claim to be tolerant of everything? Again, this will become evident as you discover what the God of the Bible requires of the individual and a nation.

Other expressions of America's war on God

Abortion

The Oxford dictionary's definition of murder is "the unlawful premeditated killing of one human being by another." I don't think there is a better description of abortion on demand. An unborn human baby can't possibly be guilty of anything that warrants it being killed before its life really even begins. The vast majority of babies killed in their mother's womb in America are for primarily convenience sake.[1] I call this murder! If that sounds harsh, the alarming reality is that it's true. If it makes me sound non-compassionate that is unfortunate, but the truth is, as Abraham Lincoln said, "No one has the right to choose to do what is wrong"—And it's not what the government or anyone else says is right and wrong—it's only what the God of the Bible says is wrong that trumps everything and everyone else.

The culprits for this infanticide are not only the mothers, the husbands, the boyfriends, and/or the families of the mothers making this choice, but American government for legislating it to be allowed carte blanche without criminal consequences. A former black slave once said that the institution of slavery ultimately destroyed both the victim and the perpetrator. This is also true of the moral evil of abortion that is contributing to the moral downfall of the individual and the nation as a whole.

Abortion for medical reasons when a mother's life is in danger has always been allowed in this country even before Roe vs. Wade. When those occasions arose, it was up to the mother, her family, and her doctor whether or not to take the life of the unborn baby to save her own. But these kinds of abortions, even according to Dr. Alan Guttmacher of Planned Parenthood, are extremely rare and statistically make up less than 1% of all abortions performed in America.[2]

So when God commands, "Thou shall NOT murder," doing so despite the Biblical command puts one at odds with God and is another way that many in America are making war against God and the Bible.[3]

Socialism/Communism/Marxism

The push in America today to replace our foundering father's trust in the Creator-God with Godless socialism is just another example of America waging war against its Creator. What makes this so egregious is that God has blessed America so much—more so than any other nation that has ever existed, but now many of our leaders want to replace Him with a system that, when fully realized, has always led to the deaths of millions of the people subject to it wherever it has been instituted and allowed to come to full fruition.

Socialism, and what it leads to—Communism, is a human-centered ideology that seeks to replace God with "enlightened" human reason. The so enlightened often turns out to be one individual, a megalomaniac of the ilk of a Mao Zedong of Red

China, or a Joseph Stalin of the former Soviet Union, or a Pol Pot of Cambodia. All of these "enlightened" individuals ordered the deaths of millions of their own people for political purposes. The implementation of socialism within a society, such as is currently being done in America with so-called nationalized healthcare, welfare, and other government handout programs, is designed to slowly replace capitalism and a market-based economy with an economy that is totally regulated and run by the state. This type of system is always made up of an oligarchy—a relative handful of elitists that takes its orders from a supreme ruler like what our current president is attempting to be. Socialism/Communism/Marxism is a system where a very small percentage of a people, a rich tyrannical class, rule over the subjugated, powerless, and mostly impoverished masses. The great statesman and former British Prime Minister, Winston Churchill, said it best, "Socialism is a philosophy of failure, the creed of ignorance, and the gospel of envy, its inherent virtue is the equal sharing of misery."

Discarding God for something vastly inferior reminds me of when in the Bible's Old Testament, the Israelites insisted upon having a king like the nations around them. This happened after God allowed them to enter the promised land of Canaan where He subsequently governed the nation using judges. The judges were essentially mediators between Him and the people and were often called upon to settle disputes between the different tribes[4] especially when the disputes threatened the unity and safety of the nation as a whole. The judges also came into play when Israel was being threatened by one or more of its enemies. God would tell the judges what the people were to do and the judges would in turn tell the people, who would then do as instructed and be delivered. It was a system that apparently worked well for over four hundred years.

But although the Israelites had a king in the person of God Himself, they did not think of Him as a king since God is spirit and as such, invisible. It was a common theme in the Old Testament for the people of Israel to continually abandon God because they could not perceive Him with their physical senses. And even though God had revealed Himself to them many times by the many miracles and amazing things He had done for them at opportune times, they still could not grasp the fact that He was always with them and looking out for them.

After several of Israel's judges turned out to be corrupt, the people collectively decided they wanted to scrap the entire system and have a mortal king that they could actually see and touch—and thereby emulate the pagan nations around them. So God gave them what they insisted upon knowing they were not just rejecting the few judges who were found to be corrupt, but because they were rejecting Him personally (I Samuel chapter 8). So God chose a young man named Saul to act as king over them instead of the proxy judges. And this is where Israel's real problems began, because Saul was flawed, as all men are, and became the first of many kings that did not do what was right in the sight of God. Indeed, Saul became the first in a long line of bad monarchs, which would lead, over the centuries, to Israel repeatedly being occupied by foreign enemies with many of its people going into captivity to some foreign power.

Now America is doing the same thing—rejecting God for an inferior system that will also ultimately lead to calamity for the nation and its people.

Removing God from School Textbooks

Another way the people of America are making war on God is by replacing school textbooks that contain references to Him and the Bible with those that do not. It seems that the architects of America's new revisionism are primarily concerned with history and science. This undoubtedly is because these secular social engineers think that if they can get rid of references to God in history and creation, they stand a better chance of keeping Him out of the consciousness of future Americans. As George Orwell wrote in his prescient novel, *1984*, "Who controls the past controls the future; who controls the present controls the past." Robert H. Bork, who will be referred to again later agrees,

"Rewritten history has always been a weapon in the struggle for control of the present and the future."[5]

Another reason the God of the Bible is being taken out of American textbooks today is because of the push toward multiculturalism in our society that began in earnest in the 1980s. Joseph Moreau in his book, *Schoolbook Nation: Conflicts over American History Textbooks from the Civil War to the Present,* cites the increasing number of various special interest groups that are responsible for reshaping the content of America's history textbooks. Multiculturalism by nature tries to pander to the beliefs of a widespread group made up of racial minorities, radical homosexuals, and others so that no one is allowed to say much at all about anything that is of much value to almost anyone. This is undoubtedly one of the major causes for the Christian worldview being omitted from America's history.

Although the reasons for changing history are myriad, including the desire by these diverse groups to assert their own political agendas over the truth, there is still a deliberate and conscious effort to remove the Christian God in particular from the national consciousness.

Anyone wondering how much the Christian God and the Bible were historically included in America's public education need look no further than William Holmes McGuffy and his series of "readers" that were published between 1837 and 1885. According to Catherine Millard in her book, *The Rewriting of America's History,* "McGuffy's readers" were used in American public schools longer than any other textbooks. She cites how, by 1963, over 125 million copies had been sold. As difficult as it is to believe today, McGuffy was honored by the now extremely liberally biased National Education Association (NEA) at the time of his death in 1873 for his, among other virtues, "conscientious Christian character." Furthermore, McGuffy has been immortalized in American history for basing his textbooks on the Bible and for teaching young minds the moral character derived from it that in turn helped shape the moral character of the nation as a whole.

One of McGuffy's textbooks, the, *Eclectic Third Reader,* for example, presented the Biblical worldview that "the Bible is evidently to give us correct information concerning the creation of all things, by the omnipotent Word of God" and that "the Scriptures [the Bible] are especially designed to make us wise unto salvation through faith in Jesus Christ." The textbook also includes an apologetic on the Bible itself and where and how it was created.

But of course by today's hollow standards of political correctness, no one's worldview should take precedence over anyone else's except with one exception, as I will now show.

Today, Christianity and the Bible have not only been removed from school textbooks, they are being replaced with the religion of Islam and its teachings from the Qur'an, the one religion that appears to be the exception to the exalted "multicultural rule."

Beginning in the early 2000s, the non-profit group, ACT! for America Education, reviewed 6th to 12th grade school textbooks published by 38 major publishers such as Macmillan/McGraw Hill and Harcourt Brace concluding that most are filled with errors, omissions, and bias that leads one to believe that there is a concerted effort underway to show Christianity and Judaism in a bad light and Islam in a good light.

I encourage the reader to explore the organization's website at: www.actforamericaeducation.com to discover just how extensive the infiltration of Muslim influence is in American school textbooks and how deceptively the material is presented.

For example, although Islam is arguably most identified with jihad, the making of war against infidels (anyone who is not a Muslim), the term is completely absent from many of the textbooks' studied. After examining a social studies textbook by Harcourt Brace, one of ACT's researchers states, "the term 'jihad' is almost never used or defined in any of the textbook's discussion of the Islamic conquests, and the reality of jihad is erased from history." This is even though the founder of Islam, Muhammad, taught that Allah commands all Muslims to wage perpetual jihad warfare against non-Muslims until Islam is supreme on the earth.

In another textbook on world history published by Holt, Rinehart and Winston, jihad is fraudulently presented as a defensive mechanism for Muslims to defend the Islamic faith when it is really used as an offensive, aggressive method to attempt to establish the dominance of Islam throughout the world.

In still another textbook by publisher Houghton Mifflin, the meaning of jihad is misrepresented as something that is merely adopted in order to "overcome" the difficulties of life such as temptation and evil or as a defensive act against aggression or persecution.

As is almost universally known by informed people in the West, Islam teaches, and its adherents dutifully practice, a horrendous treatment of woman. However, the same social studies textbook mentioned above, typical of those I looked over, falsely presents Western Civilization as being the major culprit against women's rights. The above researcher again notes that, "In stark contrast, the textbook does not devote a single word to a direct discussion of the extensive restrictions and legal disabilities imposed on Muslim women under Islamic Shari'a law. While there is one indirect reference to a restriction on Muslim women, it is obscure and oblique."

Robert Spencer, an authority on Islam, states in his book, *The Politically Incorrect Guide to Islam*, that, "As long as men read and believe the Qur'an, women will be despised, second-class citizens, subject to the heartbreak and dehumanization of polygamy, the threat of an easy and capricious divorce, and worse—including beatings, false accusations, and the loss of virtually all of the most basic human freedoms."[6]

ACT researchers also note that many of the textbooks also fail to make mention of the onerous jizya tax and other burdens and restrictions imposed on non-Muslims living under Islamic rule. As Robert Spencer sites in his book mentioned above, non-Muslims have three choices when confronting Islam: 1. Accept it and convert, 2. Pay the debilitating jizya or poll tax in order to co-exist with Muslims, or 3. Fight against Muslims in order to preserve and protect one's way of life apart from Islam.

Also being covered-up in the examined textbooks is the fact that it was followers of Islam waging jihad who attacked New York City's World Trade Center on September 11, 2001. A textbook by Glencoe/McGraw Hill titled "The American Vision" mentions only that it was "terrorists" who made the attack and that it was "the works of a man named Osama bin Laden and his organization, al-Qaeda." No mention is made of the fact that bin Laden was a Muslim or that al-Qaeda is made up of Muslims. After examining the material shown by ACT, textbooks by Macmillan/McGraw Hill, McDougal Littell and Pearson Prentice Hall all partake of the same kind of cover-up.

Replacing the God of Christianity and the Bible with a pagan god that really is no God at all is tantamount to making war against the true God and breaks His first commandment that states: *"You shall have no other gods before me."* This is exactly what got the Old Testament nation of Israel repeatedly into so much trouble, they continually abandoned God for the false gods of their enemies which were no more than graven images usually made from wood or metal. Although Muslims do not worship graven images, their god, Allah, as you will see in chapter four, is certainly not the beneficent Creator of the universe who is described in the Bible.

Removing God from Science

When Charles Darwin published *On the Origin of Species,* his ideas were presented as theory. However, today, in many classrooms across America, this theory is presented as proven fact as though there are no plausible alternatives to Darwin's hypothesis of how life developed on planet earth.[7]

What most people don't realize about Darwin's theory of Natural Selection, commonly referred to as "Evolution," is that it utilizes an outside and unnamed force that causes the natural selection process to actually occur or produce ever-evolving results. Darwin himself often refers to this mysterious cause as a "law." When something doesn't always occur randomly or there is repeated order within a seeming chaotic environment, then there must be an outside cause that is acting upon the elements within that environment. So when Darwin states: "...Natural selection acts only by taking advantage of slight successive variations; she can never take a great and sudden leap, but must advance by short and sure, though slow steps," he is talking about some invisible law of nature at work. Because when he says, "acts only," he must be alluding to a natural law that causes the something, whatever it is, to only act in a certain way.

So who wrote the law? What did Darwin or what do his followers of today think determines how natural selection chooses what to accept and what to discard? And—Who designed the process that "can never take a great and sudden leap, but must advance by short and sure, though slow steps"?

Ascribing intelligence to a purely materialistic system is prevalent within secular science in the America of today, but at the same time denying that there is any influence outside the material system or environment. Adherents of Darwinian Evolution repeatedly attribute thinking or design to a process that is supposedly "closed" and devoid of any outside influence, things that only God our Creator possesses.

So when the Bible states in Genesis 1:1, *"In the beginning God created the heavens and the earth"* and learned people and leaders in America who have thought about or studied the issue, choose the improbable theory of Darwinian Evolution for the primary reason that it doesn't involve God and then say—No He didn't—it's just another way that America is making war on God. Chapter three deals with more evidence for our universe coming from God and not from some other ethereal, unnamed force or cause.

But the main problem with secularized science as it is taught in American schools and universities today is not simply that it teaches purely material processes for how our universe and everything in it came to be, but that creationism or the idea of an intelligent designer is given no chance to be proposed much less articulated to or by students. Is this censorship by those in power really a result of their certainty that the universe and all the life in it came out of nothing or is it their fear of opposing views that may convince too many people of the evidence for God? I believe it is the latter.

Same Sex Marriage

Since homosexuality is expressly forbidden in the Bible, it only logically follows that same sex marriage is also forbidden.

The Bible only talks about one kind of marriage in the Bible. Genesis chapter 2:24 states: *"Therefore a man leaves his father and his mother and cleaves to his wife, and they become one flesh."* In Matthew chapter 19:4-5 Jesus Christ reaffirms this: *"He answered, 'Have you not read that he who made them from the beginning made them male and female,' and, 'For this reason a man shall leave his father and mother and be joined to his wife, and the two shall become one?'"*

Actually, the very idea of same sex marriage and seeking to make it lawful in America is tantamount to spitting in God's face. It is as though militant homosexuals are mocking God by saying, Not only are we going to do what we want in spite of Your rules, but we are also going to compel people to accept it by getting the government to legalize it—If that is not making war against God, I don't know what is.

The apostle Paul in the Bible book of Romans 1:18-32 describes those who practice such rebellion against God's laws, including homosexuals, in very bleak terms.

Erasing God from America's National Consciousness

Still another way America is waging war against God is by government bureaucrats subtly omitting references to Him from monuments, buildings, and in some cases, even reprinted representations of founding documents. The place where this is most apparent is in Washington D.C. at the U.S. Capitol's new Visitor's Center.

A group named Wallbuilders, an online resource for informing people about how America was founded on the Bible and Christian principles, put together a presentation called *"War On*

God in America." In it they show how the "Visitor's Center" deliberately leaves out any references to God or religion. The presentation shows how "In God We Trust" is conspicuously missing from above the American flag in a display that supposedly duplicates the Speaker of the House's rostrum inside the House of Representatives' chamber when the words actually do appear in that position inside the real House of Representatives.

The presentation reveals another area of the Center where a passage taken from Article III of the Northwest Ordinance of 1787 states: "...schools and the means of education shall forever be encouraged" when the passage actually reads: "Religion, morality, and knowledge, being necessary to good government and the happiness of mankind, schools and the means of education shall forever be encouraged."

Article VII taken from the same ordinance, has omitted the words "in the year of our Lord" from the excerpt on display which is glaring since the citation actually reads: "...done in Convention by the Unanimous Consent of the States present the Seventeenth Day of September *in the Year of our Lord* one thousand seven hundred and Eighty seven..." (emphasis is mine).

Even the relatively recently constructed World War II Memorial fails to make any mention of God even though the president at the time, Franklin Delano Roosevelt (FDR), and the Supreme Allied Commander of the European theater of war, General Dwight Eisenhower, among other prominent figures at the time, made important statements or prayers asking for God's favor in the D-Day landings of June 6, 1944, one of the most important and successful military undertakings of all time. FDRs prayer before D-Day and General Eisenhower's D-Day statement to soldiers, sailors, and airmen of the Allied Expeditionary Force before the invasion may be read in their entirety in the Appendix for chapter one of this book. After reading them, you will understand why God has so blessed America and why He now appears to be turning away from us in this age of such widespread rejection of Him, even from our highest leaders.

Roots of America's war on God

So when did this war on God start?

Some, like the late jurist and Constitutional professor of law, Robert Bork, mentioned earlier, believed that the morality of America began to falter during the time between the First and Second World Wars, then came to full expression in the 1960s with the counterrevolution made up of primarily college-age students. Bork makes a good case for his assertion in his book, *Slouching Towards Gomorrah*.

Mr. Bork is also correct in his implication that these counter-culture revolutionaries would not have been as successful as they have been, even up to today in America, had it not been for the fact that, as he puts it, "religious faith began a retreat."

Although Mr. Bork mostly lumps all religion together, I will say more specifically that—This revolution could not have been as successful as it has proven to be without first, the already diminishing convictions of many followers of Christianity and the Bible.

So then, when did the adherents to Christianity begin to waver in their faith?

To answer that question, I believe one has to understand how the universe works. The second law of thermodynamics basically states that although energy cannot be destroyed, it does change—albeit gradually—from usable to unusable, in much the same way that hot water over a period of time turns cold. The law also implies that the natural end of all things in the universe, including the universe itself, is entropy or total stagnation or degeneration. Unless some outside force acts upon the thing that is deteriorating, it will gradually go from order to disorder and eventually to chaos.

This process also occurs with human morality within nations, especially when those nations have been initially infused with morality-based religions like Christianity. It happened with the Romans and with other European countries that were at one time bastions of Christianity such as England and Germany.[8]

So by this reasoning, the natural order of all things is degradation unless some outside force causes the thing that is in the process of deteriorating to be reconstituted or made vibrant or usable again. This process is also true for the Christian Church in America.

When believers in the Bible began coming to America in 1607 they were often leaving countries where they were looked down upon or even persecuted because they didn't agree with the doctrines of the official state-mandated churches. Such was the case in England where many of America's earliest colonists originated and who opposed Anglican Church dogma. The persecution and intolerance toward believers in Jesus Christ such as the Puritans for their criticism of the teachings of the Church of England, as the Anglican Church was also called, kept these sects vibrant and vigilant.

Many of the early colonists brought that vibrancy and vigilance with them to the New World. In addition, survival in their new surroundings was precarious and caused many of them to stay close to God and rely on His word for both physical strength and spiritual sustenance.[9]

As things began to improve however, more and more people began to drift away from God, as is common with human nature. By 1741, enough had strayed from God and the Bible to cause a young preacher named Jonathon Edwards to deliver a fire-and-brimstone sermon to his congregation called *"Sinners in the hands of an angry God."* It is difficult to believe now, in this age of all but total secularism, but in those days, pastor's sermons were regularly printed in the local newspaper and soon many had read Reverend Edward's message. Many scholars credit this sermon as the beginning of the Great Awakening that brought new life and vibrancy to Christianity and many fresh converts as well. This resurgence of the Christian faith so positively affected those who would officially form America's nascent government that they were compelled to base the nation's founding documents on Biblical precepts, nature, and nature's God.

This same spiritual infusion of God and His word is the only hope for America today.

But of course, none of the above is convincing unless one learns that the Bible that teaches about this Creator-God can be trusted, that it does indeed contain His words and commands, and that it is He who has been offended by this war that is being waged against Him. And that is what the next chapter will deal with.

Chapter 2
The Judeo-Christian Bible Stands Out

Many in America today think the Bible is little more than an old book full of myths, errors, forgeries, and contradictions created long ago by sexist males. But for anyone who tries to back up any of the above claims, and are willing to do some investigation, he or she will find that the Bible is historically reliable, is about real people and events, and contains more truth, wisdom, and insight than any other book that has ever been written. Also, if the Bible cannot be shown, beyond reasonable doubt, that it is from the one true God, then there is no war on God in America since there would then be no moral absolutes and morality would be relative and subject to each individual's personal philosophy and/or experience. What I intend to show in this chapter is that the Bible *can* be demonstrated to possess compelling credentials and that it does indeed contain the true words of the Creator and Judge of the people of America and the world and that individual subjectivity is irrelevant and America is in big trouble.

Consulting the experts

When one wants to know the truth about something it is smart to consult someone who is an expert on the subject in question. This is the role that Biblical scholars play in assessing the historical reliability and truthfulness of the Bible. In 35 years of reading and studying the works of scores of Biblical scholars, I have found them to be intelligent, honest, fair-minded, and genuinely interested in discovering the truth concerning Biblical subjects that involve Biblical source documents and evidence from, history, archaeology, and prophesy—all topics I will be discussing in this chapter.

The uniqueness of the Bible

The Bible contains two main parts: the Old Testament and New Testament. The Old Testament, or Hebrew Bible as it is also called, "contains the continuous history of civilization from Creation to Roman times. It is also the only record of God's dealings with humanity through His prophets, priests, and kings. In addition, it is the only ancient religious document that has survived completely intact."[1] The New Testament contains the teachings and ministry of Jesus Christ and at least some[2] of the teachings and ministries of the apostles who were chosen by Jesus Himself to spread His gospel and grow His Church.

Old Testament and New Testament also refer to revelations made by God to man before Jesus Christ came to earth (OT), then after (NT). The reason for this delineation is because God's way to a right standing with Him was different during Old Testament times than it is today in the Christian era. In the Old Testament, God required the blood of animals to temporarily atone for believer's sins, but after the death and resurrection of Jesus Christ, only the blood of Christ can atone for believer's sins, and then permanently, for all time, by belief in Him. An important aspect that the Old and New Testaments have in common is that obedience to what God says in both of them is the only way to be reconciled to Him.

Although the Protestant Bible is thought of as one book, it is actually a compilation of 66 books (as compared with the Catholic Bible that contains additional books in the Old Testament called the Apocrypha) that were written over a period of at least 1000 years and is comprised of some 39 to 40 individual authors. In spite of this broad span of time by so many different authors from many different countries, there is a cohesiveness to the books of the Bible that makes it stand apart from any other volume that has been written and compiled by men. As such, the Holy Bible is the most unique book that has ever existed in the world.

What scholars have to say about the Bible

According to Bible scholar, Paul D. Wenger, "There is extensive manuscript evidence for the Bible, including at least 300 Hebrew manuscripts and 5,800 Greek manuscripts, as well as more than 20,000 ancient manuscripts of the Old and New Testaments written in various languages, and more than 30,000 scriptural quotations in the early church fathers [writings] which help confirm the accuracy of the Scriptures. Neither the Qur'an nor The Book of Mormon can make this claim."[3] Also: "There are, in fact, three times as many manuscripts of the New Testament within two hundred years of its composition as there are of the average classical author's work within two thousand years of its composition."[4] Wenger also adds: "The New Testament is far and away the best-attested work of Greek or Latin literature from the ancient world. Precisely because we have hundreds of thousands of variants and hundreds of early manuscripts, we are in an excellent position for recovering the wording of the original.... The task of filling in the gaps without manuscript testimony is absolutely necessary for most of Greco-Roman literature, and almost entirely unknown for the New Testament."[5]

Werner Keller in his book *The Bible as History* states: "No book in the whole history of mankind has had such a revolutionary influence, has so decisively affected the development of the western world, or had such a world-wide effect as the 'Book of Books', the Bible."

Sir Monier-Williams, a former professor of Sanskrit at Oxford University who spent over 40 years studying Eastern religious books, said after comparing them with the Bible:

> Pile them, if you will, on the left side of your study table, but place your Holy Bible on the right side, all by itself, alone, and with a wide gap between them. For there is a gulf between it and the so-called sacred books of the East which severs the one from the other utterly, hopelessly, and forever; a veritable gulf which cannot be bridged over by any science of religious thought.[6]

F.F. Bruce, a Biblical scholar who advocated the historical reliability of the Bible especially as it compares to other religious writings said,

> The Bible, at first sight, appears to be a collection of literature, mainly Jewish. If we enquire into the circumstances under which the various Biblical documents were written, we find that they were written at intervals over a space of nearly 1400 years. The writers wrote in various lands, from Italy in the west to Mesopotamia and possibly Persia in the east. The writers themselves were a heterogeneous [diverse] number of people, not only separated from each other by hundreds of years and hundreds of miles, but belonging to the most diverse walks of life. In their ranks we have kings, herdsman, soldiers, legislators, fishermen, statesman, courtiers, priests and prophets, a tent-making Rabbi and a gentile physician, not to speak of others of whom we know nothing apart from the writings they have left us. The writings themselves belong to a great variety of literary types. They include history, law, religious poetry, didactic treaties, lyrical poetry, parable and allegory, biography, personal correspondence, personal memoirs and diaries, in addition to the distinctively Biblical types of prophecy and apocalyptic visions. For all that, the Bible is not simply an anthology but there is a unity which binds the whole together.[7]

Merrill F. Unger, one of the twentieth century's greatest Bible scholars and a prolific Christian writer, says about the believability of the Bible:

> Scripture is intensely realistic. Invariably it presents a vividly true-to-life portrait of whatever it may be depicting. This is what would naturally be expected in a revelation inspired and given, as it is, in accordance with the highest standards of divine truth and inerrancy. On its pages there is no room for romanticism, or looking through "rose-colored glasses" in portraying either the character of individuals, or things, or the state of nations. People and conditions are presented as they [really] are. Good as well as evil is drawn in true color. God's

closest friends, as well as his avowed and implacable enemies, His own people Israel, as well as the heathen nations surrounding them, are photographed in "candid-camera style" and presented with remarkable life-like reality.[8]

Inerrancy of the Bible

In the above passage, Unger mentions the inerrancy issue regarding the Bible. Inerrancy is one of those terms that is often misunderstood about Bible Scripture. It does not mean that there are not transcriptural errors or other differences in the Bible, especially in its many translations. What inerrancy means is that the Bible contains no falsehoods, fraud, or deceit. Biblical scholar Douglas K. Blount explains, "The doctrine of inerrancy states that the Bible is wholly truthful."[9] Blount also quotes fellow scholars Norman Geisler and Larry Wilson: "When one speaks of inerrancy, he is claiming that the Bible is factually and actually correct (true) in what it affirms. The Bible makes no mistakes and affirms no false statements. What the Bible says is true is true; and what the Bible says is false is false."[10]

Professor Richard R. Melick Jr. says, "God so orchestrated the circumstances of the writing of Holy Scripture [in its original form] that every word participates in its context to communicate exactly and accurately what God intended to say. Since every word comes from God, and is inspired, the Bible is inerrant. It is correct in what it teaches and accurate in what it records."[11]

In regards to the discrepancies that are known to exist between manuscripts that are the basis of the various Bible translations, Bible scholar Daniel B. Wallace has this to say: "Of the hundreds of thousands of textual alterations [from thousands of manuscripts], the majority are spelling differences that have no impact on the meaning of the text. The ancient scribes did not have standardized spelling but often followed regional usage or their own whim on many words. Yet spelling differences account for about 70% of all textual variants. Thousands of these are neither viable nor meaningful, while thousands of others are viable but not meaningful."[12]

Even though there *are* meaningful and viable variants in the Bible manuscripts, Wallace adds, "They are by far the smallest category, consisting of *less than 1 percent* of all textual variations [Wallace's emphasis]."[13] And according to Bart Ehrman, a scholar in his own right and popular contemporary critic of the Bible, "Essential Christian beliefs are not affected by textual variants in the manuscript tradition of the New Testament."[14]

Wallace therefore concludes: "Suffice it to say that viable textual variants that disturb essential Christian beliefs have not been found in New Testament manuscripts."[15]

In regards to the manuscripts themselves that the Bible is translated from and into its various languages and versions, Wenger says this: "Since the earliest texts that we have agree substantially with the later ones, the changes from the autographs [original writings] to the earliest copies would be miniscule if we were to project backward to the original."[16]

This means that whatever small, mostly typographical errors or spelling variations the Bible does contain, they in no way affect major Biblical doctrines such as God's plan for man's way for redemption and salvation, which is the entire purpose of Holy Scripture.

Another important point to make is that although we do not have the original texts that the Biblical authors wrote, because they were primarily written on perishable materials such as papyrus or animal hides, scholars do have access to extremely old copies that have been reverently copied by scribes from the original texts,[17] so many in fact, that Wallace says, "In terms of extant manuscripts, the New Testament textual critic is confronted with an embarrassment of riches" when compared with "the very best that the classical world has to offer."[18]

As far as the Old Testament by itself is concerned, Biblical scholar Bruce K. Waltke in his book, *Biblia Hebraica Stuttgartensia*, which is the most recent edition of the Hebrew Bible, quotes Shemaryyahu Talmon, J. L. Magnes Professor Emeritus, of the Department of Bible Studies at The University of Jerusalem who agrees, "even the errors and textual variations that exist 'affect the intrinsic message only in relatively few instances'."[19]

In summation, according to Wallace, "most biblical scholars – –whether they are evangelical or liberal, Protestant or Catholic— believe that what we have today in all essential respects… is what the New Testament authors penned nearly two millennia ago."[20] A similar statement may be made for the Old Testament as well since Jewish scribes went to painstaking efforts to accurately transcribe the oldest and most reliable Old Testament texts.

How the Bible was written

As I began writing this book I prayed and asked God to give me ideas and direct my thoughts as I wrote so that I conveyed what He wanted and not just what I thought was important. But I quickly realized that He had been training me all my Christian life to write this book and that I really didn't need to worry too much about whether what I wrote was what God wanted me to write or not. Although I certainly wasn't creating or adding to Scripture, I well understood what I later read from the scholars below.

According to Charles L. Quarles, "Although some portions of Scripture state that they were dictated by God… this is not the exclusive means by which God gave his word to his people… Most evangelical biblical scholars today recognize that the most common mode of inspiration was a special form of divine providence in which God utilized many different circumstances to shape the mind and thought of the human authors of Scripture so that they wrote exactly what they intended to communicate to their audience and this was exactly what God intended to communicate as well."[21]

Bible scholar Wayne Grudem agrees: "In cases where the ordinary human personality and writing style of the author were prominently involved, as seems the case with the major part of Scripture, all that we are able to say is that God's providential oversight and direction of the life of the author was such that their personalities, their backgrounds and training, their abilities to evaluate events in the world around them, their access to historical data, their judgment with regard to the accuracy of information, and their individual circumstances when they wrote, were all exactly what God wanted them to be, so that when they actually came to the point of putting pen to paper, the words were fully their own words but also fully the words that God wanted them to write, words that God would also claim as his own."[22]

David Nelson and David Dockery aptly summarize: "It [the Bible] is the Word of God written in the words of men."[23] They also said:

> These men of God [the biblical writers] had known God, learned from him, and walked with him in their spiritual pilgrimage for many years. God had prepared them through their familial, social, educational, and spiritual backgrounds for the task of inscripturating his word. The experiences of Moses, David, Jeremiah, Paul, Luke, John, and Peter differ; yet throughout their lives God was working to prepare and shape them, even their own vocabulary, to pen the Scriptures.[24]

The Bible canon

As stated earlier, the Protestant Bible is made up of 66 individual books. This compilation of these books is called the canon of Scripture. These books [among many early Church writings] were decided upon by the end of the fourth century AD by the Council of Carthage that was primarily made up of prominent bishops of the early Christian Church. Paul D. Wegner, Terry L. Wilder, and Darrell L. Bock agree that: "One of the outcomes of the Council was its publication of the names of the twenty-seven books held to be Scripture by the church of Jesus Christ... it is evident that by the middle-to-late fourth century there was little or no question concerning the twenty-seven canonical books of the NT. No really serious question about this canonical list has arisen since."[25]

One of the ways the Church fathers determined what books would be included in the canon of Scripture was whether or not they contained phrases such as: "the word of the Lord [God] came to," "the Lord says," "Thus says the Lord," "This is what the LORD, the God of Israel, says," and other similar phrases where God Himself claims to be speaking. What makes this remarkable is that all the books that contain these phrases, also have a consistent message or theme that appears to come from one mind or being whom apparently transcends time and space.

On an earlier note, the reason that the Apocryphal books that are in the Catholic canon of Scripture are not in the Protestant canon is—First, as the above scholars agree, "None of the apocryphal books claim to be the word of the Lord as do many Old Testament books."[26] And secondly, "The New Testament never cites any apocryphal books as inspired; Jesus' use of Scripture suggests that only the books in the Hebrew Bible [Old Testament] were considered to be authoritative."[27] In other words, Jesus Christ never referred to any other books outside of the Hebrew Old Testament canon of Scripture and after His death and resurrection, He is considered to be the supreme authority on the Old Testament.

The above scholars therefore conclude, "that the sixty-six-book Protestant canon is well-justified. The early Christians embraced the thirty-nine books of the Hebrew Scriptures simply and rightly because these books (without the Apocrypha) were those embraced by their Lord Jesus Christ and his apostles and the Jewish community of faith in which they lived."[28] As far as the New Testament itself is concerned, the scholars add, "The NT canon was naturally grounded in the perception of apostolic authority. Believing that the apostles were commissioned by Christ to be his authoritative spokesmen, the only significant question the early church had was whether or not a book carried the apostolic imprimatur [sanction or approval]. Such authority was recognized in books that were seen to be authored or endorsed by an apostle, were consistent with apostolic doctrine, and were widely accepted in the apostolic churches. The twenty-seven books of the NT passed these tests."[29]

History and Archaeology

History and archaeology go hand in hand in proving the historical accuracy of the Bible because what experts in archaeology uncover becomes part of the historical record. In recent years archaeologists have made amazing finds in lands in and around Israel. Archaeology has substantiated many of the people, events, and places from the Bible that were once thought to be fictitious or myths such as: The Tower of Babel where God scrambled the world's one common language into many, The city of Sodom that God destroyed by fire and brimstone because of the inhabitant's extreme wickedness, And the exodus of the children of Israel out of the land of Egypt where they had been slaves. These Old Testament events and others from New Testament times have been substantiated through the archaeological discoveries of extra-Biblical writings found in the places where they happened.

For example, did you know that—A tell (an artificial mound formed by the accumulated remains of ancient settlements) called, "Tall el-Hammam," is believed by archaeologists to be the ancient Sodom, one of the "cities of the plain" that God destroyed by fire and brimstone? The site reportedly possesses a thick layer of ash from a previous habitation dated to the Biblical time of its destruction that contains charred human remains, melted pottery and sand-into-glass—all indications that the city was destroyed by a "sudden, intense, high heat [exceeding 2000 degrees Fahrenheit] catastrophic event" consistent with that from the flash of extreme heat caused by a nuclear detonation.[30]

Or, did you know—There is an ancient Sumerian inscription dated to around 6,000 years ago from an area where the Tower of Babel (where there are at least 30 remains of ziggurats like what the Tower of Babel would have been like) existed that tells of a people who spoke one common language but had it confused into many "strange tongues" by a god?[31]

And did you also know that—There is much evidence in ancient Egyptian writings for the plagues that God brought upon Egypt for the Pharaoh not releasing God's people during the time of the Exodus as recorded in the Bible?[32]

The above are just a few examples of fairly recent archaeological discoveries that are not generally known but that reveal the truthfulness of the Bible and that it does indeed contain narratives of real people and events and not myths or stories too fantastic to be true. Scholar and author of many books on Biblical theology and philosophy, Walter C. Kaiser Jr., explains that, "Archaeology has been one of the strongest allies for making the case for the historical accuracy of the Old Testament."[33]

Biblical scholars, Joseph M. Holden and Norman Geisler relate how, "Today, nearly 100 biblical figures, dozens of biblical cities, over 60 historical details in the Gospel of John, and 80 historical details in the book of Acts, among other things have been confirmed as historical through archaeological and historical research."[34] About the relationship between history and archaeology the two men further add: "The Bible itself is an archaeological document that represents the most complete and substantiated corpus of literature we possess from the ancient world."[35] And although, "Historical investigation is not a 100 percent certain procedure with absolutely guaranteed results... Nevertheless, the Bible remains the one outstanding piece of ancient literature that excels in passing historical investigations mounted by even its harshest critics."[36]

Journalist and author, Werner Keller, writes in the introduction of his bestselling book, *The Bible as History*:

> In Palestine [the land of Israel], places and towns which are frequently mentioned in the Bible are being brought back once more into the light of day. They look exactly as the Bible describes them and lie exactly where the Bible locates them. On ancient inscriptions and monuments scholars encounter more and more characters from the Old and New Testaments. Contemporary reliefs depict people whom we have hitherto only known by name. Their features, their clothes, their armour take shape before our eyes. Colossal figures and sculptures show us the Hittites with their big noses; the slim tall Philistines; the elegant Canaanite chiefs with their "chariots of iron" which struck terror into the hearts of the Israelites; the kings of Mari, contemporary with Abraham, with their gentle

smiles. During the thousands of years that divide us from them the Assyrian kings have lost nothing of their fierce and forbidding appearance: Tiglath-Pileser III, well known as the Old Testament "Pul"; Sennacherib who destroyed Lachish and laid siege to Jerusalem; Esarhaddon who put King Manasseh in chains, and Ashurbanipal the "great and noble Asnapper" of the book of Ezra. As they have done to Ninevah and Nimrud—old-time Calah—or to Ashur and Thebes, which the prophets called No-Amon, the scholars have also awakened from its ancient slumber the notorious Babel of Biblical story with its legendary tower. In the Nile Delta archaeologists have found the cities of Pithom and Raamses, where the resentful Hebrews toiled as slaves. They have laid bare strata which tell of the flames and destruction which accompanied the children of Israel on their conquering march into Canaan. In Gibeah they found Saul's mountain stronghold, whose walls once echoed to the strains of David's harp. At Megiddo they came upon the vast stables of King Solomon, who had "12,000 horsemen". From the world of the New Testament reappeared the palatial edifices of King Herod. In the heart of Old Jerusalem The Pavement was discovered, where Jesus stood before Pilate, as is mentioned in St. John's gospel. Assyriologists deciphered on the astronomical tables of the Babylonians the exact dates on which the Star of Bethlehem was observed. These breathtaking discoveries, whose significance it is impossible to grasp all at once, make it necessary for us to revise our views about the Bible. Many events which previously passed for "pious tales" must now be judged to be historical. Often the results of investigation correspond in detail with the Biblical narratives. They do not only confirm them, but also illuminate the historical situations out of which the Old Testament and the Gospels grew... The opinion has been, and still is widely held, that the Bible is nothing but the story of man's salvation, a guarantee of the validity of their faith for Christians everywhere. It is however at the same time a book about things that actually happened... the events themselves are historical facts and have been recorded with an accuracy that is nothing less than startling... Thanks to the findings of the archaeologists many of the Biblical narratives can be better understood now than ever before.[37]

Even paleontology and geology are witnesses to the reliability of the Bible, if one has the courage to look at the evidence objectively in this age of rabid, pro-evolutionary thought. Although there is evidence for a worldwide flood like that recounted in the Old Testament from the writings of more than a dozen ancient civilizations, this is not the most compelling evidence for the event. The most powerful evidence for the "flood of Noah" may be right under our noses.

Fossilization is something that is little understood by most Americans, perhaps even including the so-called experts. Most of us who have grown up in the American public education system have been told since we were small children that the earth is billions of years old and that "highly-evolved" life has existed on the planet for tens of millions of years. We have also been told that dinosaurs existed and died off millions of years before mankind "evolved" to its present state. One of the "proofs" for this, we have been taught and are still being told, is all the different strata, or layers of earth deposits in geological formations took millions of years to form. We are told that things within these layers, such as fossils and coal, have also taken millions of years to form. But when one discovers how bones and other organic bodies actually become fossilized, and examines exactly what is in substances like coal, one realizes that what we are being told is probably not true.

Way back in 1981 Josh McDowell and Don Stewart wrote a book called: *Reasons Skeptics Should Consider Christianity.*[38] In some of the chapters they make a convincing argument for how fossils are created and relate that with the known amount of sediment that is deposited around the globe by water and air each year, it would take an extremely abnormal rate of deposition to allow fossils to form like they have around the world. Although known rates of sediment deposition do not explain the creation of fossils, the authors propose that a worldwide deluge *would* create such conditions for fossilization and that all the fossils we have today are actually evidence for it.[39]

So again, the Bible is proving itself to be accurate and trustworthy in what it says.

Biblical Prophesy

Biblical prophecy is unique among the world's religions.

Josh McDowell in his book *Evidence that Demands a Verdict* quotes Wilbur Smith, considered one of the most important Biblical scholars of the 20th century. Smith said of Biblical prophecy:

> Whatever one may think of the authority of and the message presented in the book we call the Bible, there is world-wide agreement that in more ways than one it is the most remarkable volume that has ever been produced in these some five thousand years of writing on the part of the human race. It is the only volume ever produced by man, or a group of men, in which is to be found a large body of prophecies relating to individual nations, to Israel, to all the peoples of the earth, to certain cities, and to the coming of One who was to be the Messiah. The ancient world had many different devices for determining the future, known as divination, but not in the entire gamut of Greek and Latin literature, even though they use the words prophet and prophecy, can we find any real specific prophecy of a great historic event to come in the distant future, nor any prophecy of a Savior to arise in the human race. Mohammedanism [Islam] cannot point to any prophecies of the coming of Mohammed uttered hundreds of years before his birth. Neither can the founders of any cult in this country rightly identify any ancient test specifically foretelling their appearance.[40]

Unger's Bible dictionary states about a prophet of God that he is "One who is divinely inspired to communicate God's will to His people, and to disclose the future to them."

The rules for Biblical prophets were strict. If an Old Testament prophet made a prediction that he claimed to come from God and the thing didn't come to pass, he was to be put to death (Deuteronomy 18:20-22). God had a real problem with people who went around putting words in His mouth.

John Dwight Pentecost, considered one of the greatest latter day theologians on Biblical prophesy said: "A greater body of

Scripture is given to prophesy than any other one subject, for approximately one-fourth of the Bible was prophetic at the time it was written."[41] It has also been stated that over 2000 Biblical prophecies have already been fulfilled.[42]

It is safe to say that there is nothing like Biblical prophesy in the ancient or modern world. According to Robert C. Newman, the closest we get to Biblical prophesy in the classical world, which really wasn't close at all, were the Greek counterparts to the Bible's prophets called theomantes or oracles. According to Newman, these "diviners" were typically paid for their pronouncements and used methods to deceive the one seeking divine answers or divine direction. Newman tells how the diviner's proclamations were almost never just, understandable, or conclusive. Today we would call these people charlatans. He goes on to say that when answers to seekers were given, they were always ambiguous enough so as to mean more than one thing and in such a way as to be able to "predict" many or any outcomes and oftentimes, answers were given so as to have opposite meanings in order to protect the diviner from a powerful ruler or aristocrat.[43]

The predictions made by modern, twentieth century prognosticators, Edgar Cayce[44] and Jeane Dixon[45] are as equally dismal as their ancient counterparts.

Arguably, the most famous false prophet, often referred to as a seer or astrologer, was Nostradamus who lived in sixteenth century France. Nostradamus made his predictions via quatrains. A quatrain is a type of stanza or a short, but complete poem consisting of only four lines. Steve Bright, for the Christian Research Institute, writes about the predictions of Nostradamus: "There is no need to be uncritical or uninformed regarding Nostradamus's enigmatic prophecies. Beyond failing the biblical test of 100 percent accuracy, most of Nostradamus's prophecies are vague and ambiguous. His reputation as an accurate prophet rests on spurious and unjustified interpretations. His prophecies pose no real challenge to the uniqueness of biblical prophecy, which is specific and accurate." Bright quotes Peter Lemesurier who describes Nostradamus's predictions as "a massive verbal jigsaw puzzle." Moreover, Lemesurier adds, "their [the quatrains] language is often obtuse and sometimes positively arcane… the result is that a further layer of impenetrability is added to an already chaotic text." Bright also quotes John Hogue who says about Nostradamus that, "his writing is muddled enough to be taken any way one wishes… His ambiguities have kept the controversy of his prophecies alive, and even enhanced his stature as a seer in the centuries following his death (just as he predicted)." Bright also says about Nostradamus that, "His few specific or dated prophecies, moreover, have proven to be consistent failures."[46]

Compared to the inaccurate prognostications of these false prophets of ancient and modern times, God's prophets from the Bible were always 100% correct in what they prophesied and the Bible is the only book in the world that contains such proofs that it is indeed divinely inspired.

Miracles

I have put miracles after the above objective evidences because they are the least provable of all the Bible's attributes. It is my hope that since the Bible has been shown to be reliable as to historical events that the reader will believe that Biblical miracles really occurred as well.

The great Christian apologist, C. S. Lewis, defined a miracle as "an interference with Nature by supernatural power."[47] Biblical scholar, Steven B. Cowan, explains that, "A miracle may be simply defined as an event that is so unusual and contrary to the ordinary course of nature that the causal activity of God is the best explanation for the event."[48]

It is true that Biblical miracles do not provide empirical evidence for today that the Bible is the true word of God, primarily because we are so far removed from them and the people who witnessed or who were affected by them. However it is important to note that God did not cause miracles to happen at random or for no reason. He often used miracles as proof to the people in the Bible that it was indeed Him who was communicating with them.[49] God didn't expect people to just take the word of one of His representatives like Moses or one of the prophets like Elijah that they were speaking for Him. He worked miracles through them to prove it. Jesus Christ is the perfect example of this as He utilized many diverse miracles to prove He was who He said He was in order to add credence to His divine message. Charles L. Quarles says of the miracles Christ performed, "If a researcher is willing to remain open to the possibility of miracles and weigh the historical evidence, he will discover that the case for Jesus' miraculous ministry is very strong."[50]

It is also important to point out that true, bonafide miracles are conspicuously absent from most if not all non-Biblical religious writings.

Miracles are not unknown to science

It has been stated that the scientific method observes regularities and repetitions in nature and since specific miracles are one-time events, those adhering solely to the scientific method have defined them as nonexistent or impossible. This would mean that disciplines like archaeology would also have to be dismissed because archaeology studies one time events that cannot be replicated in real time since one cannot go back in time and recreate or replicate an event using all the dynamics that were involved within a specific moment in time (a one-time event that is unique to a single moment in time).[51] So the scientific method is limited in that it cannot also confirm or deny such events as the Big Bang theory for the origin of the universe or the very first living organism developing on planet earth. These facts compel us to look elsewhere for the origins and answers to well-attested-to miraculous events or phenomena and often ultimately lead us to God.

The different Bible translations

The Bible was originally written primarily in Hebrew (Old Testament) and Greek (New Testament). Words sometimes have slightly different meanings or nuances when they are translated from one language to the next. This can also be the case with many versions of the Bible within the same language where certain words or entire verses from different translations can appear to have different meanings when compared with each other. This is one of the great challenges for Bible translators: to translate the meaning of passages as accurately as possible from the original Hebrew and Greek into the modern, target language.

For example, there are at least four different words that mean love in the Greek language and only one word for love in English. The Greek words are: Agape—meaning unconditional love, like that of God's love for His people, Phileo—meaning the love between friends, Eros—meaning love with sexual overtones, such as romantic love, and Storge—the type of love that is felt between family members like, father and son, and sibling toward sibling, etc.

Hebrew too is a very precise and expressive language. Merrill Unger notes how, "In some cases, a play on words is virtually impossible to reflect in the English translation."[52] This makes it difficult for translators to accurately convey the most accurate meaning of a text in Hebrew or Greek into English. This type of impreciseness exists between all languages and can sometimes present a real problem for Bible translators, hence, the different translations or versions even within a given language like English where each translation is an attempt to more closely convey the correct meaning of the oldest, available text.

Obviously the ideal way around this dilemma would be for the reader to be fluent in Hebrew and Greek. Since it is difficult for many readers of the Bible to learn these two languages, for various reasons, many Bible study helps are available for those wishing to find the most accurate meaning of a Bible word or passage in its oldest available form. The other alternative is to find a Bible-believing, Christian church whose pastor is schooled in Hebrew and Greek who can accurately expound the word of God.

But although precise meanings of certain Biblical words or passages may take in-depth study, the major themes and principles of the Bible are clearly and accurately presented in nearly all Bible translations and versions.

Are there contradictions in the Bible?

If the Bible contained perfectly matching accounts by different authors of the same event, Biblical writers would be accused of either plagiarism or collusion. On the other hand, when Biblical stories recounting the same event differs, like those of the New Testament Gospels,[53] there are those who are quick to call the differences discrepancies or contradictions. It only goes to show that some will never accept the Bible as the word of God no matter what it says or how it says it.

Sometimes a writer of a book from the Bible didn't have all the knowledge available on a particular event or he was writing from a particular perspective with a particular theme in mind and would exclude things that weren't relevant to his reason for writing and he would primarily emphasize those things that were. The New Testament Gospels are an excellent example of this.

In the translation that I use, the Summary of Books section tells the individual themes for each of the various books of the Bible. For example, it explains that the *Gospel of Matthew* focuses on presenting Jesus Christ as the King of the Jews and seeks to show that Jesus *is* the Messiah prophesied about in the Old Testament. The Summary tells that the *Gospel of Mark* presents Jesus as a servant and highlights His ministering to the physical and spiritual needs of others. The Summary explains that the *Gospel of Luke* centers on showing Jesus as the Son of Man and His perfect humanity. Last, the Summary conveys that the *Gospel of John* emphasizes Jesus as the Son of God and His divine nature and equality with God the Father.

Professor of Biblical and theological studies at Biola University, Douglas S. Huffman, says that,

> Authors cannot write everything. They have no choice but to be selective of what they include in their accounts. The selectivity of an author is related to his purpose of writing and does not entail an absolute denial of events not selected. This is true of authors in all time periods everywhere. The truthfulness of an author's report cannot be questioned simply because it does not satisfy a particular reader's curiosity for information unrelated

to the author's purposes. For example, each of the four Gospels has information not contained in any of the others. But this does not necessitate that these records are in contradiction with one another.[54]

Huffman points out that what New Testament writers were most concerned about was "getting the message correct."[55]

John W. Haley in his book, *Alleged Discrepancies of the Bible*, says that early church father, John Chrysostom (349 to 407 AD), regarded "discrepancies as really valuable as proofs of independence on the part of the sacred writers."[56]

Also, the chronological order that stories appear in the four Gospels vary, but this does not mean that one or more of the Gospels is in error. For instance, *The Gospel According to Mark* was written by Mark, but Mark was not an apostle, he was a disciple and a kind of surrogate son to the apostle Peter (I Peter 5:13). As such, he got what he knew about Jesus, directly from Peter, who *was* an eyewitness to Jesus and His ministry, so we can't expect the events and miracles in Jesus' ministry recorded in Mark's Gospel to be necessarily chronological, nor do they need to be. The story is similar with Luke, the writer of the Gospel with his name. Luke states in the second verse of the first chapter of his Gospel that he got the story of Jesus, along with His deeds and teachings, from *"eyewitnesses and ministers of the word."* Luke goes on to say that because he had *"perfect understanding of all things* [concerning Jesus] *from the very first"* he decided to write down *"an orderly account"* of what he knew which ultimately became the *Gospel According to Luke*. So it would hardly be surprising that Luke may have gotten some of the events that happened in Jesus' ministry out of chronological order, which isn't nearly as important as the events and teachings themselves.

In summation, many books have been written in defense of the Bible concerning "alleged discrepancies." Haley, quoted earlier, covers nearly 900 in his book. If these allegations are important to you, I suggest you seek out scholarly refutations of alleged inconsistencies because as Haley points out, many are of "flimsy and disingenuous character."[57]

Are there forgeries in the Bible?

Finally, I want to address the skeptic's contention that there are forgeries in the Bible. A popular proponent for this assertion is Professor of Religious Studies, Bart D. Ehrman. In his book, *Lost Christianities*,[58] Ehrman makes a case that several New Testament epistles (letters or books) are forgeries in that they were written by someone other than whom the individual letters say they were written by. However, in my estimation, Ehrman really doesn't offer any real proof or compelling evidence for his claims, certainly not enough that any other reputable Biblical scholar has agreed with him.

According to Bible professor, Terry L. Wilder, "Those who say that forgeries exist in the Bible really need to take a closer look at the evidence. The onus of proof weighs heavily upon them… any objections to the authenticity of biblical books can be plausibly answered. The evidence we possess points to the trustworthiness of Scripture."[59]

The significance of the Dead Sea Scrolls (DSS)

In 1947, sheepherders in south-western Israel near the Dead Sea discovered caves (11 in total) where clay jars with ancient manuscripts inside them were found. These jars were later identified as put in these caves by an ancient religious sect called the Essenes. It turned out that many of these jars contained both fragmented and fully intact versions of the Old Testament as well as other texts that related mostly to the Essene culture. When it was learned by authorities exactly what was found, some, such as the late archeologist, William F. Albright, an early authenticator of the finds, called them "the greatest manuscript discovery of modern times."

It turned out that the manuscripts found represented every OT book except the book of Esther. The consensus among Biblical scholars is that all the scrolls and text fragments discovered within the various caves around the ancient Qumran-Essene community dated from the third century BC to the first century AD.

This turned out to be good news indeed because Jewish rabbis had a practice of destroying worn out copies of the Scriptures, aka The Old Testament. As a result, the earliest Hebrew texts for modern Biblical translators are relatively late, historically. Prior to the discovery of the DDS the oldest know OT manuscripts (called the Masoretic texts) were from around the end of the first millennium AD, beginning from 917 AD to be exact. According to Biblical scholar and Christian apologist, Norman Geisler, "The scrolls give an overwhelming confirmation of the faithfulness with which the Hebrew text was copied through the centuries. By the tenth-century Masoretic copies, few errors had crept in." In his book, *The Dead Sea Scrolls*, Bible scholar and leading authority on the DDS, Millar Burrows writes concerning them, "It is a matter of wonder that through something like a thousand years the text underwent so little alteration. As I said in my first article on the scroll, 'Herein lies its chief importance, supporting the fidelity of the Masoretic tradition.'"

As stated, many of the texts found in the caves of Qumran were fragmented; however, some completely intact OT books *were* discovered. For example, there were fourteen individual manuscripts of the book of Isaiah. Of this book, Bible scholar Gleason Archer observed that the two copies of Isaiah discovered in Qumran Cave 1 "proved to be word for word identical with our standard Hebrew Bible in more than 95 percent of the text. The 5 percent of variation consisted chiefly of obvious slips of the pen and variations in spelling."

This is nothing short of amazing and tells us that the Bible we have today is in all respects extremely close if not exact to what God had His, prophets, apostles, and other divinely-inspired writers to write down thousands of years ago and is proof positive that modern translations of the Bible can be trusted today to be the true words of God.

Conclusion—Is the Bible the Word of God?

In this chapter I presented a lot of objective evidence for trusting the Bible. The next logical step is for the honest, unbelieving reader to apply this knowledge as foundational reasoning for believing that the Bible contains the words of the one true God. Because if the Bible can be trusted as a reliable historical document with supernatural attributes such as fulfilled prophesy and divine miracles, it is illogical to deny that it is wrong about also containing the words of God Himself.

Some may ask—But if God does really exist, why doesn't He just show Himself plainly? Actually, God tried that approach at least twice in history, and both times it didn't work out so well. The first time was with the Israelites when He led them out of Egypt during the Exodus under Moses' command. Although God revealed Himself in a pillar of cloud (by day) and fire (by night) and worked many miracles through Moses like the ten plagues against Egypt, and provided manna and quail from heaven everyday for over forty years as well as several times getting water from rocks for the people and their animals to drink, the children of Israel still didn't trust Him. The second time God revealed Himself physically was through Jesus Christ, with mixed results, which will be discussed in depth in chapter eight.

Anyone still doubting or unsure of the accuracy of Scripture should watch the documentary, *The Star of Bethlehem* by Producer Stephen McEveety. In the film, Bible verses are utilized to discover the origins for the literal Star of Bethlehem that the wise men followed that led them to the Christ child, Jesus. It reveals how amazingly accurate the Bible is in what it reports, in this instance, where an astronomical event that occurred over 2000 years ago can be pinpointed in time by using the Bible as the primary guide.

Another documentary that is equally impressive is *The Isaiah 9:10 Judgment* by Rabbi Jonathan Cahn (also the author of the film's companion book, *The Harbinger: The Ancient Mystery That Holds the Secret of America's Future*). Cahn's two works use Bible scripture in a remarkable way to predict the judgment that is coming to America for rejecting the God of the Bible.

God's modus operandi today for getting people to believe and trust in Him is by using evidence, such as has been presented in this chapter, then requiring faith on the part of the true seeker, after he has been shown reasons to believe. The writer to the Hebrews in the New Testament explained the value of mixing objective evidences with faith when he quoted Psalm 95:7-11 in Hebrews 3:7-10 that reads in part:

Do not harden your hearts, as in the rebellion, and as in the day of trial in the wilderness, when your fathers tested Me [God]*, they proved Me, though they saw My work. For forty years I was grieved with that generation, and said, "It is a people who go astray in their hearts, and they do not know my ways," so I swore in My wrath, "They shall not enter my rest."*
(NKJV)

The writer of Hebrews then goes on to say that what the Israelites saw *"did not profit them, not being mixed with faith…"* (Hebrews 4:2).

God has given us much evidence for His existence and the reliability of the Bible, but it is up to each one of us to take that knowledge and seek after Him with a heart of faith.

And He has made from one blood every nation of men to dwell on the face of the earth, and has determined their preappointed times and the boundaries of their habitation, so that they should seek the Lord in the hope that they might grope for Him and find Him, though He is not far from each one of us.
Acts 17:26-27 (NKJV)

Chapter 3
God vs. No God

Any treatise for the Judeo-Christian God and the Bible would not be complete without addressing the secular alternative to believing in God and the Bible. And since the leading Godless opposition comes from proponents of the theory of evolution in America today, I will discuss the probability that our known universe and its living and nonliving elements came from God and not by purely unintelligent material processes.

As briefly mentioned in the first chapter, one of the battles being waged against God in America is the idea that it was not Him who created the universe and all that is in it, but some random process utilizing material whose origin secular scientists and theorists can't account for.

People who reject God as the Creator of all things are often referred to by many titles: evolutionists, Darwinian evolutionists, materialists, naturalists, modernists, etc., or some combination of these terms. For the purposes of this book, I will call this group, evolutionists, because that is how the average person knows them in America today.

People opposing the evolutionary point of view are the creationists and/or intelligent design adherents. Creationists believe that an all-powerful Creator outside the universe created it and everything within it. Adherents to the intelligent design theory don't necessarily believe in the Judeo-Christian God, but they recognize that with the mind-boggling complexity and order of all things, there had to be some super intelligence with unfathomable abilities that carefully designed and made everything. For the purpose of brevity, I will refer to these two related groups as creationists since they essentially believe the same thing.

Evolutionists typically assume that some form of matter or energy has always existed and that it somehow morphed or evolved into the natural world that we know today. They believe that what they call simple life forms evolved through natural processes into higher or more complex life forms. They also believe that nature is all there is and that there is no special purpose for it or anything else. Many of these people assert that invisible natural laws like gravity have arisen solely from random and chance chemical processes. Evolutionists also tend to marginalize adherents of creationism or intelligent design because they see the two as religious and stemming from a supernatural (outside the known, natural system) viewpoint.

Conversely, creationists believe that an eternal, all-powerful God existed before our universe and that He created it and everything in it by special design and for a particular purpose. Creationists believe this partly because the God of the Bible *says* He made all things in His word and that He *did* create everything for a purpose, especially we human beings. Creationists also believe this because they think the evidence more supports the Biblical worldview than the evolutionary view. Creationists believe too that God programmed the universe and its contents to act in a certain way and that He gave life or the animating force to all its living components, plants and animals.

Evolutionists assert that their worldview does not require any higher power or all-powerful God in order for our universe to exist. However, I contend that the belief in naturalism, otherwise known as the Darwinian theory of evolution that is adhered to by so many, requires much more faith than believing in an all-powerful God and creationism as presented in the Bible since there is much more evidence for the latter than the former.

How evolution allegedly works

To illustrate the faith issue, I will refer to former UC Berkeley law professor, Phillip E. Johnson, who quotes popular evolutionist, Richard Dawkins, who wrote *The Blind*

Watchmaker. In his book, Dawkins postulates how bats got their wings:

> How did wings get their start? Many animals leap from bough to bough, and sometimes fall to the ground. Especially in a small animal, the whole body surface catches the air and assists the leap or breaks the fall, by acting as a crude aerofoil. Any tendency to increase the ratio of surface area to weight would help, for example flaps of skin growing out in the angles of joints.... [It] doesn't matter *how* small and unwinglike the first wingflaps were. There must be some height, call it h, such that an animal would just break its neck if it fell from that height, but would just survive if it fell from a slightly lower height. In this critical zone, any improvement in the body surface's ability to catch the air and break the fall, however slight the improvement, can make the difference between life and death. Natural selection will then favor slight, prototype wingflaps. When these small flaps have become the norm, the critical height h will become slightly greater. Now a slight further increase in the wingflaps will make the difference between life and death. And so on, until we have proper wings.[1]

Evolutionists widely believe nature and the universe in which we live to be a closed system without any outside designer or maker of natural laws. They also basically believe that given enough time, molecules (whose origins they can't explain) can combine and form the building blocks of life which then eventually form into living organisms like "simple cells" (which are anything but simple), which in turn reproduce and mutate enough times to form more complex organisms some of which at least somehow perceive the need to mutate toward becoming a body with a brain and all the senses of sight, smell, touch, hearing, and a means of locomotion such as legs or wings or fins, and a need to process oxygen through either lungs or gills and other organs for various functions necessary for life. This list goes on and on and becomes ridiculous even to the most gullible unless he or she has a particular reason for believing in it such as to avoid special creation by a higher power.

In my opinion, it requires more faith to believe all of the above happening through purely material, random processes performed over millions or billions of years rather than just believing that an all-powerful entity that some call God designed and created a bat with wings that possesses other fantastic attributes as well, including radar. Johnson calls the above evolutionary process that many adhere to today as "The grand metaphysical story of science." It takes a lot of faith to believe that purely random, chance processes devoid of any programming or outside design could produce wings, legs, arms, eyes, a brain, and other highly sophisticated organs, etc. Evolution adherents also apparently believe by faith that their system suddenly stopped after the evolution of each fully developed individual species and at some point in time simply reproduced after their own kind for thousands of years without any other additional significant changes or modifications.

To say that believing the above does not require faith is to be under a delusion of the most rigorous kind.

The metaphysical aspects in the idea of evolution are absolutely inherent because—What made the "flaps of skin" in Dawkins' example evolve into complex wings instead of just devolving into non-existence? Why do things always seem to evolve in the evolutionist's world into something higher or more complex instead of the other way around? Why does the simple morph into the complex instead of staying simple or devolving and dying off? Evolutionists have no plausible answer for this. Hence something metaphysical or outside the "observable" is implied in their belief system and necessary for faith in order for them to continue to believe the manifestly improbable.

The history of the theory of evolution

So how did so many people in America come to believe such a dubious theory?

Since the Age of Enlightenment of the seventeenth and eighteenth centuries, many proponents of human reason (as being the highest authority instead of God) were looking for something to do away with the medieval way of looking at the world, especially the idea that God is the Creator of all things. Although the idea of life evolving had been around for hundreds of years, the idea really never caught on until English naturalist and geologist, Charles Darwin, added his "Natural Selection"[2] component to the idea in 1859 in his book, *On the Origin of Species*. For thousands of years before Darwin's theory, most people believed that God or a supreme god of many lesser gods created all things. Darwin's theory of Natural Selection added legitimacy to the idea of life evolving and provided, at least superficially, a somewhat plausible mechanism with scientific undertones for evolution to be a viable alternative explanation for how life came to be on planet earth. But although Darwin never really claimed to have the answers for how life began on our planet, his theory gave stimulus to those who were open to anything reasonable-sounding to replace the idea of an authoritarian-type God creating the natural world.[3] Thus, Darwin's theory of evolution was soon regarded as scientific and was linked to the scientific method that had been in use since at least the time of the Renaissance in the sixteen century with scientists such as Copernicus and Galileo, thereby fallaciously adding further legitimacy to the idea.

The scientific method

Modern day evolution gurus claim that their belief system and the scientific method are synonymous. It is interesting to note that the popular web site, Wikipedia, states that, "The scientific method is a body of techniques for investigating phenomena, acquiring new knowledge, or correcting and integrating previous knowledge. To be termed scientific, a method of inquiry is commonly based on empirical or measurable evidence subject to specific principles of reasoning." If you agree with the writer on Wikipedia, evolution must be uncommon because it is not based upon either "empirical or measurable evidence." To the contrary, the available empirical and measurable evidence does not point to nor support the theory of evolution; instead, it points to special creation by an intelligent designer.

The scientific method is limited

As I stated in the last chapter in regards to miracles, the scientific method is limited in that it cannot confirm anything as real unless it can be observed and/or tested. In fact, the web site, livescience.com states: "One important aspect of the scientific process is that it is focused only on the natural world, according to the University of California. Anything that is considered supernatural does not fit into the definition of science."

So secularists have tried to sideline supernaturalism by defining it as unworthy of consideration. Phillip E. Johnson essentially agrees: "Science does not need a good theory (that is, a theory genuinely backed by empirical testing) to defeat creationism (theistic realism). The battle has been won in the definitions, before the empirical testing even gets started."[4]

I assert that because of this, the scientific method, due to the way it is handled by secularists in so-called scientific institutions today, is extremely limited.

It is the height of arrogance to decree that anything that does not fit into the secularist's worldview is not worthy of consideration let alone debate—No one with an ounce of integrity can simply define something that he or she doesn't like or understand out of the realm of discussion. And by what or whose authority does anyone have the right to proclaim that nature is all there is? This is what happens when humanists get control of America's institutions, the opposing views of the dissenters of established dogma are relegated to "kook" status and ignored. But a big problem for those who hold to Godless mechanisms for all things related to science despite the evidence is that there will always be thinking people who will challenge the accepted ideologies of those in control especially when they aren't really based upon anything but unbridled prejudice.

Problems with the pseudo-science of evolution

Most people in America today think that evolution is a proven theory supported by evidence and facts—it is not. The facts are— there is no evidence that anything on the planet has evolved (as opposed to adaptation within a species) to form a new separate species that reproduces after its own kind while it continues to evolve into yet another new species. Species of plants and animals are not in constant flux and evolving into new biological organisms or phyla. This has never been truly observed in nature. Nor does the fossil record attest to any such thing happening in the past. Some of the problems for evolutionists are:

1. No supporting fossil evidence—There is no evidence in the fossil record of biological organisms or species evolving. No "missing links" between species or so-called "transitional" creatures have ever been found. Phillip Johnson states: "In the fossil record, paleontologists observe mass extinctions and the subsequent sudden appearance of new kinds of organisms. They do not observe new organs like bat wings in the process of gradual formation, and they do not observe one kind of organism changing into something fundamentally different through a step-by-step process. If the fossil record is a reliable guide, 'evolution' seems to be a process in which new forms of life appeared abruptly, remained fundamentally unchanged throughout their tenure on the earth and then often became extinct—not because they were gradually supplanted by improved descendants. But because they were in the wrong ecological nitch at the time of a mass extinction."[5]

McDowell and Stewart, mentioned in chapter two, agree, "Group after group appears in the fossil record without any evidence of evolutionary ancestors. Paleontology attempts to explain this fact by saying that the fossil record is incomplete and that millions of years passed between the deposition of different layers.[6] During these times, new creatures supposedly evolved. This view of an incomplete fossil record is essential if evolution is to be considered a viable theory. Darwin admits 'whole groups of species sometimes falsely appear to have abruptly developed; and I have attempted to give an explanation of this fact, which if true would be fatal to my views.' After a century of further searching and examination of the fossil record, many paleontologists are beginning to believe that the fossil record *is* complete since none of the gaps in the fossil record that [supposedly] existed in Darwin's time has been filled by subsequent study." McDowell and Stewart go on to say that "There never has been a creature found with half-formed feet or a half-formed wing or feather."[7]

2. Irreducible complexity—Another problem with Darwin's theory of evolution is, as Darwin himself states: "If it could be demonstrated that any complex organ existed, which could not possibly have been formed by numerous, successive, slight modifications, my theory would absolutely break down." Darwin said that if a complex organ was "irreducibly complex," in other words—if its complexity consisted of two or more parts that were so interconnected or intertwined in such a way that if one part didn't work, the entire organism wouldn't work, then his entire theory would collapse because evolution would have had to have all the parts evolve at exactly the same time so the organ continually functioned as it continued to evolve. This is hard to imagine let alone believe implicitly without some intelligent outside system or mind at work governing or orchestrating the processes of evolution. And although Darwin may have had little way of knowing at the time, all life *is* incredibly and irreducibly complex, even the so-called "simple cell."

3. Non-material programming—Despite evolutionist's assertions that non-material elements like gravity, instinct, emotion, thought, self-awareness, and universal concepts such as right and wrong, justice, fairness and unfairness, etc. developed out of purely chemical processes, there is absolutely no evidence for it. Nor has anything like these elements been produced in a lab. Darwinists don't even know what makes electrons orbit around the nucleus of an atom let alone all the other invisible forces that are at work in the universe including the phenomenon of life itself. This means that science is limited by what it can confirm in the world around us. Secular science has no plausible explanation for what makes things in the natural world do what they do. It has no tenable answers for such things as instinct, emotions, the life force of all living things, the complex design of all living things,

the mind, thoughts, etc., other than to hypothesize that they are all "a product of physical forces and chemical reactions."[8]

4. Mathematically impossible—The idea that the universe we live in and all the living biological organisms on planet earth coming into existence by purely chance, random processes is a mathematical impossibility.

MIT-trained physicist, Gerald L. Schroeder, in his book, *God According to God*, when talking about the "statistical unrealistic possibility that the fabrication of viable proteins (the building blocks of life) could have occurred by unguided random mutations" quotes Simon Conway Morris, professor of evolutionary paleobiology at Cambridge University. Morris states in his book *Life's Solutions*, "The number of 'blind alleys' is so enormous that in principle all the time since the beginning of the universe would be insufficient to find the one in a trillion trillion solutions that actually work… Life is simply too complex to be assembled on any believable time scale." Even the secular publication, *Scientific American*, as Schroeder recounts, admits in a 1979 article titled: *Life: Origin and Evolution* "that merely to create a single bacterium would require more time than the universe might ever see if chance combinations of its molecules were the only driving force."[9]

McDowell and Stewart agree, "One of the most difficult problems facing those who accept the natural origin of life is that the odds are against the chance formation of even the most simple organic molecules."[10]

5. Where did the material come from?—Proponents of evolution also have no plausible explanation for where the material in the universe came from to evolve in the first place. Schroeder says, "Theories of Darwinian or neo-Darwinian evolution all begin at the stage in which self-replicating organisms are present and abundant. How to get to those bits of replicating life was and is an enigma."[11]

The current scientific evidence seems to point to the universe we all live in as coming from a single event, one that is now called "The Big Bang theory" coined by astrophysicist Fred Hoyle in 1950. The theory basically implies that the universe had a beginning at a distinct moment in time and that it has been expanding ever since. This was postulated by Edwin Hubble in 1923 after he discovered that galaxies were not static as once thought, but were actually moving away from one another. The controversial part is the uncertainty over where the energy or material came from that produced or caused the Big Bang. Secularists have no persuasive answers except to say that the material could have come from another, parallel universe. The problem with that idea is there is no evidence for any parallel universes, unless one claims that our universe is proof that one or more exists because the material for our universe must have come from somewhere, in which case one would be partaking of circular reasoning where the person doing the brainstorming begins with what they are trying to end up with.

For Christians and other believers in God, the answer is simple—God provided the material or energy for the Big Bang, if that is indeed how our universe originated. The reason that this is more believable in the long run than it seems at face value is because Christians also believe that this Creator-God has communicated with us through the Bible via His prophets and has *told* us He created the universe. This is why the evidences for the Judeo-Christian Bible were discussed in the chapter just before this one, because it is the primary basis for understanding the universe and world in which we live.

If the person who rejects God has no reasonable theory for where the building blocks of the universe came from, why should anyone take seriously his or her mechanism for how these building blocks evolved, especially without any hard evidence?

6. Why do species suddenly cease to evolve?—Darwinian evolution doesn't explain why, in the case of all species, that the process of evolution appears to cease at some point in development. For example, the oldest human skeleton found in Africa is dated at 160,000 years old and looks pretty much like us.[12] There are many animal fossils from insects to fish that have

been dated at tens of millions of years old that look identical to their descendants of today. An example is a recently discovered fossilized mosquito dated at 46 million years old—*it looks just like a modern mosquito!*[13] So, why do so many creatures appear to evolve to a certain point, then stop for allegedly millions of years only to reproduce after their own kind with no perceivable differences? Evolutionist might say that an individual species reached perfection and didn't need to evolve anymore, but who or what determined that? Because, according to the evolutionist, everything is supposed to be evolving into something else. So, why hasn't the mosquito evolved into something higher or smarter, like a mammal? Evolutionists have no rational answers for any of this.

7. Evolution violates the laws of physics—As discussed in chapter one, the second law of thermodynamics essentially teaches us that everything in the known universe is slowly running down and eventually, unless acted upon by some outside force, will degrade to total stagnation or entropy. The problem with evolution is that the very notion contradicts this most basic observable law of science. Evolution, by the definition that its adherents have given it, is a closed system supposedly devoid of any outside influence. Therefore, how can the theory of evolution be compatible with a *proven* and *observable* scientific law that contradicts it? With the idea of evolution, molecules and organisms are reportedly always building up and evolving into something more complex, not breaking down as the second law of thermodynamics dictates.

8. Evolution is unscientific—True science simply examines the world and universe we live in, then reports on what is observed. Everything in our technologically advanced modern age is a result of scientists discovering how the world works. The problem with the theory of evolution is that it is unscientific because instead of its followers observing the world, then reporting on what they see, they try to impose their own rules and ideas on nature that don't fit. Darwin's theory of Natural

Selection was valid as long as he confined it to what he observed concerning the adaptation of individuals within species. Where he and others after him have gone wrong is trying to extrapolate his scant findings to formulate a vast improbable theory that is not supported by what has actually been observed. This appears to have been done for primarily theological reasons as alluded to earlier, especially by many of the proponents of the theory of evolution today. Johnson agrees: "This dogma is not science at all. None of it has been demonstrated by experiment, which is what would have to happen for it to be truly scientific."[14]

Other problems for evolutionists

Where does the life force of a living, biological organism come from? And what causes an organism to die? Why do all living biological organisms eventually cease to be alive?— especially since all the organisms' components such as organs are often still in evidence and appear undamaged as they were when the organism was alive. So why do all living things, including humans, eventually cease to be alive even when no disease or lack of nourishment is a factor? Adherents to secular science have no credible answers to these questions.

Modern evolution likened to ancient paganism

In ancient times, men formed false gods with their hands and worshipped them in place of the one true God. The reason for this is self-evident because self-made gods require nothing of its devotees that they don't want to do. These ancient false gods, also called idols, often took on the likenesses of a human being, or an animal like the infamous golden calf of the rebellious Israelites. All ancient idols were made with elements from nature such as wood, stone, or metal.

In modern times, nothing much has changed except that now, men have formed a new false god in their minds and call it nature, then rever it instead of the one true God. Men still worship the creation over the Creator. In antiquity the false gods had many names such as Baal and Molech. In modern times, the false gods have the names: evolution, naturalism, materialism, etc. Even though modern man has progressed somewhat over his ancient counterpart by using his mind to create something to replace the Creator rather than something crafted with his hands, the end result is the same—a rejection of the true God and Creator for creation itself.

Everything is not as it seems

The reality is—the evidence reveals that we don't live in a material universe at all, but a non-material or spiritual universe that is masquerading as a material one.

With all the new evidence available today from powerful telescopes and microscopes, Gerald Schroeder suggests that, "the idea, admittedly speculative, that the truth of our universe is not as we perceive it, even with the aid of the most sophisticated particle accelerators and most powerful space telescope; that from the invisible realm of the quantum to the vast reaches of space, our universe may more resemble a thought than a thing."[15]

Schroeder isn't the only scientist who thinks this. He quotes English physicist, astronomer, and mathematician, Sir James Jeans, who said, "there is a wide measure of agreement, which on the physical side of science approaches almost unanimity, the stream of knowledge is heading toward a non-mechanical reality. The universe begins to look more like a great thought than a great machine."[16]

Schroeder also recounts how Albert Einstein "discovered that matter is actually pure congealed or condensed energy in the form of solid matter."[17]

Schroeder concludes that, "We perceive the world as particulate because the personal encounters we have with the world are primarily tactile. But it is an error to confuse our perception of reality with reality itself."[18]

In the light of all this, this passage in the New Testament from nearly two thousand years ago is not only incredibly prescient, but scientific, and makes perfect sense:

By faith we understand that the worlds were framed by the word of God, so that the things which are seen were not made of things which are visible.
Hebrews 11:3 (NKJV)

Conclusion

Besides being true, the advantage to believing in the physical universe coming from God instead of from materialism, if that were even possible, is that believing in God gives meaning and purpose to life where purely material processes give no meaning or purpose to life at all. And the reality is, life and our universe as a whole are so incredibly complex and well-ordered that it defies even the most fantastic theories that try to explain it coming together merely by random chance, even if given unbelievable amounts of time.

To be sure, the invisible elements of our planet and universe cannot be explained by exclusively unintelligent, material processes. Sentience, feelings, self-awareness, etc., have no explanation apart from an all-powerful Creator. Our very existence is a miraculous wonder. Schroeder asks a valid question: "Why is there an 'is'?" In other words, he says—"Why is there something rather than nothing?"[19] Trying to explain the wonders of the world and universe we live in apart from a supernatural, all-powerful being where nothing is impossible—is pure folly, because you and I, along with our universe and world, are simply too incredibly made to exist apart from such an entity. The evolutionist's vain attempts to explain the awesomeness of our existence are ridiculously pathetic at best.

A quote by Phillip Johnson summarizes the subject of this chapter well,

> It is not that people don't have clear pointers to the true God; it is that they don't want to recognize Him as God. They want to substitute another god—an idol—that they can control... In our day, the idols tend to be the theories that come from the human mind. The theory of evolution is the latest fashion in idols. This myth of Darwinian evolution has helped a certain class of

people to become wealthy and powerful and to be able to control the whole culture. They are mostly not scientists: they are the rulers of science and culture—the ones who decide how science will be presented to the public through television and elite newspapers. Science is extremely profitable to them. That's why they spend all their efforts and resources making sure everybody believes their particular creation story and no one is allowed to consider another one.[20]

As stated earlier, secular science, among all the many answers it lacks concerning our existence, cannot explain why electrons stay in orbit around an atom's nucleus made up of protons and neutrons, but the Bible does. The Bible tells how God holds all these and all other things in our universe together:

*God, who at various times and in different ways spoke in time past to the fathers by the prophets, has in these last days spoken to us by His Son, whom He has appointed heir of all things, through whom also He made the worlds; who being the brightness of His glory and the express image of His person, and **upholding all things by the word of His power**...*
Hebrews 1:1-3 (NKJV)

By His word, God created all things, and by His Word, God holds all things together!

Chapter 4
The God of the Bible and Creation

God is such a safe term in America today. It can represent so many different things or beliefs to so many different people. One can refer to God and not really say much of anything. Furthermore, if one is thought to believe in some ethereal, nondescript "god," that can be such a wonderful, hip thing in some circles.[1] Indeed, there are ideas about God that are perfectly acceptable and non-threatening in today's post-Christian America.

But there is one idea about God that is not so benign or acceptable anymore. That one exception is the God represented in the Judeo-Christian Bible.

I'll illustrate this point with a personal story.

I once talked to a man whom I didn't know well but understood to have grown up attending Catholic Church and Catholic school. This man knew that I was a Christian and ironically, I in turn knew that he was very anti-Catholic, presumably, I thought, because of his parochial upbringing. I knew too that he had an experience once where he had felt some invisible spiritual entity sit beside him on a bed that he just thought was "weird." Because of this man's experiences, I decided I would ask him what I thought was a fairly innocuous question—I asked him what he thought about God. The reaction I received was immediate and completely unexpected. I sat dumbfounded as he jumped up from where he was sitting and almost came apart at the seams as he proceeded to go on a tirade against Christianity. I have never seen anything like this type of reaction to such a simple question before or since. Although I knew this man had problems with Catholicism, obviously I didn't fathom to what extent. But if this man experienced an encounter with a spirit of some sort, why did he react so violently when I simply asked him about God? The answer is, because he knew exactly *what* God I was referring to and it was the one he didn't want anything to do with.

The above story, leads me to my next point and that is—Most people believe in a god they have created in their own mind. Usually this fictitious god is all loving, never judgmental, accepts everyone just the way they are regardless of their religion, non-religion,[1] political bent, or sexual proclivity, and will welcome everyone into his or her presence one day when they die unless a person has done something really bad such as commit murder. But even many murderers have extenuating circumstances to many of the modern Universalists.[2] It could be that a murderer grew up in a bad environment that caused he or she to kill another human being; surely an all-loving, all-accepting god would understand that and overlook the offender's transgression, whether the offender understood what he was doing or not.

You see, the god of the average American today has no standards; he is just there, up in the sky, waiting to welcome the human race into his all-loving arms when we leave this life. Indeed, many people's ideas about God are a hodge-podge of what they have heard throughout their lives filtered through a mental sieve that separates the hearsay into two main groups: In one pile go all the things they have heard about God that fits their individual lifestyles and is comprised of things they can live with. In another pile go all the things that don't fit their individual lifestyles and that they can't live with. From that, they form their non-life-style-threatening opinion about God.

But of course not all Americans believe that God is just some giant mushball in the sky. Many Americans belong to a host of different religions or ideologies, most of which have different and differing theologies regarding their respective god or gods. But to most, none of this really matters because the god of all those religions are all still considered to be just like the one described earlier, a giant mushball in the sky who accepts everyone regardless of their spiritual or non-spiritual path in life, because as everyone knows—all paths ultimately lead to Him (or Her if you're a feminist).

Another story that demonstrates the point is a conversation I had more recently at a park where I walk my dog. A man, who I knew only casually at the time, stopped and talked briefly with me as we were heading in opposite directions. We somehow got on the topic of the sorry state the country is in and he made the passing comment that if only everyone acted more Christian, we would all be better off, implying that *he* was a Christian. I agreed with him, but added that there were too many liberals or Godless do-gooders, as I stated it, around for that to ever happen. He took exception to my generalization and implication that a liberal wasn't or couldn't be a Christian. I responded that most if not all liberals believe in abortion on demand and that the belief is incompatible with the Bible and the teachings of Jesus Christ. I explained that one can't be a follower of Christ and rightly think it's okay to kill human babies in the womb for the primary sake of convenience. He clearly didn't like my line of reasoning, then said that he really didn't believe that there was just one way to God, but that there were many ways. I told him that isn't what the Bible or Jesus teaches and that it sounded to me like he was more of a Universalist and not a Christian at all. He thought for a moment, then acquiesced that I was probably right, but appeared to have no problem with the new revelation about himself and went his way. I realized that he was a person who equated all ideas about God as referring to the same God. When shown that this was not the case, he seemed to have no problem with it, apparently comfortable that he at least believed in *some* kind of god.

This brings me to another point.

Recently my wife and I watched a movie that had a strong Christian theme to it. Then, near the end, one the characters who was not a believer in God throughout the movie came to believe––in some god. The movie never mentions what god or whose god or even Jesus Christ, something we expected considering the movie was based on a New Testament theme. The character just said that she now believed in god. So what? Whose god? The god of Islam? One of the gods of Mormonism or the Watch Tower Bible and Tract Society? The god of Scientology? The great spirit of the religions of many Native Americans? Which god does "in god" refer to? Do all these various religions along with people's individual notions really refer to or describe the same god? The answer is: Only if you believe that God suffers from multiple personality disorder.

The importance of having the right God

I think it is safe to say that most people who are interested in God or a Supreme, Higher Being are because they want to be in right standing with Him so that when they die they go to a good place, often thought of as heaven. This is why it is imperative to connect with the right God. As the reader will see, the concepts, ideas, and notions about what or who God is differ greatly among the religions circulating around America today and since one's eternal destiny literally hangs in the balance, it is of supreme importance to be seeking the right God.

The God of the Bible and Christianity

Before I begin listing the different descriptions and attributes of each of the gods that are in religions popular in America today, I think it is best to give the reader a baseline for comparison purposes of who and what the Bible says God is, because it is very specific. Also beneficial here is an explanation of what the term "Lord" means when it is capitalized in the Bible so the reader will know that it refers to the Creator-God of the Universe. According to esteemed Bible scholar, Merrill F. Unger, in his excellent reference guide, *Unger's Bible Dictionary*, "Lord [is] the rendering of several Hebrew and Greek words [the foundational languages of the Bible]." These various words for God are:

Lord—Unger explains that this title represents the master, owner, or governor of the whole earth.

Jehovah—Unger reveals that this is the proper name for God and means "He who is," referring to God's "self existence" and His need for nothing outside of Himself.

Elohim—Unger states that this name calls attention to God's divine power and refers to the plurality of God (more on the plurality of God later).

Adonai—Unger notes that many scholars believe this name again denotes the plural for "Lord."

I also want to make clear that although there are different names for the one true God, it does not suggest that they really refer to different gods in the Bible. The Bible also has many names that refer to Jesus Christ and even Satan, but it does not mean that there is more than one Jesus Christ or Satan. Different names are often used for descriptive purposes. For example, Jesus Christ is also called: The Prince of Peace and The Bread of Life, among others. And Satan is also called: the devil, the destroyer, and even the god of this world, and more.

Who and what God is

The first thing the Bible stresses about God is that He (the Bible almost always refers to God in the masculine) alone is God and that there is no other God besides Him, nor has there ever been or ever will be. The Jewish prophet Isaiah makes this fact clear when God inspired him to write:

"You are my witnesses," declares the LORD, "and my servant whom I have chosen, so that you may know and believe me and understand that I am he. Before me no god was formed, nor will there be one after me. I, even I, am the LORD, and apart from me there is no savior."
Isaiah 43:10-11 (NIV)

And again:

This is what the LORD says--Israel's King and Redeemer, the LORD Almighty: "I am the first and I am the last; apart from me there is no God."
Isaiah 44:6 (NIV)

To you it was shown, that you might know that the Lord Himself is God; there is none other besides Him.
Deuteronomy 4:35 (NKJV)

The Bible also reveals that God in His natural state is spirit:

God is a spirit: and they that worship him must worship him in spirit and in truth.
John 4:24 (NKJV)

Now the Lord is that Spirit: and where the Spirit of the Lord is, there is liberty.
2 Corinthians 3:17 (NKJV)

The Bible teaches that this God is the creator of the known universe and everything in it:

In the beginning God created the heavens and the earth.
Genesis 1:1 (NIV)

You alone are the LORD. You made the heavens, even the highest heavens, and all their starry host, the earth and all that is on it, the seas and all that is in them. You give life to everything, and the multitudes of heaven worship you.
Nehemiah 9:6 (NIV)

God is eternal. He had no beginning and will have no end:

For thus says the High and Lofty One Who inhabits eternity...
Isaiah 57:15 (NKJV)

Now to the King eternal, immortal, invisible, to God who alone is wise, be honor and glory forever and ever. Amen.
1 Timothy 1:17 (NKJV)

"I am the Alpha and the Omega, the Beginning and the End," says the Lord, "who is and who was, and who is to come, the Almighty."
Revelations 1:8 (NKJV)

God is the Judge of mankind and will judge whether individual people's deeds are good or evil:

Then all the trees of the woods will rejoice before the Lord. For He is coming, For He is coming to judge the earth. He shall judge the world with righteousness, and the peoples with His truth.
From Psalm 96:12-13 (NKJV)

...to God the judge of all, to the spirits of just men made perfect.
From Hebrews 12:23 (NKJV)

The God of the Bible is perfect:

He is the Rock, his works are perfect, and all his ways are just. A faithful God who does no wrong, upright and just is he.
Deuteronomy 32:4 (NIV)

Be perfect, therefore, as your heavenly Father is perfect.
Matthew 5:48 (NIV)

The God of the Bible is holy. *Unger's Bible Dictionary* states that: "Holiness is... a general term to indicate sanctity, or separation from all that is sinful, or impure, or morally imperfect... Holiness is one of the essential attributes of the divine nature [God]."

And they [angels] *were calling to one another: "Holy, holy, holy is the LORD Almighty; the whole earth is full of his glory."*
Isaiah 6:3 (NIV)

Who shall not fear You, O Lord, and glorify Your name? For You alone are holy. For all nations shall come and worship before You; For Your judgments have been manifested.
Revelation 15:4 (NKJV)

The God of the Bible is omnipotent or all-powerful:

I know that You can do everything, and that no purpose of Yours can be withheld from You.
Job 42:2 (NKJV)

For with God nothing will be impossible.
Luke 1:37 (NKJV)

Alleluia! For the Lord God Omnipotent reigns!
From Revelation 19:6 (NKJV)

The God of the Bible is omnipresent or everywhere and sees everything:

The eyes of the Lord are in every place, Keeping watch on the evil and the good.
Proverbs 15:3 (NKJV)

"Am I a God near at hand," says the Lord, "Can anyone hide himself in secret places, so I shall not see him?" says the LORD. "Do I not fill heaven and earth?" says the LORD.
Jeremiah 23:23-24 (NKJV)

God did this so that they would seek him and perhaps reach out for him and find him, though he is not far from any one of us.
Acts 17:27 (NIV)

The God of the Bible is omniscient or all-knowing:

His eyes are on the ways of mortals; he sees their every step.
Job 34:21 (NIV)

Nothing in all creation is hidden from God's sight. Everything is uncovered and laid bare before the eyes of him to whom we must give account.
Hebrews 4:13 (NIV)

God even knows what is in men's minds and hearts:

Then the Lord saw that the wickedness of man was great in the earth, and that every intent of the thoughts of his heart was only evil continually.
Genesis 6:5 (NKJV)

The Lord knows the thoughts of man, That they are futile.
Psalm 94:11 (NKJV)

"... and all the churches shall know that I am He who searches the minds and the hearts. And will give to each one of you according to your works."
From Revelation 2:23 (NKJV)

The God of the Bible cannot lie:

God is not a man, that He should lie.
Numbers 23:19 (NKJV)

In hope of eternal life which God, who cannot lie, promised before time began.
Titus 1:2 (NKJV)

The God of the Bible is merciful:

But the mercy of the LORD is from everlasting to everlasting on those who fear him...
Psalm 103:17 (NKJV)

Therefore be merciful, just as your Father [God] also is merciful.
Luke 6:36 (NKJV)

But to God who is rich in mercy...
From Ephesians 2:4 (NKJV)

The God of the Bible loves people:

And the God of love and peace will be with you.
From 2 Corinthians 13:11 (NKJV)

Whoever does not love does not know God, because God is love.
I John 4:8 (NIV)

And so we know and rely on the love God has for us. God is love.
From I John 4:16 (NIV)

Although in most ways God is not like His creation, since He is the Creator and we are merely His creatures, in some ways He is. For example, the Bible reveals God to have feelings—feelings of love, hate, anger, and even jealousy. God says in Genesis 1:26 *"Let us make man in our image, after our likeness."* A full, accurate exposition of all the implications of this verse is not only beyond the scope of this book, but beyond the expertise of this author. However, I can't help but think that God possessing at least some of the emotions that we, His human creatures have, may be what this verse in Genesis is at least partly referring to.

All of the above attributes of the one true God sound very clinical, but in truth, God is also a person. As such, God possesses feelings and gets angry with those who do not obey Him, especially those who should know better such as the Hebrews whom He led out of Egypt during the Exodus and to whom He revealed Himself so many times in so many powerful ways.

The Bible reveals that God has the capacity to hate. The Psalmist (Psalm 5:5) wrote that, *"You* [God] *hate all workers of iniquity."* The writer of Proverbs even lists some of the things God hates. Proverbs 6:16-19 reads:

These six things the Lord hates, Yes, seven that are an
abomination to him:
A proud look,
A lying tongue,
Hands that shed innocent blood,
A heart that devises wicked plans,
Feet that are swift in running to evil,
A false witness who speaks lies,
And one who sows discord among the brethren.
(NKJV)

The Bible also tells us that God gets jealous, usually as it relates to people to whom He has revealed Himself but reject Him for foreign gods that are really no Gods at all.

... for you shall worship no other god, for the Lord, whose name
is Jealous, is a jealous God.
Exodus 34:14 (NKJV)

But probably the greatest attribute of God, one which most of us can relate to, is that He loves people. And although on some level God loves all people, the Bible points out that He particularly loves and is pleased with those that believe, obey, and trust Him. But even though *"God so loved the world"* as the Bible says in John 3:16, it does not mean that He will let all people into heaven after they die. The reason is because He is perfect, holy, and cannot tolerate sin:

Your eyes are too pure to look on evil; you cannot tolerate
wrongdoing.

Habakkuk 1:13 (NIV)

Here we are before You, in our guilt [as a result of sin]*, though no one can stand before You because of this.*
Ezra 9:15 (NKJV)

Sin

The word "sin" is strictly associated with Christianity in this day and age and is anathema to many Americans. Non-Christians don't like it because it conveys the idea that there is something wrong with them, but only as they relate to the Christian God; so if one can avoid the Christian God, one can ignore the idea of sin. I once had a friend who used to say, "Why worry about something you can forget about entirely." That is exactly what many Americans would like to do with the idea of sin. I don't think this is an exaggeration and goes a long way to explain why so many Americans have a problem with the God of the Bible and Christianity in particular and are trying to get rid of both in America's consciousness.

Although the idea of sin originated with Judaism in the Old Testament, Jews are not evangelical like Christians and are not much interested in spreading their faith because God never really commanded them to. But Christianity is a different story; Christ commanded His followers to go into the entire world and spread His gospel that contains the message that people are sinners and in need of someone to save them from the penalty of their sins.

What sin is

Unger's Bible Dictionary says that the Hebrew word for sin means "a falling away from or missing the right path," then goes on to state:

> The underlying idea of sin is that of law and of a lawgiver. The lawgiver is God. Hence sin is everything in the disposition and purpose and conduct of God's moral creatures that is contrary to the expressed will of God. The sinfulness of sin lies in the fact that it is against God, even when the wrong we do is to

others or ourselves. The being and law of God are perfectly harmonious, "God is love." The sum of all the commandments likewise is love; sin thus in its nature is egotism, selfishness. Self is put in the place of God. Selfishness (not pure self-love, nor the exaggeration of it, but really in opposition to it) is at the bottom of all disobedience, and it becomes hostility to God when it comes into collision with his law.

We are seeing that last part being played out in America today: Many people's wants and desires are coming into conflict with God's commandments and instead of acknowledging their sin when confronted with it, they choose to insist on their own way and make war against the One who gave the commands.

From the above, we also see that God's laws are an expression to mankind of His nature, therefore to transgress against one or more of God's laws is the same as transgressing against God Himself.

How sin entered the world and human beings

Sin entered the world when Adam and Eve rejected God's command to them: *"And the Lord God commanded the man, 'You are free to eat from any tree in the garden; but you must not eat from the tree of the knowledge of good and evil, for when you eat from it you will certainly die"* (Genesis 2:16-17). At the point that Adam ate from the tree of the knowledge of good and evil, sin entered the world and mankind was in need of a savior, someone to save him and the people who would come after him from the spiritual death that was the result of sinning by breaking God's command. When Adam and Eve ate of the forbidden fruit they did not immediately die physically, so the command was primarily referring to spiritual death:

The soul who sins shall die.
Ezekiel 18:4 and 20 (NKJV)

After Adam and Eve's fall as a result of sinning, they were banished from the Garden of Eden and had to fend for themselves in the harsh outside world. And so it has since been for us as well.

The reader may think it is unfair that subsequent generations of people have suffered because of what the first man and woman did, but the truth is, all of us would have sinned like they did, sooner or later. Along with mankind's God-given ability to choose comes a propensity to choose what is not good for us. Too few seem to understand that choosing God's way instead of our own always leads to life and is always what is ultimately best for us. We live in God's world and His rules for it are designed to enable us to live in it successfully with at least a minimum amount of pain and sorrow.

God is made up of three persons

The Trinity or the idea that God is made up of three distinct personalities, but is still one God, has been problematic for many non-Christians as well as some Christians since the doctrine was formally accepted by the Church during the Council of Nicaea in the fourth century. One of the arguments against the doctrine is that the term Trinity is absent from the Bible. Although this is true, the concept, however, is not absent from the Old or New Testaments. The term "Trinity" came about when Biblical scholars from the early Christian Church tried to make sense of the fact that the Bible, New Testament and Old, clearly taught that there is only one God and that Jesus Christ revealed that this one God is made up of three persons, each with a different role in creation. Because of what Jesus revealed and taught, many passages in the Old Testament became more understandable, like Genesis 1:26 where God said, *"Let us make man in our image, after our likeness."*

So Christianity rightly teaches that the three persons that make up the Godhead or Triune God are: God the Father, God the Son, and God the Holy Spirit or Holy Ghost. *Unger's Bible Dictionary* correctly explains that,

> These three are joint partakers of the same nature and majesty of God. This doctrine is preeminently one of revelation. And

while it brings before us one of the great mysteries of revelation, and transcends the finite comprehension, it is essential to the understanding of the scriptures.

Another argument against the concept of the Trinity is that there is nothing in nature like it. To that I say—Thank God! Who wants a God that is just like His creation? If that were a reality, we all might be in even more trouble than we already are. It would mean that God may be no more equipped to run the universe than any of us.

Others might say of the idea of a Triune God is that it is proof that God suffers from Multiple Personality Disorder or Dissociative Identity Disorder, as it is called now, a condition "that... is characterized by a fragmentation, or splintering, of identity rather than by a proliferation, or growth, of separate identities."[3] Although the notion is intriguing, the definition hardly describes the God of the Bible. The New Testament reveals that God the Father and God the Son [Jesus Christ] were in constant communion and agreement with each other. Jesus says in John 5:19:

Very truly I tell you, the Son can do nothing by himself; he can do only what he sees his Father doing, because whatever the Father does the Son also does. (NIV)

Other clues in the Old Testament for a Triune God

The first verse that reveals this plurality of persons within the one God is the verse already mentioned in Genesis 1:26 when God said: *"Let us make man in our image, after our likeness."* But there are other scriptural clues as well. Genesis 3:22 states, *"And the Lord God said, 'Behold, the man is become as one of us.'"*[4] Genesis 11:7 reads, *"'...let us go down, and there confound their language.'"* The prophet Isaiah writes in Isaiah 6:8, *"And I heard the voice of the Lord, saying, 'Whom shall I send, and who will go for us?'"* Deuteronomy 6:4 further clarifies, *"Hear O Israel: The Lord our God, the Lord is one!"*

The God of Judaism

The God of Judaism is the God of the Bible, creation, and Christianity. And as such, all the attributes listed above describe the God of the Jewish or Hebrew people. The Bible's Old Testament has historically been God's divine revelation to the Jews.

Besides telling about creation, the Old Testament teaches about sin and contains God's commandments to mankind as a whole and to the Hebrew people specifically and contains much of their history up until the birth of Jesus Christ. Also contained within the Old Testament are prophecies about future events and especially those concerning the Jewish Messiah who would one day come to save not only believing Jews, once and for all from their sins, but the entire race of believing mankind as well.

The Old Testament is still relevant to both Jews and Christians today because of its history, universal commandments, principles, and wisdom, but it is also, in some ways, outdated, especially where it addresses how men and women are to deal with their sins and the salvation of their souls. The writer of the New Testament book of Hebrews explains:

God, who at various times and in different ways spoke in time
past to the fathers by the prophets, has in these last days spoken
to us by His Son, whom He has appointed heir of all things,
through whom also He made the worlds.
Hebrews 1:1-2 (NKJV)

This verse makes it clear that God no longer speaks universally to mankind through prophets like He did in the Old Testament. He now primarily reveals Himself through His Son, Jesus Christ, whose words are recorded in the New Testament.

Even though Judaism is a valid religion that represents the one true God, it has, since the death and resurrection of the Jewish Messiah, Jesus Christ, been replaced or "fulfilled" by Christianity and is now primarily a steppingstone for Jews and others to find Christ. There will be more about Jesus Christ and His unique importance to the world in chapter eight.

Other gods in America today

Considering how specific the Bible is about God, it is impossible to give much credence to the convoluted type of god or gods that the average non-Christian (and in some cases even individuals who claim to be Christian) has concocted in his or her mind. But considering that none of the other world religions have any objective proofs that they come from the one true God, none of them are really much different, and they too, are no more than the imagined inventions of mortal men.

The gods of Mormonism[5]

Mormonism is a polytheistic religion. That fact alone immediately puts it at odds with the God of Holy Scripture. The Bible teaches that there is one God (monotheism) and Mormonism teaches that there is more than one God (polytheism). In fact, Mormonism teaches that there are many gods and that individual Mormons have an opportunity to move up the spiritual ladder within Mormonism, and attain godhood for themselves one day and reign over their own respective planet.

Mormonism's founder, Joseph Smith Jr., whose questionable moral character is well documented, was born in Vermont, U.S.A. in 1805. He is reported to have been a "seer" or "peek stone" gazer and after he founded the Mormon Church, polygamist was added to his list of dubious credentials. Gazing into stones was something that Joe Smith allegedly practiced to help him find buried treasure, something that he apparently never found until, some might say, he wrote the Book of Mormon, first published in 1830. How the mental concoctions of a man like Joseph Smith could take hold and grow into a major world religion with so many seeming intelligent followers in America today is indeed an enigma.

In contradiction to the Bible, Mormonism teaches that it was a "council of the Gods" and not the single God, as the Bible reveals, that decided to create the world and the people in it.

Although the Bible teaches that God is pure spirit and that He is the Creator of the world and universe we live in, Mormonism teaches that God the Father of the Bible was once a mortal man of flesh and bone and that He eventually became a god by (apparently) following the Mormon gospel.

Although the Bible teaches that Adam is a mortal being created by God, Mormonism teaches that Adam is actually the god of the followers of Mormonism on earth—that he created the earth and once lived as a mortal on a planet like earth. This earth-god, according to Mormon theology, also does not appear to be omnipotent, omnipresent, or omniscient as is the God of Christianity and the Bible.[6]

None of this sounds much like the God that the Bible describes. So how can Mormonism and Christianity be representing the same God? They cannot.

The gods of the Jehovah's Witnesses[7]

Jehovah's Witnesses are also known as the Watch Tower Bible and Tract Society and the group's adherents are sometimes encountered handing out their pamphlets "The Watchtower" and "Awake" that promote their organization. The founder of this religion has a similar questionable past as that of Joseph Smith of Mormon fame.

The founder of the Watch Tower Bible and Tract Society, Charles Taze Russell, began his career as a spiritual leader in 1876 at around 24 years-of-age. At that time he was elected "pastor" of a Bible class he had been attending for six years in Pittsburgh, Pennsylvania. A possible reason for Russell's "congregation" to elect him pastor may have been because many within it liked the way he denounced major Christian doctrines at such a young age, perhaps causing them to think that he might make his mark on the world one day. And indeed Russell did. Wikipedia estimates total followers of Russell's organization in 2015 to be 8.2 million with 115,416 congregations worldwide. The "Society" also has billions of dollars in assets.

Despite the organization's ultimate success, a series of contemporary newspaper articles printed by The Brooklyn Daily Eagle around the time of the new religion's beginnings demonstrate Russell's questionable character.

After the "Eagle" printed a derogatory cartoon about Russell and the "Miracle Wheat" seed he and his group were selling at the time through its tract, "The Watch Tower," Russell and his budding organization brought a $100,000 libel suit against it. However, after the "miracle seed" was found by a U.S. Government analysis to be no better than any other wheat seed, the court vindicated the Eagle's depiction of Russell and he was forced to drop his lawsuit. Evidently the operators of the Eagle were so confident in the accuracy of their depiction of Russell that prior to going to court, the paper printed an article that reported, "The Eagle goes even further and declares that at the trial it will show that "Pastor" Russell's religious cult is nothing more than a money-making scheme."

After their success at exposing "Pastor Russell" in the Miracle Wheat scam, the Eagle went on to report more of Russell's character defects. The next being through another one of Pastor Russell's defamatory libel suits, one that again backfired on him. The recipient of this suit was a Reverend J. J. Ross, a real pastor of the James Street Baptist Church in Hamilton, Ontario. This suit was brought by Russell because the Reverend Ross wrote a pamphlet denouncing "Russell's theology and personal life." The pamphlet was titled: *"The Self-Styled 'Pastor' Charles T. Russell."* In it Reverend Ross reportedly exposed Russell's teachings, *"Studies in the Scriptures"* as "the destructive doctrines of one man who is neither a scholar nor a theologian" and his (Russell's) whole system as "anti-rational, anti-scientific, anti-Biblical, anti-Christian, and a deplorable perversion of the gospel of God's Dear Son." As if this wasn't enough, the Eagle went on to report that Rev. Ross added that Russell, "never attended the higher schools of learning; knows comparatively nothing of philosophy, systematic or historical theology, and is totally ignorant of the dead languages." This lawsuit backfired when Russell was unable to refute any of the allegations made by Rev. Ross in court, although he reportedly gave it the old college try by lying and perjuring himself under oath.

Anyone wishing to check the source material for this series of articles by the Eagle can find them in the Brooklyn Public Library system at: http://www.bklynlibrary.org.

Exposing a religion's founder as a fraud, if he or she has been proven to be one, is important because without any objective evidence or proof that their teachings are from the one true God, the reader has nothing else to go on but the character of the author of the doctrine.

Although the Watch Tower of the Jehovah's Witnesses deny or modify many orthodox Christian doctrines, it is what the organization teaches about God that I am most interested in and including here.

The Watch Tower's polytheistic teachings are also well documented. According to the Jehovah's Witnesses, there is one Jehovah, Almighty God, *and* there is a lesser god—His son, Jesus Christ. The Watch Tower's theology insists that Jesus Christ is a created being who is somehow, also a god. The Watch Tower's "bible," the *New World Translation*, contradicts the Judeo-Christian Bible and mistranslates John 1:1 that reads: *"In the beginning was the Word, and the Word was with God, and the Word was God."* The *New World Translation* adds the word *"a"* before the last *"God"* in the verse in an attempt to make the Word of God (Jesus Christ) to be less than Jehovah God. This is not only convoluted, but contradicts Christianity and Biblical theology as a whole because the God of the Bible has no beginning or end and any created creature cannot be God in the Biblical sense. This false teaching on the part of Jehovah's Witnesses makes the Watch Tower Bible and Tract Society a polytheistic religion and out of sync with the Bible's teachings concerning the one true God. The organization is also in error concerning many other orthodox New Testament teachings such as denying the Biblical teachings on hell and the all-sufficient atonement for sins made by Jesus Christ, among others. In conclusion, there is no way that the god or gods of The Watch Tower is or are the same God as revealed in the Bible and no one should entrust his or her eternal destiny to this group or it's teachings.

The god of Islam[8]

Who could have predicted the rise of Islam in America twenty years ago? It seems no other religion is fighting for respectability in the way Islam is in America and around the world today. But is Islam worth believing in any more so than anyone else's ideas about God apart from the Bible? Is Allah, the god of Islam, really one and the same as the God of the Bible as some assert?

Islam's founder is Muhammad ibn Abdallah ibn Abd al-Muttalib.[9] Muhammad was born in 570 AD in the city of Mecca in what is now Saudi Arabia. According to Robert Spencer in his book, *The Politically Incorrect Guide to Islam (and the Crusades),* Muhammad was a warrior by trade—busily engaged in raiding caravans, villages and towns, etc., throughout his adult life. After allegedly receiving revelations from Allah (The Arabic word for God[10]) in 610 AD, he added "prophet" to his resume although the added title didn't stop him from engaging in his life's profession. In fact, claiming to be a prophet of God seemed to add legitimacy and fervor to his widespread killing and war-waging. Indeed, Muhammad wasn't like the prophets one reads about in the Bible's Old Testament who were primarily oracles for God and mostly lived quiet, sanctified lives, occasionally working miracles.[11] No, Muhammad was a serial-style killer just like many of his followers of today who carry on his murderous tradition.

The Allah of Islam is represented in the Qur'an, the Muslim sacred book that Muhammad claimed was dictated to him by the angel Gabriel. The Qur'an reportedly contains Allah's 99 "most beautiful names." In this list Allah is described to be beneficent, forgiving, most gracious, merciful, and 95 other wonderful-sounding qualities. But although these 99 names for Allah, could be describing the God of the Bible, there is a dark side to the Islamic god that portrays him as a type of Jekyll and Hyde. On the one hand, Allah appears to be most compassionate and loving, but then, when he gives commands, it is often an exhortation to kill or subjugate anyone who does not believe in him.

Indeed, as Norman L. Geisler and Abdul Saleeb point out in their book, *Answering Islam, The Crescent in Light of the Cross,* "Muslims who take upon themselves to destroy their alleged enemies in the name of God can rightly claim to be following the commands of God in the Qur'an and imitating their prophet as their role model."

Consider these commands from Allah:

Fight those who believe not in God nor the Last Day nor hold that forbidden which hath been forbidden by God and his apostle nor acknowledge the Religion of Truth [Islam] *(even if they are) of the people of the Book* [Christians], *until they pay the Jizya* [poll tax] *with willing submission, and feel themselves subdued.*
Qur'an 9:29

...fight and slay the pagans [anyone who is not Muslim] *wherever ye find them, and seize them, beleaguer them, and lie in wait for them in every stratagem (of war)...*
Qur'an 9:5

Therefore, when ye meet the unbelievers, smite at their necks [meaning chop off their heads], *at length when ye have thoroughly subdued them.*
Qur'an 47:4

This command to wage war is called "jihad" by Muslims. Robert Spencer observes, "There are over a hundred verses in the Qur'an that exhort believers [Muslims] to wage jihad against unbelievers [non-Muslims]."

The jizya is a poll tax that is extracted from non-Muslims living in Muslim-controlled lands to co-exist with them and not be killed. As mentioned earlier, according to Islam, non-Muslims have three choices when confronting the followers of Islam: 1. Convert to Islam or, 2. Pay the heavy jizya tax to co-exist with them or, 3. Be killed outright, or if one is able, fight against them and risk being killed in the process.

Make no mistake, *this* is the same religion of "peace" that is falsely promoted by the politically-correct in America today.

Allah also teaches that there is a greater reward for his faithful followers who wage war against unbelievers than there is for those backslidden Muslims who do not fight and wage war but stay in the comfort and protection of their homes:

Not equal are those believers who sit (at home) and receive no hurt and those who strive and fight in the cause of God with their goods and their persons. God hath granted a grade higher to those who strive and fight with their goods and persons than those who sit (at home).
Qur'an 4:95

Some might assert that this is a call for *all* Muslims to wage jihad against all unbelievers, or at the very least, is a powerful incentive for the most devout of the religion to do so.

The God of the Bible does not forbid His people to befriend anyone on the basis of their race or religion, but Allah does:

O ye who believe. Take not the Jews and the Christians for your friends and protectors. They are but friends and protectors to each other. And he amongst you that turns to them (for friendship) is of them. Verily God guideth not a people unjust.
Qur'an 5:54

In contrast God tells the Israelites in the Bible:

And if a stranger sojourns with you in your land, you shall not mistreat him. But the stranger who dwells among you shall be to you as one born among you, and you shall love him as yourself; for you were strangers in the land of Egypt: I am the Lord your God.
Leviticus 19:33-34

Some say that the God of the Bible in the Old Testament commanded the same kind of warfare that is promoted by Allah in the Qur'an against unbelievers when He sent the Israelites to destroy many of the pagan nation/cities in the land of Canaan.[12]

It is true that God commanded Joshua, Moses' successor, to kill many of the inhabitants of Canaan. But it is not true that God made such a command because the Canaanites would not convert to Judaism or because they were not believers in the Hebrew God. God's reasons and motivation were totally different.

It is a fact of history that one of the languages spoken by the Canaanites was that of the Ammonites. The Ammonites had the distinction of worshipping the pagan god Molech that was, according to Unger, "honored by the sacrifice of children, in which they were caused to pass through or into the fire." To be clear—Ammonites burned their children to death by fire to appease or gain the favor of their pagan god. Since many if not all Canaanites spoke the same language as the Ammonites, it is reasonable to assume that they also adopted many of the Ammonite customs. But since we have modern archaeology, we don't have to rely only on reasonable assumptions. Excavations around present-day Palestine, or ancient Canaan, have shown that this was indeed the practice of the inhabitants of the land. Unger states in his book, *Archaeology and the Old Testament*,[13] that their (the Canaanites) "cultic practice was barbarous and thoroughly licentious" and included "sensuous nudity, orgiastic nature-worship, snake worship, and even child sacrifice." In *Unger's Bible Dictionary*, he says, "These Canaanite cults were utterly immoral, effete and corrupt, dangerously contaminating and thoroughly justifying the divine command to destroy their devotees."

Prior to the Israelites entering Canaan and knowing what they were going to be walking into, God commanded them, saying:

When you come into the land which the Lord your God is giving you, you shall not learn to follow the abominations of those nations.
Deuteronomy 18:9 (NKJV)

Therefore you shall keep My ordinance, so that you do not commit any of these abominable customs which were committed before you, and that you do not defile yourselves by them: I am the Lord your God.
Leviticus 18:30 (NKJV)

So we see that the Canaanites were not just kind, loving, guiltless people. They were totally depraved child killers and God did not want their depravity rubbing off on His people. His commanding the Israelites to utterly destroy them was totally justified and a benefit to humanity.

Although this type of action commanded by God is harsh and extreme, it is also unique and was only sanctioned during this one period of time. Whereas, Allah's commands concerning the killing and/or subjugation of people who do not believe in him is universal in Islam and applies to all unbelievers everywhere, for all time, or until the entire world is under the control of Islam.

Muhammad striking fear in the hearts of unbelievers

Although the Bible reveals that God had many prophets throughout the Old Testament, spanning several hundred years, it seems Allah used only Muhammad to be his mouthpiece, a relationship that supposedly lasted approximately 22 years or from 610 AD when Muhammad claimed to get his first revelation, to 632 AD when "the prophet" died.

The earliest biography of Muhammad, written around two hundred years after his death and later translated into English and published in 1955[14] recounts multiple times the prophet of Allah ordered the mass killings or assassinations of Jews and other "unbelievers." This is in stark contrast to most of the prophets of the Bible who primarily waited to be used by God to tell or warn one or more of His people of something or worked miracles to prove that they spoke and acted according to the wishes of the one true God as in the case of Elijah and Elisha.[15]

So as one can see, there is a stark contrast between the Muslim god Allah and the God of the Bible. Anyone who thinks the two are the same primarily because of the 99 "most beautiful names" only needs to read the Qur'an to realize that the commands and motives of the two personalities are as far apart as the East is from the West.

The gods or no gods of Buddhism

Unlike many religions, Buddhism or Zen, as it is sometimes called in America, does not say much about God.

Buddhism is based on teachings attributed to Siddhartha Gautama, commonly known as the Buddha (meaning "the awakened one"). Buddha is known by other names as well such as: Buddha Shakyamuni.

According to aboutbuddhism.org,[16] Buddha was born a royal prince in 624 BC in Lumbini that was in northern India and is now part of Nepal.

In opposition to the Bible that teaches that individual men and women live and die once,[17] Buddhism teaches reincarnation or, that we each live and die repeatedly through time, haplessly caught in an endless cycle called samsara (meaning "continuous flow" of birth, life, and death). Aboutbuddhism.org explains:

It is important to understand that as ordinary samsaric beings we do not choose our rebirth but are reborn solely in accordance with our karma. If good karma ripens we are reborn in a fortunate state, either as a human or a god, but if negative karma ripens we are reborn in a lower state, as an animal, a hungry ghost, or a hell being. It is as if we are blown to our future lives by the winds of our karma, sometimes ending up in higher rebirths, sometimes in lower rebirths. This uninterrupted cycle of death and rebirth without choice is called "cyclic existence", or "samsara" in Sanskrit. Samsara is like a Ferris wheel, sometimes taking us up into the three fortunate realms, sometimes down into the three lower realms. The driving force of the wheel of samsara is our contaminated actions motivated by delusions, and the hub of the wheel is self-grasping ignorance. For as long as we remain on this wheel we shall experience an unceasing cycle of suffering and dissatisfaction, and we shall have no opportunity to experience pure, lasting happiness. By practicing the Buddhist path to liberation and enlightenment, however, we can destroy self-grasping, thereby liberating ourself from the cycle of uncontrolled rebirth and attaining a state of perfect peace and freedom.

As one can see from the above, ordinary humans can become "gods" if the winds of karma blow beneficently in their direction. A life of trying to follow Buddhism will end with a lot of uncertainty as to where, what, or how one will end up—Not very comforting unless one likes to gamble with their eternal destiny. Also, in Buddhism, the concept of God is unlike that of the Bible and is closer to Mormon theology than Biblical theology—Unless one chooses to believe that Buddhism does not teach the concept of a Supreme Being because, according to Buddhist Studies on their web site's Question and Answer section,[18] when the question was asked, "Do Buddhist believe in a god?" the answer is "No, we do not." The site explains that there are several reasons for this: "The Buddha, like modern sociologists and psychologists, believed that religious ideas and especially the god idea have their origins in fear."

So whether there are any gods in Buddhism or not, its teachings, including reincarnation, are clearly not compatible with the Bible, its God, or Christianity and the two religions simply cannot be representing the same God.

The god of Scientology

To many readers The Church of Scientology may not seem like a religion in the traditional sense, but I include it briefly here primarily because it gets a fair amount of press in America today, although almost none of it good. For example, *Time Magazine,* in a headline, called Scientology: "The Thriving Cult of Greed and Power," with a subhead that reads: "Ruined lives. Lost fortunes. Federal crimes. Scientology poses as a religion but is really a ruthless global scam -- and aiming for the mainstream."[19]

Scientology is a cult phenomenon that has caught on in recent years primarily with people who either seem to be able to afford to belong to it or because it appears to attract celebrities and therefore carries a hip type of prestige in some social circles. According to comparative religions expert, John Weldon, "Scientology boasts over 700 centers in 65 countries and is one of the wealthiest of the new religions."[20]

The "Church" was founded in the 1950s by science fiction author Lafayette Ronald (L. Ron) Hubbard and has gained national recognition primarily because of many high-profile Hollywood celebrities that belong to it. According to the Christian Research Institute, "Although the church claims to be compatible with Christianity, the two belief structures—one rooted in science fiction, the other in soteriological [the doctrine of salvation) fact—are contradictory and cannot be harmonized."[21]

During his life, Hubbard did not write down any attributes for Scientology's god, so it is difficult to compare it with the God of the Bible or, as John Weldon explains:

> In the Church of Scientology the concept of God would appear to be panentheistic (believing that all finite entities are within, but not identical to, God), although monotheism could also be assumed. What the church refers to as "the Supreme Being" is purposely left undefined and not particularly relevant in Scientology theory or practice. It is variously implied to be, or referred to as, "Nature," "Infinity," "the Eighth Dynamic," "all Theta" (life), and so forth. Usually the individual Scientologist is free to interpret God in whatever manner he or she wishes.[22]

That last part would appeal to many people in America today who claim to believe in "a god," one that does not try to impose its will or rules on them. Perhaps that is the reasoning behind Hubbard's vagueness concerning his god.

According to Scientology's website, Scientology means "knowing how to know." And although many adherents of religion are concerned with the hereafter, or where one will go after their earthly bodies die, Scientology appears to be more concerned with the here and now and again, as such, is very nebulous regarding God.

In short, Scientology does not meet the Biblical standards for being a bonafide religion worthy to be entrusted with the words of the one true, living God.

Conclusion

As one can see, the god, gods, or religions prevalent in America today apart from Judaism and Christianity differ greatly in their concepts, attributes, and descriptions of God and do not in any way describe the same eternal, Almighty God as represented in the Bible. And if one is wrong about who or what God is and from what religion He is speaking, that person can be wrong about how to be reconciled with Him and ultimately be denied entry into heaven after death.

Chapter 5
How America is Making War on God

The Bible tells in Hebrews 1:1-2 that before Jesus Christ and his ministry, God revealed Himself to the world through Moses and the prophets, but in these last days, He has spoken through His Son. This line of demarcation between the prophets and Christ also delineates how many of God's Old Testament laws and commandments apply to people today.

Although there was a "vast legal system of [ancient] Israel," as Merrill F. Unger puts it, involving civil, criminal, judicial, constitutional, ceremonial, and moral laws, I will only be dealing with the last group in this chapter, which are generally considered to have universal application to mankind as a whole and to America today.

All God's laws and commandments of how people are to conduct themselves are contained in the Old Testament. Many of God's most important morals laws are contained in the Ten Commandments, also called the Decalogue. The Ten Commandments themselves are a short, concise set of laws that were written by God Himself on tablets of stone and given to Moses who in turn communicated them to the people of Israel. The Ten Commandments were only the first of many commandments that God revealed to Moses and were intended to immediately deal with issues that directly affected the Israeli people who, up until that time, had no written law. However, *all* God's moral laws are not listed in the Ten Commandments; there are many others listed in the books of Exodus, Leviticus, and Deuteronomy that warn the individual who is tempted to choose a more abnormal lifestyle or practice than what is addressed in the Ten Commandments.

Paraphrased, *Merriam-Webster Dictionary* defines a moral law as a general rule for right living or a group of rules conceived as universal and unchanging and having the sanction of God's will concerning mankind's moral nature, conscience, and sense of natural justice as revealed in human reason.

One way to differentiate between God's morals laws or commands and other types of laws in the Old Testament is whether or not the law contains a *"You shall not..."* or other similar phrase that denotes something one should not do before the specified command. Consider the following moral commands:[1]

"You shall have no other gods before me."
Exodus 20:3 and Deuteronomy 5:7

"You shall not make for yourself an image in the form of anything in heaven above or on the earth beneath or in the waters below. You shall not bow down to them or worship them; for I, the Lord your God, am a jealous God."
Exodus 20:4, and Deuteronomy 5:8

"You shall not misuse the name of the Lord your God, for the Lord will not hold anyone guiltless who misuses his name."
Exodus 20:7 and Deuteronomy 5:11

"You shall not murder."
Exodus 20:13 and Deuteronomy 5:17

"You shall not commit adultery."
Exodus 20:14 and Deuteronomy 5:18

"You shall not steal."
Exodus 20:15 and Deuteronomy 5:19

"You shall not give false testimony against your neighbor."
Exodus 20:16 and Deuteronomy 5:20

"You shall not covet your neighbor's house. You shall not covet your neighbor's wife, or his male or female servant, his ox or donkey, or anything that belongs to your neighbor."
Exodus 20:17 and Deuteronomy 5:21

The above are taken from the Ten Commandments, but the following are from other areas in the Mosaic law:

"Do not give any of your children to be sacrificed to Molek, for you must not profane the name of your God. I am the LORD."
Leviticus 18:21

"Do not have sexual relations with a man as one does with a woman; that is detestable."
Leviticus 18:22 (The New King James Version puts it this way: *"You shall not lie with a male as with a woman. It is an **abomination.**"* (author's emphasis))

The New King James also says in Leviticus 18:23: *"Nor shall you mate with any beast, to defile yourself with it. Nor shall a woman stand before a beast to mate with it. It is a perversion."*

There are many more "shall nots" in the Bible as well, such as a list in Leviticus 18:6-19 that forbids family members or related family members from having sexual relations with each other.

In addition to the shall nots, there are other sins listed in the Bible that God also considers abominations besides homosexuality. In the Old Testament, when God gave the people of Israel the land of the Canaanites, He did so because of the abominations that were being practiced by the Canaanites. The following is God speaking to the people of Israel:

"When you come into the land which the Lord your God is giving you, you shall not learn to follow the abominations of those nations. There shall not be found among you anyone who makes his son or daughter pass through fire [be sacrificed to a false god]*, or one who practices witchcraft, or a soothsayer, or one*

who interprets omens, or a sorcerer, or one who conjures spells,
or a medium, or a spiritist, or one who calls up the dead. For all
who do these things are an abomination to the Lord, and because
of these abominations the Lord your God drives them out from
before you."
Deuteronomy 18:9-12

God then warned the Israelites what would happen if they
ignored Him and did these things that He commanded them not
to do:

"Do not defile yourselves with any of these things; for by all
these the nations are defiled, which I am casting out before you.
For the land is defiled; therefore I visit the punishment of its
iniquity upon it, and the land vomits out its inhabitants. You shall
therefore keep My statutes and My judgments, and shall not
commit any of these abominations, either any of your own nation
or any stranger who sojourns among you (for all these
abominations the men of the land have done, who were before
you, and thus the land is defiled), lest the land vomit you out also
when you defile it, as it vomited out the nations that were before
you."
Leviticus 18: 24-28 (NKJV)

As you may remember from chapter one, Israel did indeed
violate God's commandments, over and over, and is the reason
why the Jewish people had not occupied their own land and were
dispersed, killed, and despised all over the world for nearly 2000
years.

This is all very instructive for America today if we will heed
God's warnings. If America's inhabitants continue in their
rebellion against God, His commands, and nature itself, by
continuing to practice all the above sins, God will cause the land
to get rid of the pestilence that dwells on it through plagues,
natural disasters, and foreign invaders, just like He did with Israel
when that nation sinned against Him and the land He had given
them.

The purpose of the law and commandments

While doing the research for this book I came across an excellent explanation of God's laws:

> Through the Law, God shows His interest in all aspects of man's life. Motivated by love, God instructs His people in the ways of Wisdom and knowledge. Since God's Law is given for our good, its regulations, both negative and positive are for our protection and prosperity. The Law is the revealed mind of God. His Will is His commandment, and His commandment is His Law. Thus, the Law is Divine since it comes from a Divine source. It is also perfect, as God Himself is perfect. God's Law supersedes all other laws. It transcends all other law, making it the Supreme Law of the entire earth. God's Law is also comprehensive and universal. It speaks to all areas of life, and to every living soul upon the face of the earth. The Law speaks of ceremonial truths, moral truths and dietary truths. It speaks of man's duty toward God, and man's duty toward his fellow man.[2]

The purpose of all God's laws and commands are not to keep good things from good people, just the opposite, they are rules for prosperous living so people can live long, healthy, and joyous lives in right relationships with their families and neighbors and avoid unnecessary death and warfare. At the same time, obeying God's laws makes one sanctified, or set apart for Him, to be in right standing with Him, to be worthy to be used in a holy endeavor for Him.

"For I command you today to love the LORD your God, to walk in obedience to him, and to keep his commands, decrees and laws; then you will live and increase, and the LORD your God will bless you in the land you are entering to possess."
Deuteronomy 30:16

Still another important reason for God's laws, is to show people that even the best of us cannot keep His laws all the time. This is because we all have an innate rebellious streak that the

New Testament calls a "sinful nature" that we inherited from Adam and Eve. As mentioned in an earlier chapter, the entire message of the Bible is to tell people how they can be rescued from this sin nature that separates us from God so that we can be reconciled to Him. In the Old Testament this was accomplished through Judaic ritual and animal sacrifices. Now, as revealed in the New Testament, it is through believing in God's Son who, by His death on the cross, is the perfect sacrifice for all sin, past present and future.

Paul informs us in Romans 7:7 that he *"would not have known sin except through the law."* So does this mean that had God not given us His law and commands that we would not be sinners? No, in fact, if God had not made His law known to us we would all be spiritually dead in our sins and without hope because we would not know that we have offended Almighty God and would be separated from Him for all eternity. It was God's love for us that caused Him to tell us that all was not right between us and Him and motivated Him to tell us why by making His just nature known to us through His laws and commandments.

Other purposes for God's laws

The first three commands of the Ten Commandments instruct us to have reverence for God. As God further relates in Deuteronomy 6:5, people are to: *"Love the LORD your God with all your heart and with all your soul and with all your strength."* Christ reiterated this in the New Testament when He was asked what the great commandment of the [Mosaic] law was and He replied:

"'Love the Lord your God with all your heart and with all your soul and with all your mind.' This is the first and greatest commandment. And the second is like it: 'Love your neighbor as yourself.' all the Law and the Prophets hang on these two commandments."
Matthew 22:37-40

Another purpose for God's laws is to keep evil at bay. When we break God's commands, we open the door for evil and the powers of darkness to enter into our lives that in turn causes us to be influenced to do even more evil. Breaking God's laws is an invitation to the devil. This is why the apostle Paul writes in the New Testament to not *"give place to the devil"* (Ephesians 4:27). In other words, don't give evil any handholds in your life so you can live long and be prosperous.

Still another purpose for God's laws is to ensure just and fair consequences for those involved when one or more of His laws are broken and to make sure that justice is meted out only to the lawbreaker and not to his or her family, city, or nation.

How God's laws apply today

Even though God's moral laws still apply to everyone today, they apply differently to people who believe and accept Him (also known as God's people) in comparison to those who willfully or ignorantly disobey and reject Him.

Before Jesus Christ, everyone in the world was under condemnation for breaking one or more of God's moral laws, not only the Israelites to whom they were given. This was and is still true because God made the world and the rules that govern it. Even though people who aren't Israelites, referred to as Gentiles in the Bible, may or may not be aware of God's written laws, the apostle Paul tells us in the New Testament that they essentially *are* aware of them because they are written in their consciences and as such, everyone in the world is without excuse when he or she breaks one or more of them:

... for when Gentiles, who do not have the law, by nature do the things contained in the law, these, although not having the [written] *law, are a law to themselves, who show the work of the law written in their hearts, their conscience also bearing witness, and between themselves their thoughts accusing or else excusing them.*
Romans 2:14-15 (NKJV)

Also:

For the invisible things of him from the creation of the world are clearly seen, being understood by the things that are made, even his eternal power and Godhead; so that they are without excuse.
Romans 1:20

But since Christ's resurrection, God's moral commands no longer hold the power of condemnation equally over all people.[3]

In an article written for the Christian Research Institute, Scott Klusendorf refers to New Testament professor, Douglas J. Moo, and his book, *Five Views on Law and Gospel*:

> Moo argues that the New Testament writers view the Mosaic law within this salvation-historical framework and relegate it to the period before Christ. Thus, "the entire Mosaic law comes to fulfillment in Christ, and this fulfillment means that the law is no longer a *direct and immediate* source of, or judge of, the conduct of God's people." Instead, Christian behavior is governed directly by the law of Christ.[4]

It may sound arrogant to the uniformed, but only true believers and followers of Jesus Christ are "God's people" in this post-resurrection era.[5] Although God's moral commands still *apply* to all people for how they should govern themselves, since the death and resurrection of Jesus Christ, only those who do not believe and trust in Him are under condemnation for breaking God's moral commands.

There is therefore now no condemnation to them which are in Christ Jesus, who walk not after the flesh, but after the Spirit.
Romans 8:1

As I explained in chapter four, breaking God's laws is called sin and the penalty for sin is eternal separation from God. However—Belief and trust in Jesus Christ for the penalty of one's sins is the only way to be rescued from the negative effects of breaking God's moral commands. This is why nonbelievers in the Bible's God and Jesus Christ in America today are not only still under the moral laws of God but will also be judged by them unless they repent of their lawlessness and trust in Christ. It is important to understand that Jesus did not do away with the law (Matthew 5:17-18), but instead gave it its full meaning which is to *"Love the Lord your God with all your heart and with all your soul and with all your mind"* and *"Love your neighbor as yourself"* (Matthew 22:37-39) so that people can live a truly abundant life as the law was intended to accomplish all along (John 10:10). Hank Hanegraaff from the Christian Research Institute writes:

> The apostle Paul explains the symbolism of the law has been fulfilled in Christ (Galatians 3:13-14). In his letter to the Colossian Christians, Paul underscores the Christian's freedom from adherence to Sabbath laws by pointing out that "these are a shadow of the things that were to come; the reality, however, is found in Christ" (Colossians 2:17).[6]

So we see that Jesus Christ brought not only fulfillment, but deeper meaning to the law. For example, Jesus says in Matthew 5:27-28: *"You have heard that it was said to those of old 'You shall not commit adultery'. But I say to you that whoever looks at a woman to lust for her has already committed adultery with her in his heart."* This is one of the ways that trusting in and following Christ fulfills the intent and aim of the Mosaic Law and Commandments; instead of worrying about keeping the letter of the law, the follower of Jesus Christ seeks to be pleasing to God and allows not only what he knows about God's laws, but also his conscience, to be his guide, enabling him to both please and obey God at the same time.

How Americans are breaking God's commandments

At one time in America, God's commandments were considered the highest laws of the land. In fact, America's founders knew that their new government could only work and survive the test of time if people self-governed themselves by willingly following God's laws as written in the Bible along with the laws of conscience He has written on people's hearts and minds. But sadly, over the decades, many have fallen far from the intents and hopes of America's founding generation.

You, the reader, may be someone who truly wonders how America is breaking so many of God's commandments today. To illustrate how this is being done, I will take selectively from the above list of commands. For example:

God commands, *"You shall have no other gods before me."*

Although most Americans may not literally believe in false pagan gods as the ancients did and as people still do in some cultures today, many Americans *do* believe in a false god they have concocted in their own mind as discussed in the last chapter. Many also believe in a Godless system such as evolution that has taken the place of God in their thinking. As explained earlier, whatever this made-up god is, it never requires anything from its "follower" nor does it forbid anything that the "adherent" wants to do which is sometimes something that has been forbidden by the true God of Creation. The purpose of this first command is to show that the God of the Bible should be the most important person or thing in each of our lives and that He alone should be looked to and thanked for daily provision and all the good things that come our way in life. This is why the creeping evil of socialism is so bad for America, because many government leaders want to condition people to look to them for their sustenance and prosperity instead of to God. This kind of attempted usurpation of power was the primary reason that America's founding generation wanted to break away from Great Britain in 1776, because many saw the English king and his rule over them as an attempt to take the place of God in their lives.

God commands, *"You shall not make for yourself an image in the form of anything in heaven above or on the earth beneath or in the waters below. You shall not bow down to them or worship them; for I, the Lord your God, am a jealous God."*

Some Bible translations say *"graven image"* or *"carved image"* instead of just *"image."* This image, also called an idol in the Bible, refers to the false gods that many religious people of old made from wood, stone, or metal, and worshipped in place of the one true God. One example is the golden calf mentioned earlier that was made by the Hebrews in the desert while Moses was on Mount Sinai getting the Ten Commandments from God. Although not many Americans deliberately worship graven images today, they do have all kinds of other man-made things that have taken the place of God in their lives: government, homes, cars, hobbies, even entertainment from television, sports, and the movies. Many folks are fixated on sports figures, music celebrities, TV and movie personalities and give them more time and thought than they do their Creator.

God commands, *"You shall not misuse the name of the Lord your God, for the Lord will not hold anyone guiltless who misuses his name."*

Too many people living in modern America think nothing of using God's name as an expletive in their everyday speech. Movies and TV are particularly bad. How can God look favorably upon America when His holy name is now not much more than a curse word to so many Americans? It must grieve God greatly to hear His name so thoughtlessly misused. However, God is not a hapless victim, He is the Creator and Supreme Governor of the universe, and if His creation offends Him as it did in the days of Noah, He will destroy the evil doers that so callously and with malicious intent slander His holy name.

God commands, *"You shall not murder."*

This commandment is mistranslated in Bible versions such as the King James Version where the word "kill" is incorrectly used instead of "murder" as it is here in the NIV. Even though it is permissible and justified to take a human life in such cases as in war and as the penalty for committing a capital offense such as murder, it is not permissible to take another human being's life for no reason or one that is frivolous or unjust. Murder would seem to be an open and shut case in America, but it isn't anymore. On the one hand, most Americans are opposed to one human being killing another as in the case of one adult murdering another, or even a child killing another child, but too many Americans have little or no problem with the taking of an innocent human child's life before he or she is born. This is the great evil of our day; and it is just as bad as any of the atrocities that went on in Nazi Germany during World War II. God will hold us as a people accountable for this infanticide that is taking place right under our noses.

Another way America is ignoring this commandment is by not giving it the same seriousness that God has for it. God's penalty for committing murder is that the perpetrator is to be put to death.[7] However, even though the homicide rate is extremely high in America today, numbering in the thousands each year, very few perpetrators are put to death for the crime. In fact, one can get and serve a much longer prison sentence for committing a much lesser crime in modern America. And more recently, as a result of prison overcrowding or for evil political reasons, murderers are being let out of prisons and back onto the streets to kill again by corrupt American authorities. Because we don't mete out God's just punishment for murder anymore, homicide rates are rampant as a result and there is no longer much justice in America. For a just God, this is an intolerable situation. The Bible says:

"Because the sentence against an evil work is not executed speedily, therefore the heart of the sons of men is fully set in them to do evil."
Ecclesiastes 8:11 (NKJV)

God commands, *"You shall not commit adultery."*

To illustrate how far America has fallen, people caught in adulterous situations in Old Testament times were to be put to death, that is how serious God considered marital unfaithfulness. But in present day America, adultery isn't even considered a crime anymore, let alone a capital offense. Marital infidelity is really not that big of a deal nowadays, especially if one has simply "fallen out of love" with their spouse or for any other even less-justifiable reason. With no negative social stigma and no harsh consequences for adultery, the American family has been devastated, and in the wake of the devastation, all manner of other crimes and problems have risen to epidemic proportions. For example, many children from divorced families have all kinds of psychological problems stemming from growing up without the mentoring of a father or mother. These children from broken homes often turn to drugs, crime and worse to try to fill the void of a missing parent in their lives. This is particularly a problem in minority societies where kids from single parent households often join gangs to get that feeling of family. This is exactly what one former Hispanic gang member told me while he was serving out a term in a California Youth Authority that incarcerates juveniles for crimes.

A study done in 2011 dealing with the children of divorced parents found that they were two to three times more likely to have suicidal thoughts when compared to people from stable or intact families, even into adulthood.[8] This rate must be similar or higher for people whose parents weren't married at all. CNSNews.com reported that, according to a survey produced by a conservative advocacy group, "Only 45 percent of American children have spent their childhood in an intact family."[9]

Another problem related to adultery in America today is fornication, a word that has almost fallen out of use. Otherwise known as "sleeping around" before or in place of marriage, fornication is another part of the moral sexual breakdown that is so prevalent in modern day America. Having sex with anyone and everyone, with no commitment required, is accepted as the norm today and promoted in books, the media, music, movies, TV, and elsewhere. Although fornication is not mentioned by name in the Old Testament,[10] the practice is definitely addressed:

"If a man finds a young woman who is a virgin, who is not betrothed, and seizes her and lies with her, and they are found out, then the man shall give to the young woman's father fifty shekels of silver, and she shall be his wife because he has humbled her, he shall not be permitted to divorce her all his days."
Deuteronomy 22:28-29 (NKJV)[11]

One reason wedlock after premarital sex is mandated by God is so the offspring of such a relationship or "one night stand" won't have to suffer the negative ramifications of a missing parent or broken home as explained above.

Sexual promiscuity is one of the primary reasons for the disintegration of the American family that in turn is one of the main reasons for the breakdown of America's moral fabric as a nation.

All this attests to the urgency and necessity of going back to observing and adhering to God's wise laws and commands.

God commands, *"You shall not covet your neighbor's house. You shall not covet your neighbor's wife, or his male or female servant, his ox or donkey, or anything that belongs to your neighbor."*

"Going after the American Dream" and "Keeping up with the Joneses" are two American idioms that are nearly the sole endeavor for many middle and upper class Americans today. The two phrases describe all too well the quest to essentially have what one's neighbor has. These are also the unspoken mottos of participants in the Yuppie movement that is thought to have begun in the early 1980s. Yuppyism is still prevalent in today's society where young, college-educated adults want to make a lot of money and have, as quickly as possible, all the things their parents and others have, things that used to take a lifetime to acquire. For many living in America, this goal is considered virtuous and tantamount to the purpose of life itself. Unfortunately for those caught up in this rat race, it isn't, but instead, is a trap and a delusion. Those buying into this "acquisition of things" have also become highly narcissistic which has led to them virtually ignoring anything that does not directly affect "them" and is consequentially not only leading to the destruction of their own souls, but the overall downfall of America as well.

God commands, *"Do not give any of your children to be sacrificed to Molek, for you must not profane the name of your God."*

Most people in America today would say that we don't sacrifice to idols or false gods anymore like they did in ancient or primitive cultures; we're too civilized now. Really? Then why have Americans, as of 2015, killed nearly 60 million of their unborn children since 1973?

In ancient times, people sacrificed their children to false gods in order to appease them or gain their favor so the personal life of the devotee could be easier or more fruitful.

Has anything really changed today since most women who abort their babies do so for primarily convenience sake? Thefreedictionary.com defines "convenience" as "the quality of being suitable to one's comfort, purposes, or needs." Is convenience really a necessity that warrants killing one's own child?

In the Old Testament story of when Cain murdered his brother Abel, God told Cain that his brother's blood cried out to Him (God) from the ground (Genesis 4:10). If it was for justice that Abel cried out to God after he was unjustly killed, it is unimaginable the cries for justice that rise up to God today from the millions of murdered human babies that have been sacrificed to the god of convenience in modern day America.

God commands, *"You shall not lie with a male as with a woman. It is an abomination."*

The homosexual rights movement and its encroachment upon traditional values is one of the biggest and most egregious problems America faces and its widespread acceptance could alone warrant God's judgment upon our nation. Ruth Bell Graham, the late wife of the twentieth century's greatest evangelist, Billy Graham, is reported to have said that "If God doesn't punish America, He'll have to apologize to Sodom and Gomorrah."[12] Apparently people have forgotten the seriousness of participating in homosexuality which was the vice of the inhabitants of Sodom and Gomorrah and the other five "cities of the plain" that God judged and destroyed with "fire and brimstone" as discussed in some detail in chapter two.

Although many homosexuals claim that they were born with the proclivity to be attracted to the same sex, clinical evidence does not support this assertion. Donald F. Calbreath PhD, an associate professor emeritus of chemistry, addressed the latest evidence that homosexuality is hard-wired into the human psyche via genes:

> The pressure to accept homosexual behavior is growing daily. A major argument for this acceptance is the belief that homosexuality is 'inborn.' Two major areas of research often put forth to support this position deal with genetics and brain structure. The search for a gene associated with homosexuality has not shown any reproducible findings. Studies of twins did not prove to support the idea of a genetic component to homosexuality. The contribution of genetics to this behavior appears to be minimal. Neuroscientist Simon LeVay argued in 1991 that there was a specific component of the hypothalamus that differed in size between homosexual and heterosexual men, although his research has never been replicated. More recent studies of different components of the brain show differences that might have some statistical significance, but also demonstrate a great deal of overlap between heterosexual and homosexual males. Reparative therapy (or "sexual

reorientation therapy") has been shown to be somewhat effective in changing the homosexual orientation, but is strongly opposed by most of the mental health community and by gay activists. Validation of a scientific theory requires that other researchers find the same data when performing experiments. The lack of reproducibility in biological studies on homosexuality has been a major hindrance to our understanding of this disorder. Recent research in brain plasticity suggests that brain changes could be the result of experiences and environmental input. These data also have implications for new approaches to reorientation therapy. Biological processes may *influence* behavior, but do not *determine* it.[13]

Most researchers look for physical evidence for people to be predisposed toward homosexual behavior and same-sex gender preference, but Merrill F. Unger thought the problem was more a spiritual issue and that the powers of darkness that are opposed to God can be responsible for sexual perversions such as homosexuality.[14] More about how evil and the powers of darkness influence people will be discussed in the next chapter.

Like all of God's laws, forbidding homosexuality is for the purpose of a longer and healthier life. The Christian Research Institute reports:

Furthermore, we would do well to recognize that the God of the Bible does not condemn homosexuality in an arbitrary and capricious fashion. Rather he carefully defines the borders of human sexuality so that our joy may be complete. It does not require an advanced degree in physiology to appreciate the fact that the human body is not designed for homosexual relationships. Spurious slogans and sound bites do not change the scientific reality that homosexual relationships are devastating not only from a psychological but also from a physiological perspective.[15]

God commands, *"There shall not be found among you... one who practices witchcraft, or a soothsayer, or one who interprets*

*omens, or a sorcerer, or one who conjures spells, or a medium,
or a spiritist, or one who calls up the dead."*

I make a special point to talk about this commandment
because the breaking of it is so widespread in America today and
so dangerous. All these practices are gateways to the occult and
are used by the powers of darkness to infiltrate people's lives for
evil purposes. America is addicted to evil in all its forms. Many
are fascinated by it and participate by consulting psychics,
mediums, and astrologers to watching it practiced in movies such
as the *Harry Potter* series of films and on television through
shows such as *Ghost Whisperer* and *Crossing Over with John
Edward*. This fascination is a key reason why there is so much
widespread evil in today's America.

Making a habit of willfully breaking God's laws

The danger of breaking God's laws with regular impunity
such as is being done in America today by so many is that the
practice can lead to God abandoning the nation and the sinner
forever. The apostle Paul warns:

*And even as they did not like to retain God in their knowledge,
God gave them over to a reprobate mind, to do those things
which are not convenient.*
Romans 1:28 (KJV)

Occasionally we hear of someone who is suspected of having
a "seared conscience." This kind of label is usually reserved for
someone who appears to be so incorrigible that he or she is
beyond hope of redemption or of ever straightening out his or her
life. This is a clear and present danger for anyone who knowingly
and repeatedly, and without remorse, breaks God's moral
commandments. This kind of open rebellion against God that
goes on until the perpetrator's death will lead to his or her eternal
damnation and separation from God and heaven itself, forever.

Conclusion

Genesis chapters 18 and 19 recount the story of God destroying Sodom and Gomorrah along with the other five cities of the plain. After not even ten righteous people could be found living in the combined cities, God decided they had to go. But because He told Abraham that He would not destroy the righteous with the wicked, He sent two angels to get Lot and his small family of three out of Sodom. Genesis 19:13 records what the angels told Lot: *"For we will destroy this place, because the outcry against them* [the 5 cities of the plain] *has grown great before the face of the Lord, and the Lord has sent us to destroy them."*

The Bible does not say who was making the outcry to God against Sodom and Gomorrah and the other cities of the plain. Besides the sins stated in the Bible that included homosexuality and neglecting the poor, the people living in those cities were probably involved in sacrificing to false gods as were many of the pagan nation-cities of that time. Also perhaps, the people of the cities of the plain were a brutal race like the later Assyrians of Nineveh fame and the victims of those cities' evil practices were crying out to God for vengeance. Whatever it was, we do not know, but we *do* know that the combined sins were grievous enough for God to be compelled to wipe them off the face of the earth.

America too has fallen a long way, especially since World War II when God used it to save the world from tyranny. But now, America's leaders are playing the tyrant and have left in their wake of corruption thousands of victims around the world from its unjust foreign wars and policies. We can only guess who is crying out to God for vengeance against America for the atrocities it has caused as a result of its people abandoning the very laws and commands of God that it was founded upon.

Chapter 6
The Invisible War

In many ways, this is the most important chapter of this book because it tells about schemes and plots that are going on behind the scenes in America and the world that only a relative few are aware of but are crucial to understanding the irrational conduct of an increasing number of people in America today.

Day after day in America, pundits observe and report on murders, suicides, social unrest, the teetering economy, high unemployment, wars, terrorism, unholy alliances, manmade and natural threats to the nation, etc., without ever speculating about the root causes or source of all the mayhem and nonsensical behavior. It's as if everyone is so used to the pandemonium they never give it a second thought or just assume all the upheaval and uncertainty is only a result of human flaws and weaknesses such as: greed, envy, jealousy, stupidity, power-plays, and the like.

Even when our top leaders, who live in America along with the rest of us, make deliberate policy choices that can ultimately result in America's demise such as reducing our conventional and nuclear military arsenals and at the same time enabling our sworn enemies like Iran to build a nuclear weapon, only a relative few question the ludicrous actions. Indeed, few seem to fathom that there might be an underlying cause or prime mover for all this widespread and almost universal chaos as well as the illogical, self-destructive decision-making.

For me, when things make no earthly rational sense, I look for an otherworld or extraterrestrial explanation. But by extra-terrestrial, I don't mean from another world or galaxy, I mean from another dimension—the spiritual realm.

Because of my Christian worldview, I understand that there is another theater of war raging in the world against God alongside the physical one being waged in America—an unseen war. Chip Ingram in his book, *The Invisible War*, puts it this way:

> Not only is there an invisible world, that world is in the midst of an invisible conflict... [it] is essential for us to understand: *we are involved in an invisible war, a cosmic conflict that has eternal implications.* It is real, it is serious, and it is ultimate in its consequences.[1]

This war is ancient and began before Adam and Eve were in the Garden of Eden. It is the classic "good against evil" that has been written about in countless stories that have a hero and a villain. This struggle has been chronicled in books such as Joseph Campbell's classic, *The Hero With A Thousand Faces*.

But what is evil exactly?

Succinctly put, evil is doing anything that God says not to do. *Unger's Bible Dictionary* says evil is "the comprehensive term under which are included all disturbances of the divinely appointed harmony of the universe." Evil interrupts good and, in short—good builds and evil destroys. Evil is the opposite or antithesis of good and since there is no in-between or other, third state regarding good and evil, to not do good is, by default, to do evil. Jesus Christ, the source of all truth, said, *"He who is not with Me is against Me, and he who does not gather with Me scatters abroad"* (Matthew 12:30). Here Jesus is saying that if you are not for Him, you are against Him, even if you are not actively against Him, or are even passive toward Him. By not being with Him, you fall into evil's camp and are automatically, by default, part of the evil world system that is intrinsically against God and Jesus Christ.[2]

The Bible reveals that this invisible war of good verses evil originated with a single being that we know as Satan and who is the embodiment of evil and seeks not only to destroy the good that God has created in the world, but His purposes as well.

*We know that… the whole world is under the control of the evil
one.*
From 1 John 5:19 (NIV)

*But even if our gospel is veiled, it is veiled to those who are
perishing, whose minds the god of this age has blinded, who do
not believe, lest the light of the gospel of the glory of Christ, who
is the image of God, should shine on them.*
II Corinthians 4:3-4 (NKJV)

Of course, many in America today will object to the idea of
the devil, Satan, or evil originating with and emanating from an
individual, but the Bible talks much about Satan and in specific,
certain terms.

Another reason many resist the concept of evil or a source of
evil that predates mankind is because if there is an ancient being
from which evil emanates and is promoted, then it is logical to
presume that there is an ancient or eternal source from which
good emanates—in other words, God. And for an ever-increasing
number of people in America today, belief in an eternal, all-
powerful God is simply not an option.

Satan and the beginning of the war against God

The Bible reveals that Satan was quite possibly God's greatest
created spiritual being. We know from Ezekiel 28:12-19 and
Isaiah chapter 14 that he was the greatest of God's angelic
creation. The prophet Ezekiel records:

*12 "Son of man, take up a lament concerning the king of Tyre and
say to him: 'This is what the Sovereign Lord says:' 'You were the
seal of perfection, full of wisdom and perfect in beauty.*
*13 You were in Eden, the garden of God; every precious stone
adorned you: carnelian, chrysolite and emerald, topaz, onyx and
jasper, lapis lazuli, turquoise and beryl. Your settings and
mountings were made of gold; on the day you were created they
were prepared.*

14 You were anointed as a guardian cherub, for so I ordained you. You were on the holy mount of God; you walked among the fiery stones.
15 You were blameless in your ways from the day you were created till wickedness was found in you.
16 Through your widespread trade you were filled with violence, and you sinned. So I drove you in disgrace from the mount of God, and I expelled you, guardian cherub, from among the fiery stones.
17 Your heart became proud on account of your beauty, and you corrupted your wisdom because of your splendor. So I threw you to the earth; I made a spectacle of you before kings.
18 By your many sins and dishonest trade you have desecrated your sanctuaries. So I made a fire come out from you, and it consumed you, and I reduced you to ashes on the ground in the sight of all who were watching.
19 All the nations who knew you are appalled at you; you have come to a horrible end and will be no more.'"

Bible scholars believe that since the king of Tyre in the above passage has no other connection in Scripture other than a heavenly one ("holy mount of God"), that he is a metaphor for Satan. Satan is also referred to here as a "guardian cherub." *Unger's Bible Dictionary* explains: "The cherubim (plural for cherub) seem to be actual beings from the angelic order." From the last part of verse 17 to the end of the passage is Satan's future and ultimate end that has yet to transpire.

It also must be emphasized here, as recorded in verse 15 of the above passage, that God created Satan as a perfect or "blameless" being, meaning he possessed no sin or rebellion in his heart at the time of his creation. Satan was also created with a free will, evidenced by the fact that, at some point in heaven, he chose to rebel against God and thus started a war against Him that is still raging today and will rage and even intensify until God finally does away with Satan and evil forever.

Revelation 12:7-9 gives more information about the beginning of this war against God:

7 And war broke out in heaven: Michael[3] and his angels fought against the dragon; and the dragon and his angels fought,
8 but they did not prevail, nor was a place found for them in heaven any longer.
9 So the great dragon was cast out, that serpent of old, called the Devil and Satan, who deceives the whole world; he was cast to earth, and his angels were cast out with him.

The "dragon" is another metaphor for Satan and after he was cast out of heaven and down to earth, the Scriptures reveal that he continuously wanders "to and fro" on it, now seeking humans he can manipulate, harass, lead astray, or even kill (Job 1:7 and I Peter 5:8).

In the passage below from Isaiah 14:11-15, the king of Babylon is also believed, by Biblical scholars, to be another picture of Satan. These verses talk about Satan after he was cast out of heaven and are more specific in regards to the reason for his expulsion:

11 All your pomp has been brought down to the grave, along with the noise of your harps; maggots are spread out beneath you and worms cover you.
12 How you have fallen from heaven, morning star [Lucifer], *son of the dawn! You have been cast down to the earth, you who once laid low the nations!*
13 You said in your heart, "I will ascend to the heavens; I will raise my throne above the stars [angels] *of God; I will sit enthroned on the mount of assembly, on the utmost heights of Mount Zaphon* [God's Holy Throne].
14 I will ascend above the tops of the clouds; I will make myself like the Most High [God]. *"*
15 But you are brought down to the realm of the dead, to the depths of the pit.

As you can see from all the "I"s in Satan's declaration in verses 13 and 14, he has quite an ego. Verse 14 records Satan's primary sin or trespass: *"I will make myself **like** the Most High."*

Even though Satan had such a lofty opinion of himself, and probably still does, he must have known he could not actually be *just like* the Most High in every way, since God is the Creator of all things, including Satan who is merely a creature, so there must have been another way Satan thought he could be like God.

It is reasonable to assume that when Satan said he wanted to be like the Most High, he was referring to his desire to be worshipped as the Most High. It seems Satan thought he could somehow supplant God and so be worshipped as Him by the rest of God's created beings which must have included the angels who were lower in rank than himself. Such is Satan's delusion and extreme arrogance.

It is noteworthy that the Bible reveals that Satan and his demons look to be worshipped in Scripture every chance they get, albeit through falsehoods and vicariously by sacrifices made to manmade idols. When Satan tempted Jesus in the wilderness, he told Christ that he would give Him kingdoms, riches, and power if He would worship him:

And he [Satan] *said to Him* [Jesus]*, "All these things I will give You if You will fall down and worship me."*
Matthew 4:9 (NKJV)

The Bible makes it clear that idol worship is no more than demon worship:

They provoked Him [God] *to jealousy with foreign gods: With abominations they provoked Him to anger. They sacrificed to demons, not to God...*
From Deuteronomy 32:16-17 (NKJV)[4]

But I say that the things which the Gentiles sacrifice, they sacrifice to demons and not to God.
I Corinthians 10:20 (NKJV)

Even the individual demons that rebelled along with Satan desire to be worshipped like God:

But the rest of mankind, who were not killed by theses plagues did not repent of the work of their hands, that they should not worship demons, and idols of gold, silver, brass, stone, and wood, which can neither see, nor hear, nor walk.
Revelation 9:20 (NKJV)

Let no one defraud you of your reward, taking delight in false humility and worship of angels...
From Colossians 2:18 (NKJV)

It is revealing too that in the ancient polytheistic religions of Rome, Greece, Egypt, and even Hinduism today, there are literally thousands of gods or a god over every conceivable aspect of life—myriad opportunities for demons to be worshipped.

Satan corrupts Adam and Eve

The Bible does not reveal how long Satan was on the earth before God created Adam; all it tells is that he was already in the Garden of Eden to tempt Eve probably not long after she was created by God from Adam's rib. The idea that the serpent, another metaphor for Satan, tempted Eve relatively soon after she and Adam were together in the garden is hinted at in Scripture by the fact it was only they who were expelled from Eden after disobeying God and not any of their later offspring (Genesis 3:23-24), because in the next verse after Genesis 3:24, in Genesis 4:1, Adam and Eve are out of Eden and Eve is shown having conceived and bearing their first child, Cain.

The story of Adam and Eve is important because it explains how Satan is the primary reason that sin and death entered the world. Could it have happened another way? Possibly, but it didn't. Had Satan or any other fallen angels not been in the Garden of Eden to tempt Adam or Eve with reasons to disobey God and thus inject sin into the world, perhaps mankind's earthly saga would have been far different than it has been down through the ages. Later in this chapter I will discuss how God knew all this would happen (or else why would he have cast Satan and his demons to earth if he knew He would one day start the human race there) but did it anyway.

Mankind was not meant to die

It also must be understood that when God created Adam, He never intended for him to die, physically or spiritually. From the Biblical text, it seems that God originally created Adam's physical body to last forever. This is inferred by Genesis 2:16-17 where God says to Adam: *"And the Lord God commanded the man, saying, 'Of every tree of the garden you may freely eat; but of the tree of the knowledge of good and evil you shall not eat, for in the day that you eat of it you shall surely die'."* It is reasonable to assume this means that had Adam or Eve not disobeyed God, neither would have died physically or spiritually and would not have passed that condition on to the entire human race.

It is interesting to note that today, even with modern medicine and scientific methods, doctors don't understand why people grow old and die since the human body appears to have been designed to continually regenerate and heal itself. Many recognize that something has been programmed into it to cause it to run down and eventually expire.

The dominion of the earth changes hands

When Adam and Eve heeded Satan, disobeyed God, then ate of the tree of the knowledge of good and evil, the dominion that God had given to Adam over the whole earth (Genesis 1:28) passed from Adam to Satan. The power that subsequent generations of mankind were intended by God to have over the earth and all that is in it also passed to Satan. Satan has used this power of dominion, down through the ages and even now in America, to include all the world's people as combatants in his continuing and all-encompassing war against God.

Biblical theologian Lewis Sperry Chafer in his book, *Satan*,[5] does an excellent job explaining Satan's role in the world today as well as his methods of deception and I will be quoting from it often in this chapter. Chafer also believes that Satan is not presently in hell and that his current abode is the earth and the air around it.[6]

AKA Satan

The name Satan means adversary and refers to his opposition to both God and mankind. Like God and Jesus Christ, Satan is referred to in the Bible by many different names and titles. As stated in a previous chapter, some of these references to Satan are descriptive of his tactics and character:

An angel of light – II Cor. 11:14 (NKJV)
A thief – John 10:10 (NKJV)
The evil one – I John 5:19 (NIV)
The enemy – Matthew 13:39 (NIV)
The wicked one – Matthew 13:19 (NKJV)
The destroyer – I Corinthians 10:10 (NKJV)
The father of lies – John 8:44 (NIV)
The deceiver – Revelation 20:10 (NIV)
The ruler and god of this world – John 12:31, 14:30 (NKJV)
The accuser of the brethren – Revelation 12:10 (NKJV)
A tempter of men – I Thessalonians 3:5 (NIV)
A murderer – John 8:44 (NKJV)
A great red dragon – Revelation 12:3 and 20:2 (NIV)
The prince and power of the air[7] – Ephesians 2:2 (NKJV)

Jesus said of Satan that he comes "to steal, and to kill, and to destroy" (John 10:10). Satan is also referred to as the devil (Matthew 4:1). According to *Unger's Bible Dictionary*, the term devil can mean several things, none of them good. It can refer to: a false god or idol, a slanderer or gossip-monger, or "the greatest of the fallen spirits"—Satan himself. Satan is also referred to in Scripture as: Beelzebub, Belial, and Lucifer (Isaiah 14:12). Lucifer[8] appears to be Satan's original name before he was cast out of heaven and means the "son of the morning" or "shining one."

Satan's abilities

Satan is revealed in Scripture to possess great innate abilities. As stated above, his power and authority over the earth increased immeasurably when he successfully wrested dominion over it from Adam. This is why he is called in the Bible as the prince, ruler, and god of this world.

Jesus, before He was crucified, said to the apostle Peter, *"Satan has asked for you that, he may sift you as wheat"* (Luke 22:31). The phrase "sift you as wheat" no doubt meant that Satan wished to test Peter's faith in Jesus in the same or similar way he tested Job to see how much he really trusted God. Satan must have thought this was something God might allow since God *had* allowed him to torment Job (Job 1:6-12) in order to prove to Satan that Job was an upright man and loved God more than riches or anything else of this world.

Later, probably many years after Jesus' death and resurrection, the apostle Peter warns followers of Christ to, *"Be sober, be vigilant; because your adversary the devil walks about like a roaring lion, seeking whom he may devour"* (1 Peter 5:8).

The gospels of Matthew and Luke also divulge that Satan, as the god of this world, has power to give riches, kingdoms, and authority (power) to whomever he wishes (Matthew 4:8-9 and Luke 4:5-6). This goes a long way to explain—Why do the wicked prosper?—as has been pondered through the ages and especially in the Old Testament by many of God's prophets and patriarchs.

In America today, it is not difficult to come up with many names of people who are of low, moral character and could even be said to be evil, yet are incredibly rich and well taken care of. I have no doubt that it is Satan who has made many of these types of people wealthy and that God has allowed it for His own divine purposes. Chafer essentially says the same thing: "Satan is... set forth [in the Bible] as having direct control of the physical well-being of his subjects[9] [those who reject or who do not acknowledge God]."

All this means is that Satan uses all the power at his disposal to keep people who do not believe in the Bible or its God comfortable enough in their circumstances and beliefs so that they won't be compelled to seek their Creator.

Satan can also make people sick as Job 2:7 reveals when Satan *"struck Job with painful boils from the sole of his foot to the crown of his head."* Jesus Christ also repeatedly healed individuals who were made sick by the powers of darkness (Matthew 12:22 and 17:14-18).

With his dominion over the entire earth and everything in it, Satan has power to control elements in nature. In Job 1:16, the Bible tells us that Satan caused lightening or *"fire... from heaven"* to consume Job's servants and sheep, and in verse 19, a tornado or *"a great wind"* to destroy Job's oldest son's house where all Job's sons and daughters were eating and drinking. There is also reason to believe in Mark 4:39 that the storm that tossed about the sea and boat that Jesus was in along with his disciples was caused by Satan, because Jesus didn't just tell the wind and sea to become calm, the Bible says that Jesus *"rebuked"* the wind and sea just as he did many of the demons he cast out of people possessed by them.

The Bible also reveals that Satan can speak to or influence people's minds. Such was the case with Ananias and Sapphira as recorded in Acts 5:1-10:

Now a man named Ananias, together with his wife Sapphira, also sold a piece of property. With his wife's full knowledge he kept back part of the money for himself, but brought the rest and put it at the apostles' feet. Then Peter said, "Ananias, how is it that Satan has so filled your heart that you have lied to the Holy Spirit and have kept for yourself some of the money you received for the land? Didn't it belong to you before it was sold? And after it was sold, wasn't the money at your disposal? What made you think of doing such a thing? You have not lied just to human beings but to God." When Ananias heard this, he fell down and died. And great fear seized all who heard what had happened. Then some young men came forward, wrapped up his body, and carried him out and buried him. About three hours later his wife came in, not

knowing what had happened. Peter asked her, "Tell me, is this the price you and Ananias got for the land?" "Yes," she said, "that is the price." Peter said to her, "How could you conspire to test the Spirit of the Lord? Listen! The feet of the men who buried your husband are at the door, and they will carry you out also." At that moment she fell down at his feet and died. Then the young men came in and, finding her dead, carried her out and buried her beside her husband.
(NIV)

Apparently, Ananias and Sapphira must have told the Apostle Peter that they gave all the money they got for the land to the church when in reality they secretly kept part of it for themselves. This would have been fine, as Peter says, since it was theirs to begin with. But they tried to conceal the truth about what they did, possibly attempting to make themselves look more selfless and pious than they actually were.

King David of Israel got into big trouble with God as recorded in I Chronicles 21 when he unwittingly acted on Satan's temptation to call for a count of the number of people living in Israel to find out how many fighting men the nation had. Since God was supposed to be taking care of Israel, it was irrelevant how many fighting men David had at his disposal to ward off the nation's enemies. This was a foolish move by David to attempt to replace God with his own human self-sufficiency and God didn't like it to say the least.

Satan was also able to influence Judas Iscariot to betray Jesus:

And supper being ended, the devil having already put into the heart of Judas Iscariot, Simon's son, to betray Him [Jesus].
John 13:2 (NKJV)

Although Satan cannot *make* anyone do anything, he can suggest something to a person's mind in a subtle enough way so that a person thinks the thought is coming from him or herself. But for someone to actually do the evil that Satan may suggest, the recipient of his wiles must be open to doing such an act or else they would be blameless for their actions. In other words, the person must go along with the suggestion to do evil. In Luke 6:45 Jesus explains:

"A good man out of the good treasure of his heart brings forth good; and an evil man out of the evil treasure of his heart brings forth evil. For out of the abundance of the heart his mouth speaks." (NKJV) (See also Matthew 12:34-35 and Mark 7:20-23)

Below, in Matthew 13:19, we see still more proof that Satan is able to plant ideas and thoughts of doubt and confusion into people's minds:

"When anyone hears the word of the kingdom [the Gospel of Jesus Christ]*, and does not understand it, then the wicked one comes and snatches away what was sown in his heart."* (NKJV)

Even God's people, if they are not careful to bring every thought captive to the knowledge and obedience of Christ as the Bible warns in II Corinthians 10:5, can be susceptible to Satan's negative influence.

In Matthew 16:23, after Jesus tells Peter and the other apostles that He must go to Jerusalem and suffer many things, referring to fulfilling His earthly mission, Peter rebukes Him. Then Jesus, in turn, rebukes Satan as if it was he that put the words in Peter's mind and mouth, attempting to work through him to thwart Jesus from accomplishing His divine commission.

It is imperative to understand that all of us have a propensity toward doing wrong or evil, although some more so than others. This is why it is so important that society reflect Biblical morality as a check against those who have a greater propensity toward evil due to their upbringing, environment, or other more sinister influences.

Satan appears to know his prey intimately and a lot of what most people are capable of. And he always seems to know when to tempt someone with something in just the right way and at just the right time to achieve the greatest negative impact and also to cunningly deceive the person into thinking the temptation is the right or expedient thing to do.

Satan influencing people's minds also explains why at least some of our leaders make so many irrational and illogical decisions and choices. The vast majority are either totally unaware of the devil's tactics and capabilities or they are in league with him and have a sinister agenda that comes from him. This also accounts for why so many people in America believe in a universalist, all-accepting type of god and the idea that everyone is going to heaven one day after they die. Chafer says in regards to this:

> The unregenerate, are, then, unconscious of their position in the arms of Satan, and blind in their thoughts toward the gospel of mercy and favor,—their only hope for time or eternity. Satan, like a fond mother, is bending over those in his arms, breathing into their minds the guiding balm of a "universal fatherhood of God" and a "universal brotherhood of man;" suggesting their worthiness before God on the ground of their own moral character and physical generation; feeding their tendency to imitate the true faith by great humanitarian undertakings and schemes for the reformation of individuals and the betterment of the social order. God's necessary requirements of regeneration [salvation from their sins] are carefully set aside, and the blinded souls go on without hope, having the[ir] understanding darkened, being alienated from the life of God through the ignorance that is in there, because of the blindness of their heart.[10]

Satan breathing into people's minds also explains the motivations of many murderers in America today where perpetrators have said that voices inside or outside their heads told them to do the evil they did.

This is allegedly the situation with an Oregon mother recently charged with throwing her autistic 6-year-old son off a bridge to his death. An NBC article reports that she "had been 'hearing voices' and was supposed to see a doctor to adjust her medication."[11]

Another man stabbed a perfect stranger to death for no reason. According to the news source, "He told police officers who arrested him: 'I've got voices in my head telling me to do it. I left the knife stuck in her.'"[12]

A father who admitted killing six people with a knife, including his wife and two children, was "hearing voices inside his head."[13]

In 2013, a navy yard man who murdered twelve people with a gun was "Hearing voices." The assailant reportedly said "he heard voices talking to him through a wall while at one hotel, so he changed hotels twice, but the voices followed him…. He said he feared they might harm him."[14]

This is just a sampling of related headlines in the news across America today.

Although pharmaceutical or illegal drugs may be a cause for some people or the mentally ill to hear voices, I have yet to hear of a person who claims to be hearing voices that are telling him or her to do something good. Why do the voices always seem to be telling someone to do evil?

When one understands the nature of Satan and the fact that the Bible says he is a clever and invisible tempter of men, real and powerful, a murderer, a deceiver, a liar, that he comes to kill and destroy, and can give people nefarious thoughts, the true source of many of these voices people are hearing suddenly makes perfect sense.

Demons

But the logical question to ask is—Why would Satan bother with these relatively unimportant people, doesn't he only have time to influence the Hitlers and Stalins of the world?

The answer is—because it's not only Satan who is doing all these things, he has help. The Bible says that when Satan was cast out of heaven, a third of the angels went with him. Revelation 12:3-4 reads:

Then another sign appeared in heaven: an enormous red dragon with seven heads and ten horns and seven crowns on its heads.

Its tail swept a third of the stars out of the sky and flung them to the earth. The dragon stood in front of the woman who was about to give birth, so that it might devour her child the moment he was born.

The above passage is an allegory of Satan and his demonic followers being cast out of heaven after they all rebelled against God. The dragon is Satan and although the word "stars" has several metaphorical meanings in Scripture, the stars in this passage is understood by Biblical scholars to be a metaphor for angels, or in this case, the angels that rebelled along with Satan and became demons after they were cast to earth. The "child" is the Christ-child, Jesus, and the "woman" is Mary, Jesus' mother.

Bible verses such as Matthew 8:16 and Mark 9:25 explain that demons, like Satan are evil spirit beings. In Scripture, good angels sometimes appear to people in visible form as in Genesis 19:1 and Acts 12:3-11. But with the exception of Satan having been allowed to become visible to the human eye in Scripture possibly three times, the Bible does not reveal any fallen angel as having been allowed to show itself to people in a visible form. However, this does not mean that demons *cannot* reveal themselves in a visible way to humans, even today.

Before I became a Christian, I had two experiences where I saw what I believe now to be either demons or physical manifestations of demonic activity in my life.

When I was a teenager and unfamiliar with the teachings of the Bible, I was fascinated by unexplained phenomena, things attributed to so-called ghosts, poltergeists, and paranormal activity, and I continually read books recounting such strange occurrences. One night, when I was about 16-years-old, as I lay in bed and the room was dark, I saw what looked to be an orb of light about the size of a softball hovering in the air about four feet from me and four feet off the floor. I slept in the basement of my parents' home at this time and I remember looking around at the several small, high windows near the ceiling to see if there was any light coming through them that was causing this, but there was not. I could not find anything that could create this ball of light and its appearance of hovering in mid air. Unable to explain this odd event by any rational means, I remember pulling the bed covers over my head and eventually falling asleep.

I had another episode a few years later while driving home alone in my car after work at about 3 am in the morning. I was still fascinated by occultic activity and was reading books such as *The Exorcist* by William Peter Blatty. As I drove along and stared out at the road in front of me, I witnessed, what looked like several bright, giant planets in varying distances from me, but several miles away, roll across the sky perpendicular to me and near the horizon. I remember them looking huge and I glanced around at the few cars traveling next to me to see if anyone else had seen them. It didn't appear as though anyone had and I drove on, baffled about what I thought I had seen. The entire event lasted no more than ten seconds.

To this day, whether or not there was anything actually physical in either of these two episodes or whether they were images planted in my psyche, I do not know. But after I became a Christian, I found out they were probably some kind of demonic manifestations brought on by the type of occultic material I was reading at the time. In the 35 years that I have been a Christian and stopped reading such material, I have not had any similar experiences like the ones I have recounted.

However, over the years since becoming a Christian I have had several very reliable, rational people tell me of similar encounters they have had with what they knew to be physical manifestations of demonic spirits. Because of my experiences, I have no reason to doubt them.

Principalities and powers

Biblical scholar, Merrill F. Unger, in his book, *Biblical Demonology,* had this to say about the reality of demons and how they are working in conjunction with Satan, and that few people seem to understand what is going on:

> Little should need to be said about the reality of demons, inasmuch as Scriptural testimony on this point is so clear and

unequivocal. Notwithstanding, unbelief is so widespread and the problem of incredulity so vexing in the whole field of enquiry, that a discussion of it here seems necessary. It hardly requires pointing out that the Bible doctrine of a personal devil and demons has met with a great storm of skepticism in recent years. Many, in a boasted age of science and enlightenment, dismiss the Biblical claim as a mere remnant of medieval superstition, or treat the whole matter as an amusing joke. Men in the church and out of it, blatantly assert that there is no personal devil, that the devil is only evil personified, and that whatever devil there is, is in man himself, and that there is enough of that variety to answer all theological requirements. It is also confidently declared that no longer can a respectable scholar be found anywhere who believes in a personal devil or demons. Thus, this aggressive skepticism and militant attacks demand an apologetic approach to the problem.[15]

The Bible reveals unequivocally that Satan and demons do exist and explains what is really going on behind the scenes in individual human lives and human government:

For we do not wrestle against flesh and blood, but against principalities, against powers, against the rulers of the darkness of this age, against spiritual hosts of wickedness in the heavenly places.
Ephesians 6:12 (NKJV)

The great Christian writer and apologist, C.S. Lewis, said this about demons in the preface of his classic book, *The Screwtape Letters*:

There are two equal and opposite errors into which our race can fall about the devils. One is to disbelieve in their existence. The other is to believe, and to feel an excessive and unhealthy interest in them. They themselves [demons] are equally pleased by both errors and hail a materialist or a magician with the same delight.

No one here on earth knows the total number of demons who were cast out of heaven along with Satan. They could number in the millions, billions, or even more. All the Bible implies is that there seems to be enough to negatively influence most if not all of the people living in the world today, including America.

Satan's and his demons' purpose

As I stated earlier, I believe that Satan and his demonic followers' primary goal is to be worshipped either as some kind of god or as *the* Creator-God, Jehovah. But the citizens of the kingdom of darkness have other nefarious purposes as well. Chafer explains that: "Demon influence, like the activity of Satan, is prompted by two motives: both to hinder the purpose of God for humanity, and to extend the authority of Satan."[16] To accomplish this, as Chafer further states, Satan incorporates "confusion and terror... in the world" along with his other methods such as lying and deceiving as already stated earlier.

So what is the purpose of God for humanity?

The purpose of God for humanity is for as many people as possible to find Him and His chosen way so that people can be rescued from spiritual death as a result of their sins of ignoring or disobeying God's commandments on how to live.

Although Satan must know that he cannot be completely successful at thwarting God's plans, I believe he works so hard at deceiving as many as he can primarily out of spite against God by making sure that as many people as possible die un-reconciled to Him to be condemned to an eternity away from Him just like Satan is himself.

The world system

All this is extremely important to understand because there is an invisible army of demons in the world, working clandestinely in the spiritual realm, that are encouraging people to go against God and His commands and generally do acts of evil as well as keep them from understanding God and His ways. This also explains why the war against God in America appears to be so concerted and evenly widespread. Unger has this to say about

Satan's hidden methods, especially as they relate to human governments:

> In every age of human history and in every phase of daily life demons have played a tremendous and very important role. In no realm is their activity more significant than in the sphere of human government. In this area possibly more than in any other field of their operation their activity has frequently not been clearly discerned or even partially understood. Their invisible nature, their close and inseparable identity with their visible human agents, and the supernatural character of their operations have combined to clothe them and their wicked machinations and evil enterprises in ominous mystery. Innumerable multitudes without the light of divine revelation, and other multitudes possessing the Bible, but uninitiated into the truths of the "mystery of lawlessness" (II Thessalonians 2:7), cannot get beyond "flesh and blood". They can see only the human actors upon the stage of history. Wicked rulers, ruthless dictators, tyrants, oppressors, kings, governors, and presidents are, to them, the real and only characters in the great drama of life as it affects the political realm. They have no idea at all of the unseen realm of evil personalities, energizing and motivating their human agents. "The principalities... the powers... the world rulers of this present darkness," and "the spiritual hosts of wickedness in the heavenly places" are, so far as they are concerned, mere theological nonentities with which they do not reckon.
>
> However, in the realm of human government the unseen personalities of the evil supernatural sphere are just as real and active as their visible human agents, and any deeper interpretation of human history, tracing in it a divine purpose and goal, must take into account the invisible yet very real realm of spirit. Thus interpreted, human history is seen to be not merely an account of human activities and events independent of spiritual forces, but a continuous interaction of spiritual and human personalities, in which demons play a prominent part.[17]

As you can see, Satan has done an excellent job in staying hidden in America today where all the blame for our country's woes is attributed solely to the incompetence, ignorance, or greed for money and power from human beings. Only a relative few are aware that it is Satan who is ultimately the instigator behind all the death, destruction, evil policies, evil human ambition, sensuality, and spiritual blindness, etc., everywhere. This Satanic world system that the Bible often refers to is a result of Adam's[18] disobedience and subsequent forfeiture of dominion over the world to Satan who has now modeled it after his own wicked ideals. Unger explains further:

> In this sphere Satan rules over unregenerate mankind. He secured the scepter of government in the earth from Adam by right of conquest, and has organized the present world-system upon his own cosmic principles of pride, ambition, selfishness, force, greed, and pleasure. Imposing, outwardly religious, scientific, cultured, elegant, this world-system, nevertheless, is dominated by Satanic principles, and is beneath its deceptive veneer a seething cauldron of national and international ambitions, and commercial rivalries. Satan and his elaborately organized hierarchy of evil are often the invisible agents, and the real motivating power and intelligence behind the dictators, kings, presidents, and governors, who are the visible rulers. Armed force and periodic wars, with wholesale murder and violence, are its indispensable concomitants.[19]

C.S. Lewis said "To admire Satan, then, is to give one's vote not only for a world of misery, but also for a world of lies and propaganda, of wishful thinking…"[20]

In researching this book, I came across a leaflet called the *"Leaves of the White Rose,"* that, according to Unger, was distributed by the underground anti-Hitler youth movement during the Second World War in Nazi-controlled Germany. Apparently there were some during that time who understood full well where Hitler's power and influence came from and where every other political despot's power comes from today. As you read, see if you recognize any Satanic earmarks in any of the politicians practicing their craft in America today:

Every word out of Hitler's mouth is a lie. If he says peace, he means war, and if he calls frivolously on the name of the Almighty, he means the power of evil, the Fallen Angel, the Devil. His mouth is the stinking throat of hell, and his power is fundamentally rotten. Certainly one has to fight against the Nazi terror state with rational weapons, but whoever still doubts the real existence of demonical powers has not understood the metaphysical background of this war. Behind the concrete and the perceptible things, behind all real and logical considerations, there is the irrational, there is the fight against the Demon, against the messenger of Anti-Christ. Everywhere and at all times the demons have lurked in the dark for the hour when man becomes weak, when he arbitrarily abandons his human situation in the world order founded by God for him on freedom... After the first voluntary downward step he is compelled to the second and third with rapidly increasing speed; but everywhere, and at all times of the greatest human distress, men and women who have retained their freedom have risen as prophets and saints, and called on men to turn back to God. Certainly man is free, but he is unprotected against Evil without the living God; he is like a boat without oars, exposed to the tempest, or like a baby without a mother, or like a cloud which dissolves.

Dr. Stanley Monteith in his book, *Brotherhood of Darkness*, tells how Adolph Hitler was heavily steeped in the occultic belief system of Helena Petrovna Blavatsky and read nightly her book, *The Secret Doctrine,* that is based on Satanic, occult philosophies.[21] This fact alone accounts for Hitler's evil nature and actions where millions died as a result of him knowingly aligning himself with the devil.

It is also imperative to point out from the above leaflet that any politician today who habitually uses lies and deceit to move forward his agenda, is being heavily influenced by Satan, the father of lies (John 8:44), and his demon accomplices who are also religious practitioners of their master's black arts that consist of lies and deception. Unger warns, "Rejection of truth for a lie lays one open to "wandering spirits and doctrines of demons"[22] (Job 2:2 and I Timothy 4:1).

One can see from the above how much America has fallen for and accepted the evil schemes and deceptions of the wicked one. Chafer explains:

> It may then be concluded from the testimony of scripture that Satan imparts his wisdom and strength to the unbelieving in the same manner as the power of God is imparted to the believer by the Holy Spirit... It should be further noted in this connection that this impartation of energizing power from Satan is not toward a limited few who might be said, because of some strange conduct, to be possessed of a demon; but is the common condition of all who are yet unsaved [from their sins through Jesus Christ], and are, therefore, still in the "power of darkness."[23]

Considering the explosion in America of many sexual deviancies, it is also very likely that demonism is indirectly responsible for: rampant adultery, fornication, homosexuality, pedophilia, pornography, and a burgeoning sex trade—all practices and habits God in the Bible warns against engaging in. Can it be denied that abortion "doctors" such as Kermit Gosnell also must have been heavily influenced by the powers of darkness considering how heinous were his crimes and the reportedly "filthy," "deplorable," and "disgusting" condition of his clinic when it was raided by authorities? Abortion itself is such a barbaric act upon the innocent that I am convinced that Satan is behind it all working through his wicked or naïve human proxies in the physical realm.

False religions

It is also of vital importance to understand that it is Satan and his demon followers that are ultimately responsible for all the various false religions and ideologies around the world that teach what is contrary to God's word as revealed in the Bible. A false religion or doctrine is any belief system that does not possess any objective proof that it is true or that it is from the one, true God and Creator of the universe.

The Scripture verse below explains where these false notions or doctrines come from:

Now the Spirit [of God] *expressly says that in the latter times some will depart from the faith* [of Christianity]*, giving heed to deceiving spirits and doctrines of demons.*
I Timothy 4:1 (NKJV)

The "latter times" in the above verse refers to the time that we currently live that began with Jesus Christ's first coming to earth to when He returns again at the end of this present age which many in Christendom believe is very close at hand. And as if Satan knows his time is short, he has increased his activity with stepped-up attacks on the reliability of Holy Scripture and a plethora of erroneous doctrines coming from pseudo-science, false "demonized" religions, Godless ideologies, and pseudo-Christian cults, all of which have increased almost exponentially in these last two hundred years or so.

But evil men and imposters will grow worse and worse, deceiving and being deceived.
II Timothy 3:13 (NKJV)

"Deceiving and being deceived" is a perfect analogy for the promulgators of false belief systems: Satan deceives the human founders of these fallacious ideologies and they in turn zealously deceive other humans using all Satan's devices of deception. It is truly the circle of death.

As shown in previous chapters, Darwinian Evolution and many of the pseudo-Christian cults such as Mormonism and The Watch Tower Bible and Tract Society, among many others, have all been introduced into America since 1835—relatively recent events in this Christian age that began nearly two thousand years ago.

It is easy to see how even the notion of politically correct thinking, so prevalent in America today, is also an invention of the wicked one and used as a brain-washing or mind-control technique for his diabolical schemes in association with his human puppets and accomplices in American government and the mainstream media.

Satan is not God's equal

Although the Bible reveals Satan to be powerful and possessing many abilities, he is by no means on an equal footing with God, just as something made cannot be as great as the one who made it. To be sure, Satan is God's adversary, but he is not God's direct opposite. The proof of this is the Biblical fact that Satan will be condemned to hell after God is finished using his rebellion for His own divine purposes.

Chafer sheds light on why Satan has been so universally successful on earth in driving men away from God and attracting them to his own foul ideals and methods:

> Satan, though proposing to supersede the Almighty, is not omnipotent: but his power and the extent of his activity are immeasurably increased by the co-operation of his host of demons. Satan is not omniscient, yet his knowledge is greatly extended by the combined wisdom and observation of his sympathetic subjects [demons]. Satan is not omnipresent, but he is able to keep up an unceasing activity in every locality by the loyal obedience of the Satanic host, who are so numerous as to be called "Legion."[24]

It is interesting to note here too that although Satan served as God's protective covering before sin and rebellion entered his mind, he has greatly underestimated God. For Satan to be that close to God and not fathom the extent of the Divine's power and abilities speaks more about God than it does Satan. It means that God does not make known to even the angels in heaven all His great majesty. Indeed, there is still much about Him that those closest to Him in heaven do not or cannot fathom. And how could they? They are mere creatures of an infinite Being who has no beginning or end and has existed for eons before He created either angels or men. Only God knows what He has done before He created anything in heaven and the known universe.

This ignorance concerning God by Satan is also evidenced by the way Satan spoke with so much disrespect toward The Almighty the few times Scripture records interactions between the two. The following discourse in Job 1:6-12 reveals the extent of Satan's oblivious insolence:

One day the angels came to present themselves before the Lord, and Satan also came with them. The Lord said to Satan, "Where have you come from?" Satan answered the Lord, "From roaming throughout the earth, going back and forth on it." Then the Lord said to Satan, "Have you considered my servant Job? There is no one on earth like him; he is blameless and upright, a man who fears God and shuns evil." "Does Job fear God for nothing?" Satan replied. "Have you not put a hedge around him and his household and everything he has? You have blessed the work of his hands, so that his flocks and herds are spread throughout the land. But now stretch out your hand and strike everything he has, and he will surely curse you to your face." The Lord said to Satan, "Very well, then, everything he has is in your power, but on the man himself do not lay a finger." Then Satan went out from the presence of the Lord.
(NIV)

Clearly these are the words and responses from a creature that does not even begin to understand his Maker. The words of Satan sound like the arrogant words of a rebellious child to his father.

It is also very possible that Satan did not fully understand who Jesus really was during Christ's earthly ministry. The Bible reveals that Satan and the demons knew that Jesus was the Holy One sent from God, but did Satan or his demons perceive that Jesus truly was God, the second person of the Triune Godhead, or just another created being like himself? Why else would Satan try to get Jesus to worship him as recorded in Matthew 4:9?

One last thing on the limits of Satan's abilities are aptly stated by Unger: "Satan can create nothing, nor can he perpetrate any evil, physical or moral, without Jehovah's sanction."[25]

How God uses evil

I will now explain why I believe God has done what He has done with Satan and the human race knowing both would betray and rebel against Him.

As America is an experiment by our wise founding fathers to give its citizens an opportunity to essentially morally govern themselves, God's experiment with mankind may have been along similar lines. God put His new human creation in an uncontrolled, freewill environment to see if man would be obedient to Him or go his own way without Him. Ironically, America's framers knew that the only way the country would work successfully in the short and long term was if its citizens continued to look to its Creator and stayed a morally self-governed people as many had become as a result of the first Great Awakening that began in the nascent nation around 1741. As we see from history, neither vision has worked out as originally hoped.

But unlike America's framers, God *knew* his plan wouldn't work out from the beginning. So why would God begin the world with a sinless, innocent man along with Satan, the promulgator of evil, both in the same place the way He did?

First of all, I believe one of the reasons God did it was so He could show His sentient creations that neither humans nor even the angels in heaven can live successfully apart from Him. And not only can God's freewill creatures not live successfully, but their lives will also end badly, even tragically, without Him.

It is also important to note that God knew before He created Satan, that he would rebel against Him. But remember, it was only a minority, or a third of the angels that chose to rebel against God and not the majority whom, it is reasonable to assume, also possess freewill but choose to remain loyal and obedient to God. So Satan was not unduly singled-out or compelled by God to do what he did.

The second reason I believe God has allowed Satan and evil in the world was to create a race of beings that freely chose Him over their own desires and interests. To accomplish this, God needed to allow man to have complete freedom. He partly did this out of love and respect for another sentient being who, in many ways, were much like Himself, and as something necessary in order to realize His ultimate goal. As mentioned, man's freedom came with the ability to choose, so he could choose between what he liked and that which he did not like or want. But God also wanted to give man moral choice, to obey his Creator or disobey Him. To accomplish this God needed a simple exact opposite from which man could clearly choose. When God allowed Satan to tempt Eve, He was allowing her a clear-cut choice to either obey Him and not taste of the forbidden fruit because she revered Him above all else or disobey Him to fulfill her own selfish desire to taste of the forbidden fruit despite His command not to do it. Satan tempted Eve, but Eve, out of the selfish desires of her own heart, as too did Adam later, heeded the temptation and had her own way instead of God's.

Nothing much has changed down through the centuries. Mankind, for the most part, still heeds Satan's temptations and chooses his own way over God's.

God has always hoped people would freely choose Him over their own selfish desires, but except for a relative few, this has not happened.

It is a curious fact of history that after Adam and Eve chose their own way over God's, God did not stop trying to raise up a race of people who would want to choose Him one day. Down through history, He never stopped giving mankind an opportunity to choose and obey Him over other earthly, temporal interests. Job was one of those first righteous men who chose God above all else. The patriarch Abraham was another when he chose and obeyed God even when faced with killing his only beloved son, Isaac. Because of Abraham's great faith and obedience, God chose to raise up a nation from his seed. The plan was, God would choose and reveal Himself to these Hebrew offspring of Abraham, and they would in turn, hopefully choose Him back.

But it was not to be. As the Old Testament reveals, the Hebrews, the nation of Israel, was a "stiff-necked" people and constantly chose evil and their own ways over God's commandments even though God had revealed Himself to them with many signs and miracles. Even Israel today, although they are still God's chosen people and He still has a plan for them, have not embraced their Messiah, Jesus Christ, and are still primarily a secular race of people.

It wasn't until God sent His own Son that God successfully chose for Himself, out of all the Gentile nations on earth, a people who chose Him back—the believers and followers of that same Jewish Messiah, Jesus Christ, whom the Jewish people and most of the rest of the world, have largely rejected.

Summary

Chafer thus summarizes Satan and his role in today's war against God in America:

> Satan is thus revealed as having been first created as perfect in all his ways, mighty in power, and full of beauty and wisdom. While thus privileged, he proposed a stupendous project in his heart – himself to become like the Most High. Though cast down and yet having access to God, he is seen wresting the world scepter from man [Adam]; and ruling as the god of this world, until the judgment of the Cross;[26] and after that he still rules as a usurper. At the end of the age he is cast out of his access to heaven, into the earth; from thence to the pit; and, finally, is banished to the lake of fire forever... After Satan rebelled, humanity, too, was thrown into an abnormal and almost universal attitude of independence toward God; and this continues beyond the Cross with increasing confusion and darkness, to the end of the age. The only exception to this rebellion is the little company of believers; and how terribly real is the tendency of the self-governed life of the old nature, even among these! When Satan is cast out of heaven and is limited to the earth, there is tribulation upon the earth, of which Jesus speaks in Matthew 24:21, and which is also referred to in Daniel 12:1. When Satan is bound and put in the pit, and the

promised Kingdom of Christ has come, there is a peace covering the earth as water covering the face of the deep. Can it be doubted that this mighty being is a living power, acting directly in the affairs of men, even in this self-glorying age?[27]

Conclusion

This chapter began with the verse from I John 5:19, *"We know that... the whole world is under the control of the evil one."* It is Satan who has the entire world under a delusion and God allows it because of the world's, including America's, wholesale rejection of Him (Romans 1:28).

Because superstition is so much a part of demonology in all the world's religions and belief systems outside Christianity, Unger states in *Biblical Demonology* that: "the New Testament... constitutes the only true basis for understanding and evaluating strange and bewildering phenomena which have perplexed both the ancient and the modern world" and that "So far from satisfying an idle curiosity, or pandering to a morbid imagination, its [the Bible's] chaste reticence is indicative of its high aim to enlighten and warn the unwary against the ever-impending peril of evil supernaturalism, and point the way to deliverance and victory."[28]

In concluding this chapter it is vitally imperative to understand that the fallen world we live in is greatly influenced by the powers of darkness. Most if not all the events and actions on the part of men only make sense when one understands that there are malevolent beings in the invisible spiritual realm that are bent on murder, mayhem, and deceiving the human race into destroying God's world and testimony, and ignoring God Himself.

For the Christian reading this book, Satan and demons are not to be feared. However, it must be understood that they are powerful and deceptive, and as stated earlier, it is crucial for the true follower of Jesus Christ to question every thought that contradicts what he or she knows to be true about the Bible and the person of God and Jesus Christ. Satan and his cohorts in the spiritual realm will do all they are allowed to derail the true child of God from his or her earthly mission for Christ and His kingdom.

For the unbeliever it is especially essential that you understand that there is an invisible adversary in the world who is working overtime to deceive you into thinking that the Bible and its God and especially Jesus Christ are irrelevant. It is Satan's and his demons' untiring mission to keep you from knowing, understanding, and following the truths that are presented in Holy Scripture. The only protection against the powers of darkness is to believe in God's chosen Son, the only way to salvation, the Lord Jesus Christ.

None of us can take credit for anything that we possess: our intelligence, our talents, even our accomplishments—because they all come from God. Even the time in history and part of the world we are born into are ordained by God for reasons known only to Him (Acts 17:26). The only thing we can claim as our own—is our will, our ability to choose. And this is where the real battle is being waged today in America—in people's minds. Satan wants Americans, as he does everyone else in the world, to choose to believe his lies and deceptions and God wants us to believe in Him and His words as revealed in the Bible.

Chapter 7
The America That Once Was

Despite how the deniers and deceivers in politics, the major media, and academia try to propagandize people to the contrary, America was indeed founded as a Christian nation and the evidence is available for all to see and read. In fact, it is this belief in the Bible and Christianity that has made America the greatest nation on earth and nothing else.

Indeed, what has made America great is not the land itself or even what is indigenous to the land. Alexis de Tocqueville, mentioned in the introduction to this book, discovered in 1831 what the cause of America's greatness was:

> I sought for the greatness and genius of America in her commodious harbors and her ample rivers – and it was not there . . . in her fertile fields and boundless forests and it was not there . . . in her rich mines and her vast world commerce – and it was not there . . . in her democratic Congress and her matchless Constitution – and it was not there. Not until I went into the churches of America and heard her pulpits aflame with righteousness did I understand the secret of her genius and power. America is great because she is good, and if America ever ceases to be good, she will cease to be great.[1]

What made America great began in the colonies of Jamestown (1607) and Plymouth (1620) that survived and grew when others (such as Roanoke) didn't can be attributed to the great faith these colony's predominantly Christian inhabitants exercised in God. By 1630, Christians known as Puritans, because they wanted to purify the official Church of England of what they deemed to be un-Biblical practices absorbed from Roman Catholic dogma, began coming to America from Great Britain in small fleets of sailing ships. So many emigrated that it became known as "The Great Migration." The un-Biblical practices the Puritans objected to had been publically identified in 1517 by a Catholic priest in Germany named, Martin Luther, and involved many erroneous doctrines that included an individual making a monetary contribution to the Church to lessen one's punishment in the afterlife. Catholicism also decreed that the Holy Scriptures could not be understood by the ordinary layman and required a Catholic priest or the pope himself to correctly interpret them for the masses. For Puritans, one of the most un-Scriptural and egregious practices of the papacy, at that time, was its teachings that salvation from sin came by a combination of faith in Jesus Christ and a system of works, even though the Bible, without the "priestly" interpretation, taught that salvation came by God's grace and through faith in Christ alone. Luther's call for a return to Biblical principles ultimately led to the Protestant Reformation movement in many European countries like Great Britain where it especially took hold.[2]

One of the changes that came out of the Protestant Reformation was the way Christians viewed earthly government. At the time, most European countries like Britain and France were ruled by kings or queens who could be benevolent or dictatorial, depending upon the disposition of the individual monarch. British monarchs, like most monarchs of the day, also believed they ruled by the direct will of God and were the final authority over their subjects, something Puritans disagreed with since they believed God and the Bible to be the ultimate authority over men. A bad disposition from a king or queen could lead to the persecution, death, and even mass killings of Christians who didn't agree with the monarch's so-called divine right or the teachings of his or her official church. As a result, many Christians in these groups, especially the Puritans, began emigrating to the wild and dangerous land of the New World in North America—a place where they could be free from religious persecution and practice their Biblically-based faith without the oversight of a tyrannical king, queen, or state-sanctioned church.

One of the leaders of the "People of the book" as Puritans were sometimes called, that came across the Atlantic Ocean from England in 1630 was John Winthrop. It was Winthrop who made the now famous reference to America "as a city upon a hill." This proclamation was a reference to Christ's words in the Bible from the Sermon on the Mount where He preaches, *"You are the light of the world! A city that is set on a hill cannot be hid."* Winthrop and his fellow Puritans founded the Massachusetts Bay Colony where he entreated his co-inhabitants "to love the Lord our God and to... walk in His ways and keep His commandments."[3]

Visible and written testimonies to America's Christian faith

One visible testimony that America was founded upon Christian beliefs is *The National Monument to the Forefathers* in Plymouth, Massachusetts. Dedicated in 1889, long before Godless humanism began to take over the nation, the monument was built to honor the Christian virtues that were possessed by the Pilgrim colonists who not only founded Plymouth Colony but whose counterparts also established the other colonies along the eastern coast of North America in the seventeenth century. This monument is particularly noteworthy because it depicts the major tenets that are identified with Christianity: faith, the Holy Bible, morality, the Ten Commandments, prophecy, evangelism, justice, mercy, and religious liberty, among others. Another nearby memorial is a granite figure known as, The Pilgrim Mother, with an inscription that reads: "They brought up their families in sturdy virtue and a living faith in God without which nations perish." These and other such memorials testify to the strong Christian faith of America's first European immigrants.

These original colonists and establishers of the New World also left much written evidence of their Christian beliefs that dominated everything they did and participated in, including government. For example, when the Pilgrims first arrived in the New World, even before they disembarked from their ship, the Mayflower, their leaders drew up a constitution, later known as the *Mayflower Compact*, for the purpose of properly governing the new colony. The Compact began early with the words:

"Having undertaken, for the Glory of God, and advancements of the Christian faith…"[4]

Quaker[5] William Penn was responsible for establishing the Pennsylvania colony and the town of Philadelphia. In a letter announcing his arrival to the indigenous people living near the land he intended to occupy, he began:

> My friends—There is one great God and power that hath made the world and all things therein, to whom you and I, and all people owe their being and well-being, and to whom you and I must one day give an account for all that we do in the world; this great God hath written his law in our hearts, by which we are taught and commanded to love and help, and do good to one another, and not to do harm and mischief one to another.[6]

The letter goes on to say, "but I desire to enjoy it [the land] with your love and consent, that we may always live together as neighbours and friends…" Penn assured the natives that he would not treat them disrespectfully as he had heard other "people of these parts of the world [probably Europe] had." Although it may seem arrogant for Penn or any other colonist to suddenly lay claim to land that technically belonged to someone else, it was not the intent of many of the early Christian colonists to displace the native people but instead, to live in harmony with them.

All of America's first thirteen colonies contained language that attested to the people's general belief in the Christian God. Historian, Rod Gragg, author of *Forged in Faith*, lists their founding documents:

> The Massachusetts Bay Colony's charter recorded an intent to spread the "knowledge and obedience of the only true God and Savior of mankind, and the Christian faith," much as the Mayflower Compact cited a commitment to "the Glory of God, and Advancement of the Christian faith."
>
> Connecticut's Fundamental Orders officially called for "an orderly and decent Government established according to God"

that would "maintain and preserve the liberty and purity of the Gospel of our Lord Jesus."

In New Hampshire, the Agreement of the Settlers at Exeter vowed to establish a government "in the name of Christ" that "shall be to our best discerning agreeable to the Will of God."

Rhode Island's colonial charter invoked the "blessing of God' for "a sure foundation of happiness to all America."

The Articles of Confederation of the United Colonies of New England stated, "Whereas we all came into these parts of America with one and the same end and aim, namely, to advance the Kingdom of our Lord Jesus Christ and to enjoy the liberties of the Gospel..."

New York's Duke's Law prohibited denial of "the true God and his Attributes."

New Jersey's founding charter vowed, "Forasmuch as it has pleased God, to bring us into this Province...we may be a people to the praise and honor of his name."

Delaware's original charter officially acknowledged "One almighty God, the Creator, Upholder and Ruler of the World."

Pennsylvania's charter officially cited a "Love of Civil Society and Christian Religion" as a motivation for the colony's founding.

Maryland's charter declared an official goal of "extending the Christian Religion."

Virginia's first charter commissioned colonization as "so noble a work, which may, by the Providence of Almighty God, hereafter tend to ...propagating of Christian Religion."

The charter for the Colony of Carolina proclaimed "a laudable and pious zeal for the propagation of the Christian faith."

Georgia's charter officially cited a commitment to the "propagating of Christian religion."[7]

With this kind of evidence, it is the height of dishonesty and deception to claim that America was not founded as a Christian nation.

The need for a spiritual re-awakening

By 1741 a pastor named Jonathon Edwards had been watching the people in America and felt they were lax in holding fast to the great Christian principles their forefathers had instilled in the colonies the century before. Apparently, he was not alone in this observation. Gragg writes:

> The Judeo-Christian worldview was still the consensus philosophy of Colonial America, but many Christian leaders feared that America's foundational faith was faltering. Prosperity, security, and the distractions of a progressive culture had dulled Christianity in the Colonies, they believed, and the American people had grown lukewarm in their faith. The frontier lacked churches and clergy, and was notorious for its rowdy lifestyle. America's cities were little better, some believed. Among the urban elite, deism—with its view of a disinterested, impersonal God—was growing fashionable, and the squalor and hardship of slum neighborhoods bred secular indifference. Throughout the Thirteen Colonies, eighteenth-century Americans seemed to be drifting from the faith of their fathers. "In short, the old established religious habits and customs were crumbling under the impact of changing social conditions," historian Carl Bridenbaugh would later write, "and secularism was slowly, almost imperceptibly, filtering into the minds and actions everywhere..." A Pennsylvania pastor fretted that "the people were very generally through the land careless at heart, and stupidly indifferent about the great concerns of eternity." A minister from Vermont concurred: "The difference between the church and the world was vanishing away," he lamented. "Church discipline was neglected, and the growing laxness of morals was invading the churches."[8]

It is uncanny how much the above sounds like the spiritual place of America today. And it was against this worsening national condition in 1741 that the reportedly non-flamboyant, yet authoritative Edwards gave his famous sermon called, *Sinners in the Hands of an Angry God,* to a crowd in Enfield, a town within the Colony of Massachusetts. Edward's prominence in the area had grown over the years due partly from his unbending belief in sound, Biblical doctrine. For example, he believed that one had to be a "born-again" believer in Jesus Christ in order to be saved from one's sins. Edwards was also coming into the public's view for the mini-revival that had been taking place for several years in his home town and surrounding areas where he regularly preached. Gragg recounts Edward's description of the transformation that he observed was already taking place as a result of this regional revival that was going on even before he delivered his most memorable sermon:

> Our assemblies were then beautiful. Our public praises were greatly enlivened. Our young people, when they met, were wont to spend their time talking about the love of Jesus Christ.... They had now abandoned their frolicking, their night-walking, their impure language and lewd songs. And among all, whether young or old, there was seen to be a change in their habits of drinking, tavern-haunting, profane speaking and extravagance of apparel. Notoriously vicious persons have been reformed. The wealthy, the fashionable, the great beaus and fine ladies, have relinquished their vanities.[9]

It is amazing that despite years of technological change in modern America, human nature has remained the same.

It has been reported that *Sinners in the Hands of an Angry God* had been "delivered soberly and with his [Edwards'] characteristic gentle and precise eloquence—but," according to Gragg, "it fell upon its hearers like the gust of a mighty wind"[10] and had a lightening effect on the colonies. The sermon had been not only directed at non-believers but to regular churchgoers as well and spread like a wildfire through the colonies. Gragg writes:

Beginning at Enfield that summer evening in 1741, a mighty wind of change swept through New England, then to other colonies, and, eventually, to all thirteen. It was the greatest spiritual revival in American history, and became known as the "Great Awakening." It would reinvigorate a biblical faith for decades to come in Colonial America, affecting the common and the affluent alike, and permeating city, town, village, and frontier. "The Great Awakening," asserted Pulitzer Prize-winning historian Vernon Parrington, "was the single movement that stirred the colonial heart deeply during three generations." The revival was unleashed full-force that night at the Enfield meetinghouse, but it arose almost simultaneously in various locations. A similar swell of Christian conversions had occurred in the Middle Colonies through the preaching of evangelists Theodore Frelinghuysen and Gilbert Tennent, and other outbreaks of revived faith occurred elsewhere. Meanwhile, the Great Awakening's most famous evangelist was also at work—and through him, the revival would sweep across Colonial America like a mighty gale.[11]

Another staunch believer and advocate for the "new birth" spiritual experience was Reverend George Whitefield. Whitefield was a powerful orator who preached in America and England during the same time as Jonathon Edwards. But as Edwards was more a pastor to a specific congregation, Whitefield was an evangelist to the masses and attracted tens of thousands of listeners to his many crusades during his lifetime. As a result of pastors like Edwards and evangelists like Whitefield, America was changing for the better and being turned back to the God of the Bible. Gragg recounts the words of Benjamin Franklin, an observer of the changes coming over the people in Philadelphia in particular:

It is wonderful to see the change soon made in the manners of our inhabitants... From being thoughtless or indifferent about religion, it seem'd as if all the world were growing religious, so that one could not walk thro' the town in an evening without hearing psalms sung in different families of every street.[12]

In short, the Great Awakening was changing the hearts and minds of people living in eighteenth century America. Gragg writes:

> While it encouraged denominational diversity, the Great Awakening also established an extraordinary unity of faith in Colonial America. Despite denomination differences, essential Christianity reigned throughout the land. "In kindling the religion of the heart in the great mass of plain people," historian Merle Curti would conclude, "the revivals gave a broader base to the Christian heritage. Thus the intellectual life of the colonists—their views of the universe, of human nature, and of esthetics, their social and political ideas—was shaped in large measure by Christian patterns of thought." Americans came to expect biblical values to be reflected in the institutions of the day—church, education, the arts, business, law, and government. "The key principle," American scholar Daniel Dorchester would note, "was that the government, civil and ecclesiastical, is constituted and administered upon the Bible as the source of knowledge and authority...." Philosophically in the mid-nineteenth century, Protestant, Catholic, and Jewish Americans alike had a common consensus—the Judeo-Christian worldview. It was the cultural glue that united Colonial America's melting-pot culture.
>
> In renewing the influence of the biblical worldview, the Great Awakening also increased Americans' awareness of the biblical principle of equality before God—and the God-given inalienable rights that Higher Law bestowed on every individual. Many Americans—especially the New Light[13] multitude in the dissenter denominations[14]—began to apply biblical principles to Colonial American politics. For the free exercise of their Great Awakening faith, they were willing to resist London-based Colonial authority throughout the Thirteen Colonies. Likewise, when authorities with the government's [England's] national church sought to install an American bishop, Americans blocked it with outspoken intercolonial opposition. "For the first time," historian Harris Starr would write, "the American people...sought to limit ecclesiastical and political authority and advocated freedom of conscience and individual liberty."

Due largely to the Great Awakening, the political base in Colonial America on the eve of the American Revolution was not some secular organization—it was the local church. Likewise, Colonial America's most influential leader was not a politician, merchant, banker, journalist, or performer—it was the preacher of the local church. The church was the center of family life in eighteenth-century America, and the direction of the local pastor was generally heeded with respect. Unlike the French Revolution, with its humanistic hostility to Christianity and clergy, its lawless violence, and its inevitable reign of terror, the American Revolution would be a genuine quest for liberty that was fueled, disciplined, and restrained by the rule of law— the Higher Law of the Bible. "God hath given to every Man," said New England minister Solomon Paine, "an unalienable right...and hath blessed them that appeared to stand uprightly for the Liberties of Conscience...."[15]

It was in this national climate that the signers of the *Declaration of Independence* and framers of America's *Constitution of the United States* were raised.

The faith of the 1776 generation

From the time the first colonists arrived on the east coast in 1607, the Christian faith was by far the dominant religion and belief system in Colonial America. And when the first Continental Congress met in 1774, Gragg tells that, according to John Adams, the second president of the United States, the delegates from the thirteen colonies were mostly comprised of Protestant Christians from Presbyterian, Congregationalist, Baptist, Lutheran, German Reformed, and Anglican denominations. Adams said that only a very few delegates held beliefs outside those of Christianity, such as those of deists or atheists.

It is also interesting to note that eight of America's most prestigious colleges and universities were founded by Christians from various protestant denominations prior to the Revolutionary War and many of them as a result of the Christian revival that began in the 1740s under Edwards and Whitefield. It is tragic that these academic institutions of higher learning such as Yale and Harvard Universities, and Dartmouth College that once taught from the Bible and were established by people of Christian faith are now bastions for Godless ideologies and thought.[16]

Although there were many writings by secular philosophers from the Enlightenment Era available to people like founding father Thomas Jefferson, it was not these that most influenced them. Instead, according to Gragg, it was other works such as those of Puritan legal scholar Sir Edward Coke and his book *Institutes of the Law of England*, which "placed God-given inalienable rights above the authority of the monarchy." Gragg says that Jefferson believed, "as did others of his day, that the foundation of English law was on the higher law of Scripture—which had inspired... English common law."[17] Gragg tells of other writings that were high on the list of influencing Colonial politicians such as Jefferson:

> Jefferson and his peers in Congress were also influenced by other English thinkers—especially John Locke's *Second Treatise of Government* and *The reasonableness of Christianity*. The view of Natural Law commonly held by Jefferson's generation was based on Locke's view that the "Laws of Nature and of Nature's God" were God's general revelation to man, inscribed in the human heart. "That God has given a rule whereby men should govern themselves."[18]

Gragg continues:

> Also influential among lawmaker's of Jefferson's day was the Scot philosopher Henry Home, also know as Lord Kames. Home's work was required reading for any law student and taught that a God-given sense of morality encouraged "an equal pursuit of the happiness of all." Most influential, perhaps, was an Oxford professor acclaimed as the eighteenth century's leading expert on English law—Sir William Blackstone. In his *Commentaries on the Laws of England*, Blackstone defined an entire set of criminal acts as actions that "offend God, by

openly transgressing the precepts of religion, either natural or revealed."[19]

The "equal pursuit of happiness" and "Laws of Nature and of Nature's God" were words and concepts that would appear in the United States' founding documents such as *The Declaration of Independence.*

George Washington

The belief in and adherence to the Christian faith of some of America's founding fathers such as Thomas Jefferson and George Washington has been called into question in recent years by secularists. And, as if to create their own reality about America's patriarchs, much of the truth about them that contradicts their areligious notions is omitted.

To illustrate my point, not long ago I read a biography on George Washington published in 2003 that made little mention of Washington's faith or belief in a personal God. In fact the author, Joseph J. Ellis, said, "Never a deeply religious man, at least in the traditional Christian sense of the term, Washington thought of God as a distant, impersonal force, the presumed well-spring for what he [Washington] called destiny or providence."[20] The author provided no evidence in the form of written statements by Washington or others for his assertions however, and although he told of Washington's many virtues, he made no mention as to how he came by those virtues.

However the truth is, during his first term as President of the United States, Washington said:

> I am sure there never was a people who had more reason to acknowledge a divine interposition in their affairs than those of the United States, and I should be pained to believe that they have forgotten that agency, which was so often manifested during our Revolution, or that they failed to consider the omnipotence of that God who alone is able to protect them.[21]

Does the above sound like a man who believed God to be a "distant, impersonal force"?

When Washington used the term "providence," as he often did in his writings, he meant, as did his peers, Almighty God's personal divine intervention; a God who appeared to be intimately interested in the nation's founding and well-being, especially since America's founding generation held God in the highest esteem and went to great lengths to obtain His favor.

Congress too frequently used the word providence in its correspondence that, according to Gragg, was part of the vernacular of the day.[22] It has already been shown that Congress's membership primarily came from the major Christian denominations of the day.

Also, since Washington had been schooled by an Anglican minister and studied the *Anglican Book of Common Prayer*,[23] his meaning for God could be none other than the Christian God of the Bible and his upbringing. The facts are that many if not most of Washington's early influences were from either Christians and church, the Bible itself, or Bible-based writings—all of which molded him into a person of true virtuous character. Gragg writes:

> In adulthood, George Washington emerged as a man whose personal theology, character, and actions were securely founded on a biblical faith. He was a sincere, low-church Anglican of Virginia's plantation gentry. Unlike New England's seventeenth century Puritans, or the Presbyterians and Baptists of his day, he was reserved in his verbal declarations of faith, although his writings were consistently laced with biblical allusions and expressions of the Judeo-Christian worldview. According to those closest to him, Washington believed that actions, not words, were the most meaningful expressions of faith. "For no man," he once wrote, "who is profligate in his morals, or a bad member of the civil community, can possibly be a true Christian...." Observed his granddaughter Nelly Custis: "He was a silent, thoughtful man.... I never witnessed his private devotions. I never inquired about them. I should have thought it the greatest

heresy to doubt his firm belief in Christianity. His life, his writings, prove that he was a Christian."[24]

None of this is mentioned or intimated in Ellis's biography of George Washington, thereby giving a warped and incomplete picture of the man in a perceived attempt to blot out his Christian beliefs and faith in the God of the Bible.

To be sure, if Washington were in a position of governmental authority today he would be under constant assault and ridicule by the forces of darkness and their legion of human surrogates in American politics and the mainstream media.

Thomas Jefferson

The secularists in modern-day America also cover up the truth about Thomas Jefferson's faith in God and Christianity. Although Jefferson did not seem to have the more obvious faith of Washington, he still considered himself a Christian. Like Washington, as a child Jefferson was tutored by Anglican ministers.[25] But for a time, at least, it seems he questioned his Christian upbringing and, according to Gragg, "plunged into the works of secular English philosophers." Gragg writes:

> Although he developed a conflicted personal theology, dabbling at times in Unitarianism[26] and deism, his personal philosophy remained rooted in the Judeo-Christian worldview… he continued to read the Bible as an adult and appears to have considered himself a Christian throughout his life. "I am a Christian," he privately wrote in 1803, during his presidency, "in the only sense in which He wished anyone to be, sincerely attached to His doctrines, in preference to all others."[27]

According to Gragg, Jefferson also advocated for the national seal of the United States to be "the children of Israel in the wilderness led by a cloud by day and a pillar [of fire] by night."[28] If you remember from chapter two, this allusion is from the book of Exodus in the Old Testament where it tells how God led the Hebrews out of Egypt and to Canaan, the promised land.

Again, all this hardly sounds like a man who was steeped in secular humanism to the point of the exclusion of Christianity.

John Adams

Although John Adams, the second President of the United States, has been accused of being a Unitarian or a deist, according to Gragg, he "professed to be a Christian all his life" and also that he "firmly fashioned his life and his politics on the Judeo Christian worldview." Gragg writes about Adams:

> He dismissed classical works of philosophy as a "disappointment," and recorded "disgust" at some of Plato's thinking. His favorite work was *Paradise Lost* by Puritan John Milton, and at one point he studied the Bible by copying its chapters into a daily journal. He was always eager to hear a well-prepared sermon, and while in Philadelphia for the Continental Congress, he tried to attend several worship services every Sunday. "The Christian religion is," he once wrote, "above all the religions that ever prevailed or existed in ancient or modern times, the religion of wisdom, virtue, equity, and humanity... it is resignation to God, it is goodness itself to man." He fancied the English theologian William Paley, an eighteenth-century apologist whose works included *Evidences of Christianity*, and he also followed latitudinarian theology which held that truth was best determined by human reason and the revelation of Scripture.[29]

According to Gragg, even the noted twenty-first century biographer and historian, David McCullough, who is not a professing person of faith, admits that Adams was "a devout Christian and an independent thinker."[30]

Other founding fathers

Other leaders of Colonial America such as Patrick Henry and Samuel Adams were also representative of the strong Christian faith of the founding generation.

Patrick Henry of "give me liberty or give me death" fame was another who was raised by Anglican Christians and, according to

Gragg, became a "devout Presbyterian who made sure he worshipped regularly..."[31] Gragg says that Henry once wrote about his faith in Jesus Christ and said it was something "I prize far above all this world has, or can boast."[32] Gragg adds that:

> At home, Henry routinely read to his family from the works of Thomas Sherlock, a leading eighteenth-century Christian apologist, whose works, Henry vouched, "removed all my doubts about the truth of Christianity." Alarmed to see French-style humanism becoming fashionable among some of Virginia's young legislators, he once reprinted and distributed Christian apologist Soame Jenyns's *View of the Internal Evidence of the Christian Religion*. As for the faddish deism in which a few of his contemporaries dabbled, Henry dismissed it as "but another name for vice and depravity" that faded before the truth of Scripture. "I am," he said, "much consoled by reflecting that the religion of Christ has, from its first appearance in the world, been attacked in vain by all the wits, philosophers, and wise ones, aided by every power of man—and its triumph is complete." Of the Bible he once said, "Here is a book worth more than all the other books that were ever printed."[33]

It was Henry who led the opposition in 1765 to the Stamp Act, one of Britain's first aggressive attempts to subdue the American colonies and make them subservient to the crown of England. It was also what led to the famous decree by Samuel Adams, "No taxation without representation." According to Gragg, "The Stamp Act of 1765 was the latest and most controversial action by [British] king and Parliament—a direct tax on all thirteen colonies even though America had no representation in Parliament."[34]

Samuel Adams was another of America's prominent founding fathers and, according to Gragg, "was the best-known champion of liberty in Colonial America" and that "Eventually, generations of Americans would know him as the 'Father of the Revolution.'"[35] Samuel Adams was the cousin of John Adams, a descendant of Puritan emigrants, and an evangelical Christian.[36] Gragg writes of him:

> Adam's inspiration, if not his influence, came from his faith—he was the embodiment of a Puritan warrior from the days of Cromwell and Charles I. Fearless and relentless on the political stage, he was devout and mild-mannered at home. His children reportedly idolized him, and his loyal wife described him as a "tender husband." His political opponents would have been incredulous to witness his nightly ritual when home: there, according to an early biographer, he would habitually gather his family in a "little circle each night [to] listen to the Divine Word." He was devoted to the faith of his fathers, and to the apostolic cry of the early church: "We must obey God rather than men!" Sam Adams, it was said, was "the last Puritan."[37]

It was Sam Adams' patriot protestors, dressed up as American Indians, who dumped ninety thousand pounds of British tea from British ships into Boston Harbor during the now famous Boston Tea Party incident in 1773.

The Colonial Church

So far, all the men mentioned above were either from military or political backgrounds or both. But a case could be made that America's true founding fathers weren't from either of these two professions at all, but were clergymen. Gragg writes:

> Ministers were often the best-educated people in their communities, and many Americans were exposed to the issues of their day from Sunday sermons and the shared knowledge of the pastor. "It was the parson who lived among books and directed the current of thought" according to [historian Frank] Child. "He [the typical pastor] was a spirited man, living in close fellowship with his Master. Strong in body and mind, compelled to be practical and disciplined in spirituality, the parson... became on many occasions the great political force... always pressing with disinterested purpose toward such issues as he deemed wisest and best."[38]

Indeed, the Colonial Christian Church bears little resemblance to the Church of Christ in America today. Unlike the modern church, Gragg says that the Colonial Church was the center of American life and it was to the local church that people went to pray in times of crisis.[39] America's Colonial pastors were among the most highly thought of persons in the community and because of this, preacher's sermons were often published in newspapers so what they thought and taught were printed and available for everyone to read. This is why ministers such as Jonathon Edwards drew large crowds outside of his immediate congregation.

Other prominent clergymen such as Presbyterian preacher Samuel Davies and Congregationalist pastor Jonathan Mayhew were also representative of the kind of Christian leaders who watched over their communities and the nation as a whole in Colonial America.

It was the dynamic New Light preacher Samuel Davies who not only greatly influenced young Patrick Henry, but according to Gragg, "shaped the thinking of an entire generation of Americans on the eve of the [American] Revolution."[40] According to Gragg, Davies' "sermons were widely published and generated a huge following throughout Colonial America. In them, he emphasized the biblical obligation of believers to selflessly serve the public good and resist tyranny." Gragg writes of Davies' beliefs:

> Christians were to be the "salt" and "light" that preserved society and lit its way with loving leadership, he taught. Without biblical direction and discipline, he counseled, political freedom would eventually dissolve into sinful self-indulgence... In a sermon titled "The Curse of Cowardice" Davies denounced the "sly hypocritical coward" who would seek public service for self-enrichment or self-promotion. Genuine, unselfish patriotism could only be inspired, he preached, by a heart that was yielded to Jesus Christ and motivated by "the agency of the Holy Spirit." Christians were therefore morally obligated to provide the leadership necessary for effective "publick Spirit and Piety."[41]

Reverend Jonathan Mayhew was another man of the cloth who was influential in shaping public opinion and action in Colonial America. During the Stamp Act crisis, a sermon that Mayhew had previously preached titled: *"A Discourse Concerning Unlimited Submission and Non-Resistance to the Higher Powers"* was reprinted in Colonial newspapers and, according to Gragg, "dramatically influenced American opinion."[42] In the sermon, Mayhew preached:

> "We may safely assert these two things in general, without undermining government," Mayhew pronounced. "One is, that no civil rulers are to be obeyed when they enjoin things that are inconsistent with the commands of God.... [D]isobedience to them is a duty, not a crime.... Another thing that may be asserted with equal truth and safety is, that no government is to be submitted to at the expense of that which is the sole end of all government—the common good and safety of society." To obey an ungodly law, Mayhew concluded, "'tis treason against mankind, 'tis treason against common sense, 'tis treason against God."[43]

It was Christian leaders such as Mayhew and others who were so influential in getting the Stamp Act and other taxes and decrees rescinded by Great Britain's Parliament and its king, King George III. Gragg says that Mayhew's *"Unlimited Submission"* sermon in particular had far-reaching affects and "would become known as 'the morning gun of the Revolution,' and it would echo from countless other American pulpits."[44]

During the Revolutionary War it was the American pastors and ministers that Britain feared even more than Washington's Continental Army, calling them the "Black Regiment"[45] for the black robes many of them wore. This was because it was the American clergy who fired up the people and called on them to resist tyranny of the kind that ignored God and sought to usurp His laws and commandments. According to Gragg, it was American clergymen who "reminded Americans that their first priority was the Higher Law of God." Gragg says that on the eve of the Revolution, "the collective call from America's pulpits was

an age-old cry of Bible-based resistance: 'No king but Jesus.'"
And in 1774 when a knowledgeable member of British
Parliament tried to explain the American mind-set to his fellow
lawmakers, he said, "If you ask an American who is his master,
he will tell you he has none, nor any governor, but Jesus
Christ."[46]

In a well-documented article, writer Joel McDurmon tells of a
custom that began at least as early as 1631 in the American
colonies where parishioners were required by law to bring their
guns to church on Sunday so they could practice using them.
Although this custom may or may not have originated with the
church, it stemmed from common sense to ensure that everyone
was able to effectively resist any threat whether it be from an
individual, a foreign invader, an insurrection, or a tyrannical
government. McDurmon tells that in 1644, a law from the
Massachusetts colony required that: "every freeman or other
inhabitant of this colony provide for himself and each under him
able bear arms a sufficient musket and other serviceable piece" as
well as "two pounds of powder and ten pounds of bullets." Those
who neglected this duty could receive fines up to ten shillings.[47]
McDurmon writes:

> The legacy of arms and freedom as Christian virtues continued
> into the American Revolution. The Lutheran pastor John Peter
> Muhlenberg is perhaps the most famous of the "fighting
> parsons." He answered George Washington's personal call to
> raise troops using his own pulpit and Ecclesiastes 3 to do so.
> Other ministers of the gospel were well known to preach with
> loaded guns in the pulpit with them. Pennsylvania preacher
> John Elder provides a great example: "Commissioned a captain
> by the Pennsylvania government, he led a company of rangers
> and was accustomed to preach with his loaded musket across
> the pulpit." Likewise, Rev. Thomas Allen, a later collaborator
> in writing the Massachusetts State Constitution, himself fired
> the first shot at the Battle of Bennington. In the context of the
> War for Independence, ministers saw guns as tools of liberty
> and defense against tyranny.[48]

Presbyterian and Congregational ministers also formed a Clergyman's Congress with the aim to protect America's religious and political liberties. According to Gragg, "Eventually, Congregationalists and Presbyterian clergy from a majority of the colonies would attend the congress, or serve on its committees of correspondence."[49]

Congress

Something that would seem extremely out-of-place in America today is if Congress called for a national day of fasting, humiliation, and prayer. But this is exactly what the Continental Congress regularly declared, beginning in 1776 and throughout the Revolutionary War. According to Gragg, by placing public notices in newspapers, the Congress would, during occasions of special crisis before and during the War, call for and "recommend that Americans everywhere beseech God for his protection 'through the merits and mediation of Jesus Christ.'"[50]

This practice actually began in the Virginia Colony in its House of Burgesses[51] when the British Navy closed and blockaded the seaport of Boston to any shipping going in or out. Gragg writes:

> In Virginia, the news from Boston arrived as the colony's House of Burgesses was convening. Patriot leader Richard Henry Lee hastily assembled an impromptu caucus of like-minded legislators that included Patrick Henry and a young lawyer named Thomas Jefferson. Huddled in the capitol's empty legislative chamber, the determined band plotted a strategy to assist Massachusetts and defend American liberty. Their solution: a day of "Fasting, Humiliation and Prayer" in Virginia on June 1, the day Boston's port would be closed. Henry and Jefferson researched Puritan fast day proclamations from a century earlier and used them as a model for the resolution... In its final, Puritan-inspired language, the resolution called on Virginians everywhere "devoutly to implore the Divine Interposition for averting the heavy Calamity, which threatens Destruction to our civil Rights,

and… to give us one Heart and one Mind firmly to oppose, by
all just and proper Means, every Injury to American Rights."[52]

Can you imagine the outcry from America's modern
multicultural society largely void of Judeo-Christian morals if
anyone even *suggested* Congress decree such a thing today?
Hence, the mess and mortal danger America is in.

Conclusion

With the exception of Ronald Reagan, few of America's
current rabble of present-day politicians are as wise as were
America's founding fathers. In fact the concept of wisdom is
another one of those terms that has fallen into disuse in modern-
day America and few seek anyone who possesses it.

The Congress of the United States whose members once
called for national days of prayer, fasting, and humiliation in
order to obtain God's favor in the American colonists' fight for
independence from Great Britain, the mightiest military power on
earth at the time, is now primarily made up of elitists on the order
of King George III who live by their own set of rules and reject
Christianity's God and His laws. John Adams said long ago:
"Our Constitution was made only for a moral and religious
people. It is wholly inadequate to the government of any other."

Today, America is in trouble because, except for a remnant of
Christian holdouts against the evil of the day, its citizens are no
longer a moral and religious people. The words of Reverend
George Duffield from 1779 offered a prescient warning:

America shall remain a city of refuge for the whole earth,
[unless] she herself shall play the tyrant, forget her
destiny, disgrace her freedom and provoke her God.

Chapter 8
Who the War is Really Against

People had a problem with Jesus Christ nearly two millennia ago and they still have a problem with Him today in twenty-first century America.

Part of this stems from misunderstanding and confusion as is shown from a Christmas card I once read that essentially said that the purpose for Jesus coming to earth was to "give the world a kiss."

But most of the problem, along with a distinct dislike comes from Jesus' well-understood and "intolerant" teachings about Him claiming to be the only way to heaven and eternal life along with His preaching that there is a place called hell with a lake of fire where people who reject Him go after they die.

Certainly, some in America today think that Jesus Christ was just a good man or a prophet of some ethereal god who said some things long ago that really don't matter much now.

Others believe Jesus to be just an ancient sage who told wise stories like those of the Greek storyteller, Aesop, of Aesop's fables fame or the Chinese philosopher, Confucius. Still others think that the idea of Christ as the Savior of mankind is only a fabrication stolen from ancient myths and that He didn't really exist at all.

But many *do* understand perfectly well Jesus' claims and teachings and not only don't like Him for them, but as so many did during His earthly ministry, reject Him because of them. Only a relative few living in America in this day and age truly believe that Jesus Christ is who He says He is: the eternal God incarnate, the Second Person of the Trinity, the Creator of all things, and the only Savior of mankind from the penalty of sin.

In this chapter, I will address, one by one, some of the misconceptions about Jesus, then provide evidence that He is who He claims to be.

Is Jesus Christ just a myth?

Some in America today have the idea regarding Jesus Christ that He was not a real person at all but a fictitious character in a made-up story taken from mythical figures from the Near East such as Horus, Osiris, or Mithras. Professor of apologetics Mary Jo Sharp asks: "Did Christians invent a religion based on first-century pagan myths?"[1] Sharp writes:

> Good sources are of the utmost importance because these indicate whether an argument has weight—and thus, whether it should be given credence. Once primary sources are obtained and comparisons are made between the two types of texts [from known myth and alleged fact], one may find that [in this case] the alleged similarities do not exist.[2] An expert in literature and mythology, C. S. Lewis was struck by the profound contrast between mythology and Scripture, so much so that his own comparison of the two actually moved him toward Christian faith. Lewis self-identified as an atheist at one point in his life, in part because the story of Jesus, with its savior-god theme, seemed to have the same structure as myth. But as Lewis began to study the Bible, he observed that it had a distinct writing structure. He said of the book [gospel] of John: "I have been reading poems, romances, vision literature, legends, myths all my life. I know what they are like. I know that not one of them is like this."[3]

Sharp posits why myths may arise in the first place by referring again to Lewis and summarizing his idea that: "Mythological stories express man's yearning for contact with God."[4]

Twentieth century scholar F. F. Bruce said: "Some writers may toy with the fancy of a 'Christ-myth,' but they do not do so on the ground of historical evidence. The historicity of Christ is as axiomatic for an unbiased historian as the historicity of Julius

Caesar. It is not historians who propagate the 'Christ-myth' theories."[5]

My question is—If the story of Jesus Christ is a myth, why then did a thriving worldwide religious movement spring from Him that has transcended nations for nearly two thousand years and against so many who have tried to eradicate it when the religions that contained mythical figures all but passed away when the respective civilizations that adhered to them died off?

Non-Biblical documentary evidence for a historical Jesus

One may say—Since Jesus Christ is not a myth or a character in ancient fiction, then one would have to assume that He was a real person and of some prominence since an entire religion arose because of Him. So is there any evidence of His existence outside of the Bible? The answer is—The person of Jesus Christ as the promised Jewish Messiah who lived at the beginning of the first century around Jerusalem in Judea (Israel) is well attested to in non-Biblical, historical writings.

Josh McDowell in his book *Evidence That Demands a Verdict* recounts no less than a dozen ancient Jewish and non-Jewish references to both Jesus Christ and His followers who were called Christians.

As Paul Barnett states, "Very few historians deny the historical evidence of Jesus. Non-Christian and hostile writers, Josephus, Tacitus, and Pliny… leave us no doubt that Jesus was, indeed, a true figure of history."[6]

Research professor of New Testament Studies at Dallas Theological Seminary, Darrell L. Bock, in his book, *Who is Jesus*, says: "near contemporary non-Christian sources, such as the first-century Jewish historian Josephus, or the early second-century Roman historians Suetonius and Tacitus, who together testify multiple times to the fact that Jesus lived in first-century Galilee[7] and died at the hands of Rome."[8]

In *The Popular Handbook of Archaeology and the Bible*, published in 2013, the authors, Holden and Geisler, write:

[A]rguments denying the existence of Jesus of Nazareth have fallen out of favor due to the growing body of documentary evidence from Jewish and Greco-Roman sources that speak of Jesus and the events surrounding His life and ministry. From these early non-Christian sources (Flavius Josephus, the Babylonian Talmud, Pliny the Younger, Tacitus, Mara Bar-Serapion, Suetonius, Thallus, Lucian, Phlegon, and Celsus) we may reconstruct the salient features of the life of Christ without appealing to the New Testament. These features include the following:

1. Jesus lived during the reign of Tiberius Caesar.
2. He lived a virtuous life.
3. He was a wonder-worker.
4. He had a brother named James.
5. He was claimed to be the Messiah.
6. He was crucified under Pontius Pilate.
7. He was crucified on the eve of the Passover.
8. Darkness and an earthquake occurred when He died.
9. His disciples believed he rose from the dead.
10. His disciples were willing to die for their belief.
11. Christianity spread as far as Rome.
12. Christian disciples denied the Roman gods and worshipped Jesus as God.

… From these discoveries emerge over 30 New Testament individuals (including Jesus) mentioned in Scripture who have been corroborated as historical figures by non-Christian sources...[9]

The ancient sources

The Jewish historian Flavius Josephus who wrote in the second half of the first century tells of a Jesus who lived at the same time of Pontius Pilate, the Roman procurator who condemned Him to be executed by crucifixion, the same story with some of the same details as related in the New Testament. Josephus wrote:

Now, there was about this time Jesus, a wise man, if it be lawful to call him a man, for he was a doer of wonderful works – a teacher of such men as receive the truth with pleasure. He drew over to him both many of the Jews, and many of the Gentiles. He was [the] Christ; and when Pilate, at the suggestion of the principle men among us,[10] had condemned him to the cross, those that loved him at the first did not forsake him, for he appeared to them alive again the third day, as the divine prophets had foretold these and ten thousand other wonderful things concerning him; and the tribe of Christians, so named from him, are not extinct at this day.[11]

Josephus also tells the story of James' death by stoning who he says was, "the brother of Jesus, the so-called Christ."

Roman historian Cornelius Tacitus who was born around 53 AD writes of "Christians" who were "punished with the most exquisite tortures" whose religion was from "Christus, the founder of the name, [who] was put to death by Pontius Pilate, procurator of Judea in the reign of Tiberius [Caesar]."[12]

McDowell writes of Plinius Secundus, also known as Pliny the Younger. He says Pliny was governor of Bithynia located in Asia Minor in the early second century AD and wrote a letter to the Roman emperor Trajan asking him how he should treat Christians. According to McDowell, Pliny:

Explained that he had been killing both men and women, boys and girls. There were so many being put to death that he wondered if he should continue killing anyone who was discovered to be a Christian, or if he should kill only certain ones. He explained that he had made the Christians bow down to the statues of Trajan. He goes on to say that he also "made them curse Christ, which a genuine Christian cannot be induced to do." In the same letter he says of the people who were being tried: "They affirmed, however, that the whole of their guilt, or their error, was, that they were in the habit of meeting on a certain fixed day before it was light, when they sang an alternate verse a hymn to Christ as to a god, and bound themselves to a solemn oath, not to do any wicked deeds, but never to commit any fraud, theft, adultery, never to falsify their word, not to deny a trust when they should be called to deliver it up."[13]

Holden, Geisler, and McDowell all recount the words of several ancient writers who mention the darkness and earthquakes that accompanied the crucifixion of Christ as told in the book of Matthew 27:45-54 (also Mark 15:33-39) from the New Testament. McDowell tells of early third century AD historian Julius Africanus who quotes first century AD historian Phlegon, whose original work, *Chronicles*, has been lost. According to Africanus, Phlegon talks about the "eclipse [of the sun] which took place during the crucifixion of the Lord Christ... during the full moon."[14] McDowell then quotes Africanus again, when Africanus muses over what first century historian, Thallus, whose original works have also not survived the centuries, wrote about this event:

> Thallus, in the third book of his histories, explains away this darkness as an eclipse of the sun – unreasonably, as it seems to me (unreasonably, of course because a solar eclipse could not take place at the time of the full moon, and it was at the season of the Paschal full moon that Christ died).[15]

Holden and Geisler quote Africanus as well, who again refers to Thallus:

> On the whole world there pressed a most fearful darkness; and rocks were rent by an earthquake, and many places in Judea and other districts were thrown down.[16]

So we see in secular history that not only is Jesus Christ attested to, but the extraordinary events surrounding His crucifixion are as well.

Archaeological Evidence

Although there is admittedly only a small amount of archaeological evidence that directly supports the person of Jesus Christ,[17] what does exist is compelling.

Such is the "James Ossuary" that came into the public eye in Israel in 2002.[18] The Gospels of Matthew (15:55) and Mark (6:3), tell us that Jesus had four brothers (actually half-brothers): James, Joses, Simon, and Judas, and at least two half-sisters (Mark 6:3). Jesus' "stepfather" of course was Joseph, since Christ's divine conception required no earthly, biological father. But of all Jesus' half-brothers and sisters, we are only told in the Bible that James became one of His disciples. Although Jesus' half-brother James was not one of the two James mentioned among the twelve apostles who were chosen by Jesus, according to Unger, he became very prominent in the Jerusalem Church[19] after Christ's resurrection and was also the author of the epistle in the New Testament that bears his name.

Concerning Jewish ossuaries, they were typically made out of limestone, measured approximately eighteen inches long, and were used to store the bones of the deceased after the flesh had decomposed. This was allegedly done to save space, so that more human remains could be interred within tombs that possessed limited space. Ossuaries were reportedly in use in Israel for only a short time, from about the second century BC to 70 AD. The ossuary of James, (who was reportedly martyred around 62 AD in Jerusalem), fits well within this time frame.

The transliteration of the full inscription on the James Ossuary reads: "Jacob (or James), son of Joseph, brother of Jesus."

At first it was thought by authorities that the "brother of Jesus" was added at a later date, but as the result of a long, drawn-out court trial and much forensic investigation, the last three words were deemed to be authentic as was the first part of the inscription. Although all three names could be part of Jesus Christ's earthly family, all three names were reportedly very common in first century Israel and may not be. However, at the very least, the ossuary and its inscription does prove that the names and associations as recorded in the New Testament are historically accurate.

Although archeology has uncovered some other evidences for Jesus Christ, His Church, death by crucifixion, and other prominent figures from Christ's time, to me, none are as captivating as the James Ossuary.

Jesus Christ—Lord, liar, or lunatic?

Okay, so Jesus Christ is a real person of history, but who was or is He really? Was He a prophet as some who belong to religions other than Christianity claim? Yes, Christ was a prophet of the one true God in the sense that He correctly foretold of things that were to come,[20] but He was also much more than a prophet in the Old Testament use of the term, since He also claimed to be God in the flesh. And this is one of His claims that many people in America today seem to have a real problem with.

Although some understand that Jesus claimed to be God, others say that Jesus never really made such an assertion. However, this is not correct, Jesus *did* claim to be God *and* to be equal with the Father who He said He was in constant communication and unity with. As recounted earlier, Jesus says in John 5:19: *"the Son* [Jesus] *can do nothing of Himself, but what He sees the Father do; for whatsoever He does, the Son also does in like manner,"* then later He says in chapter 10, verse 30 that, *"I and My Father are one."* In John 12:45 Jesus states: *"And he who sees Me sees Him who sent me."* In John 10:37-38 Jesus tells the Jewish religious leaders who did not believe in Him: *"If I do not do the works of my Father, do not believe Me; but if I do, though you do not believe Me, believe the works, that you may know and believe that the Father is in Me and I in Him."*

In both of these last instances, the Jews attempted to seize Jesus for blasphemy because they understood full well that He was making Himself equal with God; after Jesus' words in John 10:30, verse 31 reads: *"Then the Jews took up stones again to stone Him."*

But Jesus not only claimed to be equal with God, He claimed to be God Himself.

In Exodus 3:13-14 of the Old Testament, Moses said to God who was in the burning bush: *"Suppose I go to the Israelites and say to them, 'The God of your fathers has sent me to you,' and they ask me, 'What is his name?' Then what shall I tell them? God said to Moses, 'I AM WHO I AM. This is what you are to say to the Israelites: **I AM** has sent me to you.'"* [author's emphasis]

Fast forward to the New Testament to the Gospel of John, chapter 8. In verse 52, as part of an ongoing conversation between the Jewish religious leaders and Jesus that began at the start of the chapter, the religious leaders accuse Jesus of being possessed by a devil. Compare what God said at the end of the Exodus passage with this:

At this they exclaimed, "Now we know that you are demon-possessed! Abraham died and so did the prophets, yet you say that whoever obeys your word will never taste death. Are you greater than our father Abraham? He died, and so did the prophets. Who do you think you are?" Jesus replied, "If I glorify myself, my glory means nothing. My Father, whom you claim as your God, is the one who glorifies me. Though you do not know Him, I know Him. If I said I did not, I would be a liar like you, but I do know Him and obey His word. Your father Abraham rejoiced at the thought of seeing my day; he saw it and was glad." "You are not yet fifty years old," they said to Him, "and you have seen Abraham!" "Very truly I tell you," Jesus answered, "before Abraham was born, I am!"(NIV) [author's emphasis]

In this passage, Jesus not only equates Himself with Jehovah, the eternal God, He claims that He *is* the eternal God. If this seems fantastic, Jesus' apostles and disciples, those closest to Him, understood exactly who Jesus is.

In John chapter 20, after Jesus was resurrected from the dead, He showed Himself to the apostles. All were present except Thomas. Later, after Jesus was gone, when the other apostles told Thomas they had seen Jesus alive, he doubted them. When Jesus showed Himself to the apostles again eight days later, including Thomas this time, Jesus singled him out: *"Then He said to Thomas, 'Put your finger here; see my hands. Reach out your hand and put it into my side. Stop doubting and believe.'"* At this, John says that Thomas proclaimed to Jesus: *"My Lord and my God!"*

Furthermore, all the writers of the New Testament understood full well that Jesus is God come in the flesh. John explains in his Gospel that Jesus Christ, before His incarnation, was called the Word of God. John 1:1-3 reads:

In the beginning was the Word, and the Word was with God, and the Word was God. He was in the beginning with God. All things were made by Him, and without Him nothing was made that was made. (NKJV)

Verse 14 then says:

And the Word became flesh and dwelt among us, and we beheld His glory, the glory of the only begotten of the Father, full of grace and truth. (NKJV)

The apostle Paul also thoroughly understood who Jesus was and is. In his letter to the Christian church in Philippi, he wrote:

Let this mind be in you which was also in Christ Jesus, who, being in the form of God, did not consider it robbery to be equal with God, but made Himself of no reputation, taking the form of a servant, and coming in the likeness of men. And being found in appearance as a man, He humbled Himself and became obedient to the point of death, even the death of the cross. Therefore God also has highly exalted Him and given Him a name which is above every name, that at the name of Jesus every knee should bow, of those in heaven, and of those on earth, and that every tongue should confess that Jesus Christ is Lord, to the glory of God the Father.
Philippians 2:5-11 (NKJV)

Paul adds in his letter to the Church at Colosse: *"For in Him* [Jesus] *dwells all the fullness of the Godhead bodily"*, (Colossians 2:9) and to his disciple Titus: *"*[We should live] *looking for the blessed hope and glorious appearing of our great God and Savior Jesus Christ."* (Titus 2:13)

Jesus' followers also worshipped Him as God and Jesus did not forbid them or tell them not to: Matthew 14:33 says, after Jesus stilled the wind when He and the apostles were in the boat that was in danger of sinking, that the apostles *"came and worshipped Him, saying, 'Truly You are the Son of God.'"* And again after Christ's resurrection, Mary Magdalene and Mary the mother of Joses, *"came and held Him by the feet and worshipped Him"* (Matthew 28:9). Again in Luke 24:52 the apostles *"worshipped Him."* Even the wise men, when they found the baby Jesus, *"fell down and worshipped Him"* (Matthew 2:11).

Other Biblical proofs that Jesus Christ is God

Other, less known, corroborations within the Bible itself between the Old and New Testaments also reveal Jesus Christ to be Almighty God.

The prophet Daniel in the Old Testament describes God in a vision as the "Ancient of Days." He writes in Daniel 7:9-10:

"I [Daniel] *watched till thrones were put in place, And the Ancient of Days was seated; His garment was white as snow, And the hair on His head was like pure wool. His throne was a fiery flame, Its wheels a burning fire; And a fiery stream issued And came forth from before Him, a thousand thousands ministered to Him; Ten thousand times ten thousand stood before Him. The court was seated, And the books were opened."* (NKJV)

Compare the above with the vision that the apostle John received which became the book of Revelation (1:12-15) in the New Testament:

Then I [John] *turned to see the voice that spoke with me. And having turned I saw seven golden lampstands, and in the midst of the seven lampstands One like the Son of Man, clothed with a garment down to His feet and girded about the chest with a golden band. His head and His hair were white like wool, as white as snow, and His eyes were like a flame of fire; His feet were like fine brass, as if refined in a furnace, and His voice as the sound of many waters.* (NKJV)

Now compare the above verse in Revelation with the words of the prophet Ezekiel in the Old Testament who also saw God in a vision:

And behold, the glory of the God of Israel came from the way of the east. His voice was like the sound of many waters; and the earth shone with His glory."
Ezekiel 43:2 (NKJV)

In the above passages, God, whom the prophet Daniel saw and Jesus, whom the apostle John saw, both had a head and hair like white wool. And God, whom the prophet Ezekiel saw, and Jesus, whom the apostle John saw, both had a voice like "*the sound of many waters.*" These people must all be seeing the same person.

In the Old Testament book of Isaiah, God tells the prophet "*I am the First and I am the Last; Besides Me there is no God.*" (Isaiah 44:6) Isaiah recounts two other times (also Isaiah 41:4 and 48:12) that God essentially said the same thing about Him being "*the first and the last.*" In Revelation 1:17, the apostle John writes that the "*Son of Man*" says the same words of Himself. After the Son of Man lays his right hand on John, He tells him: "*Do not be afraid; I am the First and the Last*" then adds: "*I am He who lives, and was dead, and behold, I am alive forevermore.*" At the end of the Book of Revelation, the Son of Man concludes in chapter 22 verse 13 with: "*I am the Alpha and the Omega, the Beginning and the End, the First and the Last,*" then in verse 16 He plainly identifies Himself as "Jesus."

There can be no doubt that Jesus Christ *is* God Almighty!

Since I demonstrated in chapter two that the Bible is the trustworthy word of God, the question you, the reader, must ask yourself is—Are the words of Jesus Christ in the New Testament those of a liar, a lunatic, or from someone who knew exactly who He was and who He claimed to be and His disciples knew Him to be—the Great God and Savior, the eternal Lord of all?

Did Jesus really die on a cross?

Now that it has been established that Jesus Christ is indeed a historical figure, it is not difficult to believe that He was crucified just like the Bible says, especially since it is almost commonly known that Rome used the practice for many years as the ultimate punishment for criminals and other less-desirables in their society.

Bock says: "One of the best-attested events in Jesus' life is his crucifixion."[21] And Werner Keller writes:

> The descriptions of the trial, sentence and crucifixion in the four Gospels have been checked with scientific thoroughness by many scholars and have been found to be historically reliable accounts even to the last detail. The chief witnesses for the prosecution against Jesus have been indirectly attested and the place where sentence was pronounced has been accurately ascertained by excavations. The various incidents in the course of the trial can be verified from contemporary sources and modern research.[22]

Although it seems of little importance, some have said that Jesus wasn't really nailed to the cross as the New Testament relates because the Romans used to tie their victims to crosses with ropes and didn't use nails. Although it is reportedly true that Romans also tied victims to crosses, the discovery of the Yehohanan Ossuary proves that it was also customary to nail the victim to a cross as well. Holden and Geisler write:

> That Christ died by crucifixion, and that the Romans practiced this form of capital punishment in the first century AD during the life of Christ, is now well-attested. This is supported by our understanding of history spanning from the sixth century BC to the fourth century AD; namely, that this type of punishment was used by the Persians, Carthaginians, and the Romans, only to be abolished in the fourth century by Emperor Constantine. Moreover, a limestone ossuary... was discovered in Jerusalem

in 1968 that contained the bones of a first-century AD crucifixion victim named Yehohanan ben Hagkol. Upon examination, the right heel and wrist bone still contained the Roman seven-inch spikes intact, thus attesting the Roman practice during the first century when Christ was reported to have been crucified.[23]

Even though many skeptics will concede that Jesus was crucified, they claim that He didn't really die on the cross, but merely "swooned" or fainted. They say that this is why He was able to later show Himself alive to hundreds of people as the New Testament tells. However, for those who believe the Bible accounts in the New Testament, as well they should, concerning the beating and flogging that Jesus received even before He was crucified as told in the Gospels, there is no possible way Christ merely fainted on the cross only to show up three days later, alive and well.

Author Lee Stroble, in his book, *The Case For Easter*, interviewed Alexander Metherell, a medical doctor with a PhD because, as he says, he had heard that Metherell possessed the medical and scientific credentials to explain the crucifixion of Christ. In the book Stroble quotes Metherell telling what a Roman flogging and crucifixion was like in Jesus' day:

Roman floggings were known to be terribly brutal. They usually consisted of thirty-nine lashes but frequently were a lot more than that, depending on the mood of the soldier applying the blows. The soldier would use a whip of braided leather thongs with metal balls woven into them. When the whip would strike the flesh, these balls would cause deep bruises or contusions, which would break open with further blows. And the whip had pieces of sharp bone as well, which would cut the flesh severely. The back would be so shredded that part of the spine was sometimes exposed by the deep, deep cuts. The whipping would have gone all the way from the shoulders down to the back, the buttocks, and the back of the legs... One physician who has studied Roman beatings said, "As the flogging continued, the lacerations would tear into the underlying skeletal muscles and produce quivering ribbons of bleeding flesh." A third-century historian by the name of Eusebius described a flogging by saying, "The sufferer's veins were laid bare, and the very muscles, sinews, and bowels of the victim were open to exposure." We know that many people would die from this kind of beating even before they could be crucified. At the least, the victim would experience tremendous pain and go into hypovolemic shock.

Metherell then explains what "hypovolemic shock" is:

Hypo means "low," *vol* refers to volume, and *emic* means "blood" so *hypovolemic shock* means the person is suffering the effects of losing a large amount of blood... This does four things. First, the heart races to try to pump blood that isn't there; second, the blood pressure drops, causing fainting or collapse; third, the kidneys stop producing urine to maintain what volume is left; and fourth, the person becomes very thirsty as the body craves fluids to replace the lost blood volume. Jesus was in hypovolemic shock as he staggered up the road to the execution site at Calvary, carrying the horizontal beam of the cross.

Metherell then relates what the Gospels say, that Jesus finally collapsed, and a Roman soldier ordered a man named Simon to carry the cross for him. Metherell continues:

Because of the terrible effects of this beating, there's no question that Jesus was already in serious to critical condition even before the nails were driven through his hands and feet.

[On Calvary] He would have been laid down, and his hands would have been nailed to the outstretched position to the horizontal beam. This crossbar was called the *patibulum*, and at this stage it was separate from the vertical beam, which was permanently set in the ground.

Metherell then tells that Jesus would have been nailed to the "horizontal beam" and that the Romans used iron spikes tapered to a sharp point and were five to seven inches long:

They were driven through the wrists... This was a solid position that would lock the hand; if the nails had been driven through the palms, his weight would have caused the skin to tear and he would have fallen off the cross... And it's important to understand that the nail would go through the place where the median nerve runs. This is the largest nerve going out to the hand, and it would be crushed by the nail that was being pounded in. The pain was absolutely unbearable... In fact, it was literally beyond words to describe; they had to invent a new word, *excruciating*. Literally, *excruciating* means "out of the cross." Think of that: they needed to create a new word because there was nothing in the language that could describe the intense anguish caused during the crucifixion.

At this point Jesus was hoisted as the crossbar was attached to the vertical stake, and the nails were driven through Jesus' feet. Again, the nerves in his feet would have been crushed, and there would have been a similar type of pain... his arms would have immediately been stretched, probably about six inches in length, and both shoulders would have become dislocated--you can determine this with simple mathematical equations. Once a person is hanging in the vertical position... crucifixion is essentially an agonizing slow death by asphyxiation. The reason is that the stresses on the muscles and diaphragm put the chest into the inhaled position; basically, in order to exhale, the individual must push up on his feet so the tension on the muscles would be eased for a moment. In doing so, the nail would tear through the foot, eventually locking up against the tarsal bones. After managing to exhale, the person would then be able to relax down and take another breath in. Again he'd have to push himself up to exhale, scraping his bloodied back against the coarse wood of the cross. This would go on and on until complete exhaustion would take over and the person wouldn't be able to push up and breathe anymore. As the person slows down his breathing, he goes into what is called *respiratory acidosis*--the carbon dioxide in the blood is dissolved as carbonic acid, causing the acidity of the blood to increase. This eventually leads to an irregular heartbeat. In fact, with his heart beating erratically, Jesus would have known that he was at the moment of death, which is when he was able to say, "Lord, into your hands I commit my spirit." And then he died of cardiac arrest. Even before he died--and this is important too--the hypovolemic shock would have caused a sustained rapid heart rate that would have contributed to heart failure, resulting in the collection of fluid in the membrane around the heart, called a *pericardial effusion,* as well as around the lungs, which is called *pleural effusion.* Because of what happened when the Roman soldier came around and, being fairly certain that Jesus was dead, confirmed it by thrusting a spear into his right side. It was probably his right side, that's not certain, but from the description it was probably the right side, between the ribs. The spear apparently went through the right lung and into the heart, so when the spear was pulled out, some fluid—the pericardial effusion and the pleural effusion--came out. This would have the appearance of a clear fluid, like water, followed by a large volume of blood, as the eyewitness John described in his gospel. John probably had no idea why he saw both blood and a clear fluid come out—certainly that's not what an untrained person like him would have anticipated. Yet John's description is consistent with what modern medicine would expect to have happened. There was absolutely no doubt that Jesus was dead.[24]

It is also important to add here that, according to the Gospels of Luke and John,[25] two criminals were crucified at the same time as Jesus and near Him. The apostle John tells how the Jews (the religious leaders) did not want the bodies to remain on the crosses on the Sabbath and asked Pilate *"that their legs might be broken, and that they might be taken away."* The legs of victims were broken so that they could no longer push themselves up in order to breathe as told above. After the legs were broken, a victim would die within minutes. But John says that after the soldiers came and broke the legs of the two criminals because they must have been clearly alive, they stopped at Jesus, because, as John testifies, they *"saw that He was already dead."* Although they didn't break Jesus' legs, just to make sure He really was dead, one of them *"pierced His side with a spear,"* after which John tells, *"blood and water"* came out of the wound. Because of this, it is obvious the soldiers knew for certain Jesus was dead since they still did not break His legs.

All of the above is to show that there is no way Jesus survived or *could have* survived any of the physical abuses done to Him and that He indeed died on the cross at Calvary.[26]

Was Jesus' tomb really empty?

Now comes the part of the story of Jesus Christ where things start to heat up.

Albert Henry Ross writing under the pen name of Frank Morison set out to do a thorough investigation of the facts surrounding the death and resurrection of Jesus Christ. In his classic treatise, *Who Moved the Stone,* Morison says:

> In all the fragments and echoes of this far-off controversy that have come down to us we are nowhere told that any responsible person asserted that the body of Jesus was still in the tomb.[27]

According to Scripture, Jesus' body was claimed by one of His disciples, a wealthy man named Joseph from the city of Arimathea. Joseph got permission from Pilate to take down the body of Jesus after which he placed it in his own tomb, one that the Bible says had never been used before. John in his Gospel tells that the Pharisee, Nicodemus, the one whom Jesus had told must be born again in order to see the kingdom of God (John 3:1-3), had come with Joseph who also may have been a fellow Pharisee, although neither had been in on the plot against Jesus.[28] Even though the details of what happened next differ slightly from the four gospel writers, what is clear is that at least two of Jesus' female disciples, *"Mary Magdalene and Mary the mother of Joses,"*[29] had followed Joseph and Nicodemus and saw where they interred the body of Jesus. They must have also seen that although Jesus had been wrapped in a *"clean linen cloth,"* He had not been buried properly with *"spices and fragrant oils"* according to Jewish custom. This may have been because it was by this time so late in the day and was dark or getting dark. At some point before they left the scene, Joseph, together with Nicodemus, must have rolled the stone in front of the tomb entrance, essentially sealing Jesus' body inside. Then, the two women apparently left as well, with a plan to come back after the Sabbath and properly prepare Jesus' body. At some point too, before Joseph and Nicodemus left the tomb, Roman guards[30] arrived to watch over it to make sure that Jesus' disciples could not *"come by night and steal Him away, and say to the people, 'He has risen from the dead'"* as the religious leaders warned Pilate (Matthew 27:64), causing him to order soldiers to stand watch. What also probably happened is that the soldiers helped Joseph and Nicodemus roll the very large stone over the tomb entrance after witnessing that Jesus' body was indeed inside the tomb.

The Bible then says that the two women arrived at the tomb once more the morning after the Sabbath. And again, Gospel stories differ, but what is probable is that they: met an angel, saw that the stone sealing the tomb had already been rolled away exposing the entrance and, that the inside of the tomb was empty and devoid of Jesus' body. The Roman guards were also witnesses to at least some of what happened at the tomb that morning because they went almost immediately (Matthew 28:11) and told the Jewish religious leaders what they saw. Matthew tells in his Gospel that the guards told the *chief priests all the things that had happened.* This must have included seeing the stone sealing the tomb rolled away by the angel (Matthew 28:2-4) and possibly Jesus exiting it alive because Matthew tells how the "chief priests" later bribed them with money and told them to say: *His disciples came at night and stole Him away while we slept.* This was tantamount to an admission that the disciples had *not* stolen the body, because if they had, why *pay* the soldiers to tell the truth, which they probably would have done.[31]

And this is where the real controversy begins.

Many skeptics and unbelievers today say that Christ's tomb could not have been empty, that the Biblical accounts of His burial are false because people simply don't come back to life after being dead for three days so there must be another natural explanation for the absence of Jesus' body.

Morison, who investigated all these possibilities as to what happened to Jesus' remains says:

> It is the complete failure of anyone to produce the remains, or to point to any tomb, official or otherwise, in which they were said to lie, and this ultimately destroys every theory based on the human removal of the body.[32]

And:

> I am convinced that no body of men or women could persistently and successfully have preached in Jerusalem a doctrine involving the vacancy of that tomb, without the grave itself being physically vacant. The facts were too recent; the tomb too close to that seething center of oriental life. Not all the make-believe in the world could have purchased the utter silence of antiquity or given to the records their impressive unanimity. Only the truth itself, in all its unavoidable simplicity, could have achieved that.[33]

The only explanation for the empty tomb appears to be that Jesus Christ had indeed risen from the dead just as the soldiers had most likely witnessed and the evidence is in what happened with the apostles soon after.

The evidence for the resurrection of Jesus Christ

It is amazing to me that people believe in any religion that has no objective proof from its founder or otherwise to prove that he or she or it, as in the case of visions or alleged appearances of otherworldly entities, are speaking for the one true God. Both the Old and New Testaments tell of how God has always used miracles to prove His words and involvement in human affairs. Jesus too, used miracles to prove that He is who He said He is and that what He said is true. The ultimate miracle or proof was Christ raising Himself from the dead (John 2:19-21). No other religion in the world can boast of such a certification of authenticity since all other religious founders are dead and in their graves: Buddha, Muhammad, Joseph Smith, Charles T. Russell, L. Ron Hubbard, etc. The resurrection of Jesus Christ is the greatest human event of all time and the greatest proof that Christianity is the only revelation in the world today that is from the one true God. One of the evidences for the resurrection of Jesus Christ is in the changed lives of the apostles and other disciples of Jesus. Frank Morison writes:

> When we remember the swinging around of the disciples from panic fear to absolute certitude... the extraordinary rapid adhesion of converts in Jerusalem, the strange absence of administrative vigor on the part of the authorities, the steady growing of the church, both in authority and power, until the whole situation blew up into the frenzied attempts at suppression under Saul, we realize that we are in the presence of something far more tangible than the psychological repercussion of a fisherman's dream.[34]

Stroble quotes Christian apologist and philosopher, James P. Moreland, who says:

When Jesus was crucified, his followers were discouraged and depressed. So they dispersed. The Jesus movement was all but stopped in its tracks. Then, after a short period of time, we see them abandoning their occupations, regathering, and committing themselves to spreading a very specific message— that Jesus Christ was the Messiah of God who died on a cross, returned to life, and was seen alive by them. And they were willing to spend the rest of their lives proclaiming this, without any payoff from a human point of view. They faced a life of hardship. They often went without food, slept exposed to the elements, were ridiculed, beaten, imprisoned. And finally, most of them were executed in torturous ways. For what? For good intentions? No, because they were convinced beyond a shadow of a doubt that they had seen Jesus Christ alive from the dead.[35]

Biblical scholar, Paul Barnett writes,

The texts of the New Testament throb with the conviction that Jesus rose alive from the dead. So comprehensive and pervasive is the resurrection of Jesus that, historically speaking, the onus is on the skeptic to overturn it... There is no single alternative theory to the resurrection of Jesus that has been advanced to explain the historical data. Some say it was a hoax; others say that the Romans crucified the wrong man (the Qur'an), or that Jesus did not actually die on the cross (the "swoon theory"), or that the disciples stole the body, or that the women went to the wrong tomb, or that eastern mystery religions suggested the idea. It is striking that those who reject the resurrection of Jesus have not settled on one major objection to its historicity.[36]

Almost all the apostles of Jesus and many of His immediate disciples died horrible deaths for their belief in the resurrection of Jesus Christ and the teaching of His gospel.

The late, William Steuart McBirnie, who had a long list of degrees and credentials, went to great lengths to uncover the fates of the twelve apostles, even traveling to the lands of their individual deaths to learn as much as he could about the oral traditions surrounding them. In his book, *The Search For The*

Twelve Apostles, McBirnie, chronicles the life of each apostle up to the time of his death, then tells by what means each died. In the case of the apostle Peter, He tells that, according to tradition, the apostle was crucified upside down because "He refused to die in the same manner as our Lord, declaring he was unworthy."[37] In the case of the apostle Paul, he tells how, after a long and fruitful ministry, the apostle was eventually beheaded in Rome. McBirnie sites that both Peter and Paul spent time incarcerated in the infamous, "horrible, fetid prison of the Mamertine," located in Rome. Concerning Mamertine prison, McBirnie relates that:

> Never before or since has there been a dungeon of equal horror. Historians write of it as being the most fearsome on the brutal agenda of mankind. Over three thousand years old, it is probably the oldest torture chamber extent, the oldest remaining monument of bestiality of ancient Rome, a bleak testimony to its barbaric inhumanity, steeped in Christian tragedy and the agony of thousands of its murdered victims.[38]

McBirnie tells how Peter spent nine months down in the hole of Mamertine prison manacled to a post, "enduring monstrous torture." He says that Paul too spent time in the prison. Many, if not all, the apostles endured, at one time or another similar tortures and imprisonment.

According to C. Bernard Ruffin, in his book, *The Twelve*, all except possibly two apostles died violent and/or torturous deaths. Most were killed by various methods: crucifixion, flaying alive and crucifixion, impalement, sawn into pieces, stoning, stabbing, and decapitation.

Up until their last breath, all these men preached the Gospel of Jesus Christ that included His death and resurrection, many of them traveling thousands of miles to various countries in order to fulfill Christ's "Great Commission" to *"Go therefore and make disciples of all the nations"* (Matthew 28:19).

Indeed, all of the apostles were convinced that Christ was made alive again after His death on the cross and that they too would be raised again to life in heaven after they died or were killed.

Now why would each of these men do all this for what he knew to be a lie? The answer—They wouldn't, no one would!

Still other evidence for the resurrection of Jesus Christ from the dead is the absolute silence of any first century writings that contradict the Biblical narrative. Morison makes the observation:

> Yet in all the varied literature from that far-off time, written under different skies, by men of varying temperaments, possessed by obviously divergent theories of the true course of those memorable events, there has come down to us no hint or suggestion that the facts about the grave were other than those substantially recorded in the Gospel according to Mark. However disconcerting the fact may be, the literary verdict is unanimous and must at least be given its due weight by the impartial mind... I mean the extraordinary silence of antiquity concerning the later history of the grave of Jesus. It is strange––this absolutely unbroken silence concerning a spot that must have been a very sacred place to thousands of people outside the circle of the Christian believers themselves.[39]

The New Testament doesn't claim that just one or two, or only a handful of people saw Jesus after He rose from the dead, it tells that *many* people saw Him alive. The apostle Paul says in I Corinthians 15:6 that *"He was seen by over five hundred brethren at once, of whom the greater part remain to the present."* Since Paul's letter was reportedly written to the Corinthians between 55 and 57 AD, less than 25 years after Jesus' crucifixion, it would have been easy for someone to have complained to someone in authority that what Paul wrote was a lie. If this had been the case, surely some contemporary source would have recorded it and there is a good chance we would know about it today. But this is not the case. In fact, Lee Stroble quotes "resurrection" expert, Gary Habermas, as saying:

> Now stop and think about it, you would never include this phrase [I Corinthians 15:6] unless you were absolutely confident that these folks would confirm that they really did see Jesus alive, I mean, Paul was virtually inviting people to check it out for themselves! He wouldn't have said this if he didn't know they'd back him up.[40]

So we today aren't expected by God to believe that only one or even just a few witnesses saw Jesus alive after being dead, but hundreds, enough in fact that there were ample opportunities for doubters to contradict any one of them by exposing them as frauds by producing evidence to the contrary. But there is no record of any person living during that time who did this.

The Jewish Messianic prophesies fulfilled by Jesus Christ

In chapter two I talked about how prophecy is unique to the Bible. That makes it also unique to Christianity. No other religion has any predictions of its founder's birth, lineage, and details of his death, hundreds of years before he was born.

Thompson's Chain-Reference Bible lists thirty-eight Old Testament prophecies concerning the Jewish Messiah, all of which were fulfilled by Jesus Christ. The prophecies start in the first book of the Bible (Genesis) and range from the lineage or ancestry that Christ would come from, His time and place of birth to—that He would be born of a virgin and would be crucified and raised from the dead by God. Twelve prophesies alone address the details surrounding the Messiah's false arrest, subsequent death by crucifixion, and ultimate resurrection from the dead. Thompson's Bible shows each original prophecy in the Old Testament, then how Jesus in the New Testament fulfilled each one.

Another interesting source for understanding what some contemporary Jews living at the time of Jesus believed about the Messiah is in the Dead Sea Scrolls discovered between 1946 and 1956. New Testament scholar, Charles L. Quarles, tells what they expected:

Isaiah 61 is a prophesy about the Messiah or anointed one. A
text from the Dead Sea Scrolls (4Q521) confirms that first-
century Jews saw these texts as Messianic and thus expected
the Messiah to perform a variety of miracles. Jesus' widely
accepted Messianic claims thus cohere with his miraculous
ministry.[41]

So we see that even Jesus as a worker of miracles, healing the
sick and lame and freeing people from demonic influence, was
foretold in the Old Testament.

Although history informs us that there were many people in
Palestine before and after Jesus who claimed or were thought by
some to be the Jewish Messiah, none came even remotely close
to fulfilling the Old Testament Messianic prophesies like Jesus of
Nazareth.

Is Jesus really the only way to eternal life?

As I said in chapter two, the main purpose of the Bible is for
God to show mankind His plan for redemption and salvation. As
also stated earlier, the sacrifice of animals in the Old Testament
and the shedding of their blood as atonement for man's sin was a
yearly and temporary solution. God says this in Exodus 30:10
about the relationship between blood and atonement for sin:

Once a year Aaron [the first Jewish priest] *shall make atonement
on its horns. This annual atonement must be made with the blood
of the atoning sin offering for the generations to come. It is most
holy to the LORD.*

God said in Leviticus 17:11:

*"For the life of a creature is in the blood, and I have given it to
you to make atonement for yourselves on the altar; it is the blood
that makes atonement for one's life."*

This decree by God to use the blood of animals such as lambs
and goats as sacrifice for sin lasted approximately fifteen-

hundred years or from the time of Moses, to whom God gave His laws, up to the time of John the Baptist who ushered in the Jewish Messiah, Jesus Christ.

The writer to the Hebrews essentially says in chapter 9 verses 11-14 that the imperfect blood of animals where a symbolic offering for the one making it that sanctified or preserved that individual until the perfect sacrifice for sin by the Messiah would be made in the future.[42] The apostle Paul says in Romans 3:25: *"God presented Christ as a sacrifice of atonement, through the shedding of his blood—to be received by faith."* And the apostle Peter adds, *"but with the precious blood of Christ, a lamb without blemish or defect."* (I Peter 1:19)

Permanent redemption for mankind has come through the blood sacrifice of Jesus the Messiah, who is God Himself, who made perfect atonement for man's sins once and for all—for all who believe in Him.

Francis S. Collins, one of the world's leading scientists, wrestled with these concepts in his book: *The Language of God*, he writes:

> But His resurrection had to be more than a demonstration of magical powers. What was the real point of it? Christians have puzzled over this question for two millennia. After much searching, I could find no single answer--instead, there were several interlocking answers, all pointing to the idea of a bridge between our sinful selves and a holy God. Some commentators focus on the idea of substitution—Christ dying in the place of all of us who deserve God's judgment for our wrongdoings. Others call it redemption—Christ paid the ultimate price to free us from the bondage of sin, so that we could find God and rest in the confidence that He no longer judges us by our actions, but sees us as having been washed clean. Christians call this salvation by grace. But for me, the crucifixion and resurrection also provided something else. My desire to draw close to God was blocked by my own pride and sinfulness, which in turn was an inevitable consequence of my own selfish desire to be in control. Faithfulness to God required a kind of death of self-will in order to be reborn as a new creation. How could I

achieve such a thing? As had happened so many times with previous dilemmas, the words of C. S. Lewis captured the answer precisely:

> "But supposing God became a man--suppose our human nature which can suffer and die was amalgamated with God's nature in one person--then that person could help us. He could surrender His will, and suffer and die, because He was a man, and He could do it perfectly because He was God. You and I can go through this process only if God does it in us; but God can do it only if He becomes man. Our attempts at this dying will succeed only if we men share in God's dying, just as our thinking can succeed only because it is a drop out of the ocean of His intelligence; but we cannot share God's dying unless God dies, and He cannot die except by being a man. That is the sense in which He pays our debt, and suffers for us what He Himself need not suffer at all."

Before I became a believer in God, this kind of logic seemed like utter nonsense. Now the crucifixion and resurrection emerged as the compelling solution to the gap that yawned between God and myself, a gap that could now be bridged by the person of Jesus Christ.[43]

The teachings of Jesus Christ

Many people are familiar with Jesus' words in John 3:16-17:

"For God so loved the world that He gave His only begotten Son, that whoever believes in Him should not perish but have everlasting life. For God did not send His Son into the world to condemn the world, but that the world through Him might be saved."

This is absolutely true and often quoted, but what many are less familiar with is what Jesus says right after those two verses:

"He who believes in Him is not condemned; but he who does not believe is condemned already, because he has not believed in the name of the only begotten Son of God. And this is the

condemnation, that the light has come into the world, and men loved darkness rather than light, because their deeds were evil. For everyone practicing evil [i.e. breaking God's commands] *hates the light, because their deeds were evil."*

Some might say—How narrow-minded and bigoted for God to condemn people just because they choose not to believe in His Son. Notice in the above verse that it said, *"he who does not believe is condemned already."* Too many people in America think that believing in Jesus is an option and if they decide not to believe and trust in Him that they'll still be okay, because as everyone knows—there are lots of other roads and religions that lead to heaven. But as I demonstrated in chapter four and the Bible makes clear, there *aren't* any other roads or ways that lead to heaven.

When the Bible says to "believe" in Jesus, it doesn't just mean to believe that He once existed, that He was a person of history—it means to believe that His blood shed on the cross is for all mankind's sin and that you, the reader, must accept His sacrifice for your own sin or face God's condemnation and judgment.

And this is what many people *do* understand and have a problem with because most *don't* believe they have done anything so wrong to deserve condemnation from God and eternal separation from Him and because of this, they don't think they have to believe in Jesus Christ as a sacrifice and atonement for their sins. These same people don't like Bible verses such as the one in Romans 3:23 that says: *"For all have sinned and fall short of the glory of God"* which is why they don't like the Bible either.

John the Baptist said of Jesus in John 3:36: *"He who believes in the Son has everlasting life; and he who does not believe the Son shall not see life, but the wrath of God abides on him."* The apostle John concurs: *"He who has the Son has life; he who does not have the Son of God does not have life"* (I John 5:12).

When the Bible says someone will not see or have "life" it is talking about life in heaven with God and that instead of seeing or experiencing a wonderful life in heaven, they will be condemned to eternal death in hell.

And this leads to one of the other reasons many people in America today don't like Jesus Christ and the Bible or its God— Because of their teachings on hell and eternal torment for unbelievers and wrongdoers.

Jesus confirmed His belief in eternal torment for those who reject Him when He told the story of the rich man and Lazarus in Luke 16:19-31. Although it is true that when Jesus came to earth during His incarnation, He did not come to condemn, as John 3:17 states—but Jesus *did* teach eternal damnation in hell for all those who reject Him. In Matthew 13:24-30 Jesus teaches the parable of the wheat and tares. In verses 36 through 42, He explains the parable:

"He who sows the good seed is the Son of Man [Jesus]. *The field is the world, the good seeds are the sons of the kingdom, but the tares are the sons of the wicked one. The enemy who sowed them is the devil, the harvest is the end of the age, and the reapers are the angels. Therefore as the tares are gathered and burned in the fire, so it will be at the end of this age. The Son of Man will send out His angels, and they will gather out of His kingdom all things that offend, and those who practice lawlessness, and will cast them into the furnace of fire. There will be wailing and gnashing of teeth."*
From Matthew 13:37-42

As shown earlier, the One speaking to the apostle John in the book of Revelation is none other than the risen Jesus Christ. Revelation 21:5-8 reads:

Then He who sat on the throne said "Behold, I make all things new." And He said to me, "Write, for these words are true and faithful." And he said to me, "It is done! I am the Alpha and the Omega, the Beginning and the End. I will give of the fountain of the water of life freely to him that thirsts. He who overcomes shall inherit all things, and I will be his God and he shall be My son. But the cowardly, unbelieving, abominable, murderers, sexually immoral, sorcerers, idolaters, and all liars shall have their part in the lake which burns with fire and brimstone, which is the second death."

Revelation 14:10-11 adds:

...he himself [those listed above in Rev. 21:8] *shall also drink of the wine of the wrath of God, which is poured out full strength into the cup of His indignation. And he shall be tormented with fire and brimstone in the presence of the holy angels and in the presence of the Lamb* [Jesus]. *And the smoke of their torment ascends forever and ever; and they have no rest day or night.*

The Bible mentions the lake of fire for those who reject Jesus Christ six times in the book of Revelation. Now, considering how compelling the evidences are for the Bible being God's written word to mankind, is it really prudent not to take these verses seriously? To simply dismiss these passages in the Bible as irrelevant for today is dangerous to say the least and the height of foolishness.

Conclusion

So to be perfectly clear—Jesus Christ is the one person, the only Savior whom God has appointed to whom we must submit and believe in to be saved from our sins. No other religion in the world today possesses the credentials and proofs of divine origin as does Christianity and its founder Jesus Christ. And yet, many ignore it for all manner of baseless doctrines and individuals who fraudulently claim to have the truth about God and eternal life.

Jesus Christ is absolutely unique among men and gods! And anyone wondering what God is like need only examine the life of Jesus Christ. His life exemplified God's essence as a healer of men, a patient teacher of truth, one who loved the individual no matter what faults he or she possessed. But let us never forget that Jesus Christ is none other than God Himself, the final judge of men's souls and all who reject Him.

Chapter 9
Modern-Day Laodicea

In the Bible book titled: The Revelation of Jesus Christ, Christ addresses seven Christian churches that existed in Asia at the time that He appeared to the apostle John near the end of the first century AD. Christ describes each church as having its own unique character as well as positive and negative attributes. Christ's analysis of these seven churches is thought by many Bible scholars to represent not only the churches that were in existence at that time, but also the different personalities and conditions of churches in every generation and nation since.

The church of Laodicea in particular was characterized as being at the same time both prosperous and apathetic and is thought by some to be an accurate description of the Christian Church as an institution in America today. Part of what Jesus said to the Laodicean church was:

"I know your works, that you are neither cold nor hot. I could wish you were cold or hot. So then, because you are lukewarm, and neither cold nor hot, I will spew you out of my mouth. Because you say, 'I am rich, have become wealthy, and have need of nothing'—and do not know that you are wretched, miserable, poor, blind, and naked...'"
Revelation 3:15-17 (NKJV)

When Jesus tells the Laodiceans that they were *"wretched, miserable, poor, blind, and naked,"* He most likely meant that although they were rich in material possessions, they were poor spiritually because they deemed material wealth to be more important than their faith and spiritually motivated actions and character. And when He says, *"have need of nothing,"* He probably meant they thought that with all their material wealth and security, what did they really need God or Christ for?

The same allegations could be made against the Christian Church as an institution in present day America.

It is interesting that even back in 1740s Colonial America many Church leaders of the era felt that prosperity had weakened the Christian zeal of many of the people who identified with Christ. Certainly, since the end of World War Two, modern America has experienced another unprecedented time of prosperity and its Christian Churches again have been primarily preoccupied with the American Dream and its prospects of temporal earthly mammon.

The evidence for this obliviousness on the part of members of the organized Church to things outside the sphere of personal gain is the current sad state our nation is in morally, particularly in the political realm.

Ploys by secular humanists to silence the church

Merriam-Webster Dictionary defines secular humanism as a "humanistic philosophy viewed as a nontheistic religion antagonistic to traditional religion" and "as a system of values and beliefs that are opposed to the values and beliefs of traditional religions." Oxford Dictionary defines it as "the belief that humanity is capable of morality and self-fulfillment without belief in God."

The separation of church and state ploy

Somewhere along the line, at least in the past 60 years or so, the Church of Jesus Christ in America has bought into the notion that politics is dirty business and has largely left its workings up to secular practitioners. Perhaps it became a convenient excuse when in 1947 the secular humanists in the U.S. Supreme Court deceptively misquoted Thomas Jefferson's 1802 letter that mentioned the "separation of church and state."[1] The clause has become famous by its seeming implication that religion has no place in government. Of course, when the Court used the word "religion," it really meant Christianity since it had always been the most prominent religion in America and its adherents had always been the most active in government. This new interpretation of a 150-year-old document was highly ironic since humanism had already been declared in 1933, in the first Humanist Manifesto signed by famous educator John Dewey and others, to be the new "religion" of America. So even though religion, according to the humanists, has no place in government, they themselves, adhering to a religion, albeit a Godless one, have not only participated in government and politics but have made public policy that has often replaced long-standing statutes that reflected Godly, Biblical principles. Furthermore, whereas Biblically based laws are based upon tried and true precepts, thousands of years old, these new secular mandates are derived from the ever-changing, so-called "living," whims of fallen human beings who are in open rebellion against their Creator.

The most stunning recent example of this replacement of traditional Biblical values is in the 2015 ruling by the U.S. Supreme Court that redefined the ageless, God-given definition of marriage from a God-blessed union between one man and one woman to a farcically sexually motivated relationship between two or more of any unnatural combination of God's creatures.

The tax-exempt ploy

Another method the secularists have used in modern America to silence the Church of Jesus Christ was the passage of the 1954 Internal Revenue Act which deceptively contained the 501(c)3 section instigated by mega-corrupt politician and humanist, Lyndon Baines Johnson. Although the First Amendment already exempted churches from having to pay income taxes, Johnson, then a U.S. Senator, introduced the IRS 501(c)3 mandate that masqueraded as protecting churches' tax-exempt status when no such legislation was needed. But knowing Christian Churches and clergy had always been involved in shaping public policy, then Senator Johnson determined to try to silence them by deceptively offering them the 501(c)3 statute. Sadly, Protestant churches have fallen for the scheme and been largely silent in the political arena ever since. According to Peter Kershaw in his book, *In Caesar's Grip*, instead of benefiting churches, the new 1954 tax code meant:

> 501c3 churches are prohibited from addressing, in any tangible way, the vital issues of the day. For a 501c3 church to openly speak out, or organize in opposition to, anything that the government declares "legal," even if it is immoral (e.g. abortion, homosexuality, etc.), that church will jeopardize its tax exempt status. The 501c3 has had a "chilling effect" upon the free speech rights of the church. LBJ was a shrewd and cunning politician who seemed to well-appreciate how easily many of the clergy would sell out.[2]

Even as of 2015, the IRS tax code for churches that obtain a 501(c)3 reads:

> To be tax-exempt under section 501(c)(3) of the Internal Revenue Code, an organization must be organized and operated exclusively for exempt purposes set forth in section 501(c)(3), and none of its earnings may inure to any private shareholder or individual. In addition, it may not be an *action organization, i.e.,* it may not attempt to influence legislation as a substantial part of its activities and it may not participate in any campaign activity for or against political candidates... Section 501(c)(3) organizations are restricted in how much political and legislative (lobbying) activities they may conduct.[3]

Unfortunately for America, the vast majority of Protestant Churches[4] and their pastors have fallen in line behind this deception and have obediently refrained from informing their congregations regarding political issues for fear of losing their "tax-exempt" status.

Where is the outrage?
In the time leading up to the Revolutionary War, Americans exercised their perceived God-given right of free speech even when it meant arrest or prosecution for speaking out against

things they didn't like, especially from the British Government. And since the ratification of the First Amendment in 1788, the right of free speech has been protected by the U.S. Constitution. This has been one of the unique aspects about America that our founding fathers gave us as a means to thwart evil or destructive policies coming from government. But Christians in the last several decades have largely not utilized this right to stand up and fight for Godly, Biblical values, but have instead looked the other way while those values have been usurped by immoral, corrupted bureaucrats or now, out-and-out apparatchiks who are bent on excluding God and trying to create a full-blown communistic society.

For example, where was the outrage from the Christian Church when in 1961 the Supreme Court declared both humanism and atheism to be religions, thereby putting the two Godless ideologies in the same category as Christianity? And what did the majority of Christians do after the Supreme Court in 1963 disallowed prayer and Bible reading in public schools? And except for relatively small pockets of resistance, why wasn't the vast majority of Christian men and women protesting and holding their political representatives feet to the fire after the Supreme Court in 1973 created the legal mandate for a mother to kill her own unborn baby for no reason? And where were the voices of opposition from millions of Christians when in 1980 the courts began ruling that municipalities are no longer allowed to display God's Ten Commandments in public places? And where were the masses of Christian fathers and mothers when in 1987 the Supreme Court again defied Almighty God and declared that Creationism can't be taught alongside Godless evolution in public schools? And most recently, where is the promised civil disobedience on the part of the Church of Jesus Christ after the Supreme Court fraudulently redefined marriage?

Except for a relative few voices, there has been no mass public outcry over the decades from Christians and pastors and other Christian leaders against any of these overreaches of government and the Godless humanists that now control it.

Insidious teachings from within the Church of Jesus Christ

There are four particularly pernicious and specious teachings that have infiltrated and taken root to varying degrees and in various combinations within a substantial number of Christian churches across America today. These false doctrines, outlined below, have done more than anything else to cause people identifying with Jesus Christ to be apathetic towards the evil that has encroached upon our nation.

The faith movement

When I first became a Christian in 1980, one of the biggest heresies going around the Church was that one of the reasons that Christ died on the cross was so His followers could be healthy and wealthy. There were many prominent promoters of this "gospel of greed" as it is sometimes called within orthodox Christian churches and there still are today.

Although many within the Church have resisted this kind of carnal teaching that exalts the flesh over the spirit, it has had a trickle-down affect and caused many true Christians dedicated to Christ to think that God indeed wants His people prosperous, especially in America, if for no other reason than so Christians can fund evangelistic and missionary endeavors to those in less fortunate countries. But although this last reason may have some merit, it is often more of a justification for pursuing hedonistic pleasures at the expense of spiritual character and involvement in much more important societal endeavors.

What is certain is that not all participants at gatherings purporting to be Christian are true followers of Jesus Christ. For example, for those caught up in the faith movement, many are not listening to nor following the words and instruction of the Biblical Jesus Christ. Instead, they are primarily disciples of the false teacher who always promises that the hearer will materially prosper if he or she will simply give money to the false teacher's "ministry." These promoters of what is, in essence—themselves, falsely teach that the believer in the "other Jesus" they are promoting, is entitled to earthly prosperity and physical wellness. What this really means is that the sacrifice of Jesus Christ on the cross for sin so that the true believer can be reconciled with God and live in heaven for eternity, just isn't enough. This kind of teaching is nothing more than one of the "doctrines of demons" that the Bible warns about in I Timothy 4:1.

But of course, this isn't what the real Jesus Christ taught at all, nor does the New Testament reflect any such doctrines or teachings. In fact, people who believe this stuff or are considering it should question whose gospel they are listening to.

Hank Hanegraaff, president of the Christian Research Institute (CRI), an apologetic organization committed to orthodox Christian doctrine, had this to say about the promulgators of the faith movement in his book *Christianity in Crisis*:

> The true Christ and the true faith of the Bible are being replaced rapidly with diseased substitutes offered by a group of teachers who belong to what has been labeled the "Faith movement"... The dispensers of this carcinogenic diet have utilized the power of the airwaves, as well as a plethora of pleasantly packaged books and tapes, to lure their prey to dinner. The unsuspecting have been called not to love the Master [Jesus Christ], but to love what is on the Master's table.[5]

Hanegraaff adds that, "Faith teachers ridicule the biblical Christ and replace Him with a creation of their own imaginations."

Of course, for anyone who studies the Bible, none of this should be a surprise because Jesus and the apostles warned of people who in the form of false prophets and teachers would preach another Jesus and gospel other than the one they had given that will deceive many. Jesus Himself said:

"Watch out for false prophets. They come to you in sheep's clothing, but inwardly they are ferocious wolves."
Matthew 7:15

The apostle Paul warned in his second letter to the church at Corinth:

For if someone comes to you and preaches a Jesus other than the Jesus we preached, or if you receive a different spirit from the Spirit you received, or a different gospel from the one you accepted, you put up with it easily enough.
II Corinthians 11:4

And again to the Christians in Philippi, Paul said:

For, as I have often told you before and now tell you again even with tears, many live as enemies of the cross of Christ. Their destiny is destruction, their god is their stomach, and their glory is in their shame. Their mind is set on earthly things.
Philippians 3:18-19

Paul warned the elders of the Church at Ephesus as well:

Keep watch over yourselves and all the flock of which the Holy Spirit has made you overseers. Be shepherds of the church of God, which he bought with his own blood. I know that after I leave, savage wolves will come in among you and will not spare the flock. Even from your own number men will arise and distort the truth in order to draw away disciples after them.
Acts 20:28-30

The apostle Peter too warned the true followers of Jesus Christ of heretical teachings:

But there were also false prophets among the people, just as there will be false teachers among you. They will secretly introduce destructive heresies, even denying the sovereign Lord who bought them—bringing swift destruction on themselves. Many will follow their depraved conduct and will bring the way of truth into disrepute. In their greed these teachers will exploit you with fabricated stories.
From II Peter 2:1-3

So instead of being vigilant and on guard against false teachings and studying their Bibles to know the true Gospel, too many people who call themselves "Christian" are really disciples of these spurious mystics and are focused more on their own worldly gain than heavenly treasure.

But of course, in reality, many of these people are not part of the true spiritual Church of Jesus Christ at all, but are witting followers of erroneous doctrines much like the followers of Mormonism, Islam, and all the other spurious religions of the world.

So to summarize, this counterfeit gospel of earthly self-indulgence has hijacked to varying degrees much of the Church of Jesus Christ in America today and has contributed to many of its members to be uninvolved bystanders while the wolves of society have been slowly but steadily allowed to take over and create a culture that is now in opposition to God and in mortal danger of His judgment.

The pre-tribulation rapture

The Bible undoubtedly teaches that Jesus Christ will return to earth a second time at the end of this present era. The first time, Christ came as a servant to show people that He was the only way and means by which mankind could obtain forgiveness for their sins from God and have eternal life in heaven. The Bible teaches that the second time Jesus comes, it will be with power and glory to destroy the enemies of God and His Gospel. Revelation 19:11-16 describes the transformed Jesus:

I saw heaven standing open and there before me was a white horse, whose rider is called Faithful and True. With justice he judges and wages war. His eyes are like blazing fire, and on his head are many crowns. He has a name written on him that no one knows but he himself. He is dressed in a robe dipped in blood, and his name is the Word of God. The armies of heaven were following him, riding on white horses and dressed in fine linen, white and clean. Coming out of his mouth is a sharp sword with which to strike down the nations. He will rule them with an iron scepter. He treads the winepress of the fury of the wrath of God Almighty. On his robe and on his thigh he has this name written: KING OF KINGS AND LORD OF LORDS.

This time of the end when Christ returns to earth a second time is known in Christendom as: The Great Tribulation.[6] Although tribulation for believers in Christ is often predicted and even promised in the New Testament, the Great Tribulation is told by Jesus in Matthew chapter 24 to be of the kind *"such as has not been since the beginning of the world."* It will be so bad in fact, that Jesus says, *"And unless those days were shortened, no flesh would be saved."* (From Matthew 24:21-22)

These verses are certainly frightening to say the least and have caused many within the Church in more recent years to reinterpret the verses that point to the events surrounding the Great Tribulation differently than they have been traditionally down through the centuries.

I believe this has been sought for several reasons, the main one is because so many Bible prophesies have been fulfilled in the last six or seven decades that point to the soon approaching end of the world as we know it. Some important as well as telling prophecies in particular have come to pass concerning Israel becoming a nation again.[7] In 1948, after nearly two thousand years of dispersion, the Jewish people returned to their ancient homeland and reestablished themselves once again as a nation.

These prophecies about Israel have become a countdown of sorts because Jesus said in Matthew 24:33-34: *"when you see all these things,[8] know that it* [the time of the end] *is near, at the very doors. Assuredly, I say to you, this generation will by no means pass away till all these things are fulfilled."*

Luke says in chapter 21, verse 32 of his Gospel that at this time of the end, *"all things are fulfilled,"* implying either all the remaining unfulfilled prophecies of the Bible are fulfilled at this "end of the age," or all the remaining unfulfilled prophecies concerning Jesus are fulfilled at this time.

So Jesus has essentially said that the generation of people on earth that witnesses the people of Israel return to their homeland

and become a nation again will not completely die off before He returns to earth a second time and also that this end of the age will be preceded by a time of great tribulation where many, including God's own "elect," will be persecuted, and killed.

The question is—how long is a generation? There is every reason to believe that when Jesus uses the word, He is referring to a literal human generation. Estimates of the length of a human generation range of from 40 to 120 years in the Bible. Since the average lifespan for people in westernized nations today is approximately 80 years, Jesus could be saying that He will return to earth within 80 years of Israel becoming a nation again. So, we may indeed be living near the time of the Great Tribulation. This assertion can also be justified by other events that are currently transpiring around the world which appear to be fulfilling many other Biblical prophecies besides those concerning only Israel.

It is this perilous age in which we live that has caused many in the Church to think that some really bad times are just ahead. This has also caused many to look for Scriptural justification that they will be rescued from the really bad times before they transpire. Which leads to the idea of a rapture for the Church of Jesus Christ.

This peculiarly Christian term "rapture" refers to Christians being caught up to *"meet the Lord in the air"* as stated in I Thessalonians 4:15-17 at the time of the Great Tribulation.[9] It is interesting that the idea of the Church in America being rescued from difficult times coincides perfectly with its increasing worldliness in this post World War II era. But the verses that some now say point to a rapture have traditionally been understood by Bible scholars to apply to the resurrection to eternal life for believers in Jesus Christ and not to a physical escape from terrible tribulation.

My purpose here is not to make a case for or against the concept of a rapture for the Church of Jesus Christ, but to show how a certain aspect of the belief has minimized the impact of believers in post-Christian America.

Like the word Trinity, one won't find the word "rapture" in the Bible. However, unlike the doctrine of the Trinity, a special rapture or catching up into heaven for believers in Jesus Christ immediately before the Great Tribulation is difficult to prove with any certainty using Biblical texts. Nevertheless, this has not stopped many pastors, teachers, and evangelists within the Church to promote it as not only fact, but also as an important Christian belief. And this is why I believe it has done much to compromise the Church of Jesus Christ in America.

Admittedly, even among rapture adherents, there is controversy as to when a rapture of the Church may actually occur. Some say it won't happen until the end of the Great Tribulation and that Christians will have to go through it and suffer. Others believe that the rapture will occur in the middle of the "Tribulation" just before God's wrath is poured out against the unGodly and those who reject Jesus Christ. But it is the thinking of a rapture happening just before the Great Tribulation that is the most problematic. The motivation here is obvious: so the Church of Jesus Christ living today, especially in America, won't have to experience anything really unpleasant.

It is this thinking of a pre-tribulation rapture, as it is called, that I believe to be most dangerous and has contributed to causing so many within the Church of Jesus Christ to become apathetic and take on the resemblance of the Lukewarm Church that existed at the time that the apostle John wrote the book of "Revelations," as The Revelation of Jesus Christ is often called.

If one believes that he or she will be rescued from persecution and tribulation resulting from an ever-increasingly immoral society that is in open rebellion against God, what is the incentive for working hard to save souls for Jesus Christ and try to promote and preserve Christian values within that society, especially if one is busy chasing the American dream? It is one thing to consider such an idea as a pre-tribulation rapture, but the danger is in believing it *absolutely* as if it is actual fact and that it will happen in the way one hopes. And sadly, far too many modern Christians in America *do* believe this to be an absolute truth of Christianity.

Dispensationalism

Today, dispensationalists are typically called cessationists. Around the beginning of the twentieth century some very fine and reputable Bible scholars within the Christian Church recognized that God worked differently in human affairs at particular times down through history. The Scripture often refers to these times as "ages" and some of these Bible scholars began referring to them as dispensations. For example, the age that we currently live began with the coming of Jesus Christ and is sometimes referred to in the Bible as the "Time of the Gentiles." A Dispensationalist would call this—the dispensation, or age of the Gentiles. Before this age of the Gentiles, God primarily revealed Himself to the world through His chosen people, the Israelites. Dispensationalists would call this age that began with Moses and the Mosaic Law and ended with the coming of John the Baptist and Jesus Christ as—the dispensation of the Jews.[10]

The idea that these and other times can be identified as different "dispensations" of how God has worked down through history with each having its own beginning and end is reasonable and valid and does not engage in creating major doctrines. But where modern Dispensationalists go too far is to say that the kind of signs, wonders, and miracles wrought by the apostles of Jesus and His disciples during the first century ended with the death of the last apostle. A Dispensationalist calls this era—the apostolic age. However, saying that these gifts *ended* with the demise of the apostles is creating new doctrine and one that is not in accordance with Scripture.

This overstep of Dispensational teaching may be because, in western culture at least, these kinds of God-induced, metaphysical phenomenon, called spiritual gifts, don't appear to legitimately occur very often in many if not most Christian circles. But instead of trying to find out why, or considering it as a symptom of an increasingly worldly Church, many Dispensationalists have simply defined spiritual gifts away as not for today.

Another reason many within the Church reject spiritual gifts is because counterfeit gifts have occasionally been exercised in some churches and Christian gatherings, especially in some that have adopted the ways of the charismatic movement that began in the early 1970s. However, the charismatic movement is a legitimate, Bible-based faction that has arisen within the Church of Jesus Christ. Charismatics believe that the spiritual gifts imparted to believers by the Holy Spirit as specifically addressed in I Corinthians chapter 12 are indeed for today as they were in the first century Church that was under the guidance and teachings of the apostles. But because some abuses of these gifts have been found within the charismatic renewal, as it is sometimes called, reputable Bible scholars such as Merrill F. Unger have attributed them to the powers of darkness, even saying that the seeking of them can open the door to demonic influence. Certainly this can be a legitimate concern, but instead of advocating that the gifts be sought and used in accordance with sound, New Testament teachings, many otherwise good men of God such as Unger have defined them away under the guise of Dispensationalism. This is highly ironic in my view because it appears as if people such as Unger, as studied as some of them were or are today, have bought into the very kind of Satanic deceptions they seek to avoid, without even realizing it. Unger also thought that God's word, the Bible, was a substitute for the necessity of the power of the Holy Spirit, although he probably wouldn't have phrased it that way. But by saying we don't need the power and gifts of God's Holy Spirit since the creation of the Canon of Scripture, is essentially saying just that. The truth is— We need the full function of the Holy Spirit, also called the "baptism of the Spirit," as much today as Jesus' apostles and disciples did in their day—when they waited for it in the upper room on the day of Pentecost—and when they received it, turned the first century world upside down with the Gospel of Jesus Christ.

But to be clear, the gifts or filling of the Holy Spirit are not to be confused with the *teaching of the Holy Spirit* which is a function of God the Holy Spirit as He resides within every believer in Jesus Christ. Having the Holy Spirit as one's teacher or "Comforter"[11] as Jesus explains in John 14:26 is different than being filled with the Holy Spirit. A believer in Jesus Christ receives the Holy Spirit as an indwelling teacher when He or she accepts Christ, but the filling of the Holy Spirit is separate and must be asked for by the believer. In Luke 11:13 Jesus said: *"...How much more will your heavenly Father give the Holy Spirit to those who ask Him!"*

This is exactly what Jesus told the apostles and disciples to do just before He ascended into heaven when He told them to wait in Jerusalem for the *"Promise of the Father"* where they would be *"baptized with the Holy Spirit"* and *"receive power when the Holy Spirit has come upon you."* (Acts 1:4-8)

In Acts 19:1-6 the apostle Paul encounters Christians who had obeyed Jesus' call to believe in Him, but had only heard of John the Baptist's baptism of water. Read how Paul instructs them on the Holy Spirit:

And it happened, while Apollos was at Corinth, that Paul, having passed through the upper regions, came to Ephesus. And finding some disciples he said to them, "Did you receive the Holy Spirit when you believed?" And they said to him, "We have not so much as heard whether there is a Holy Spirit." And he said to them, "Into what then were you baptized?" So they said, "Into John's baptism." Then Paul said, "John indeed baptized with a baptism of repentance, saying to the people that they should believe on Him who would come after him, that is, on Christ Jesus." When they heard this, they were baptized in the name of the Lord Jesus. And when Paul laid hands on them, the Holy Ghost came upon them, and they spoke with tongues and prophesied.

We can see from the above that believing in Jesus Christ and receiving the Holy Spirit in power are two separate events. So to say that the gifts of the Holy Spirit are not for today causes deep and far-reaching problems.

For example, Charles Finney, the famous nineteenth century evangelist who led revivals in towns and cities in the northeastern part of the United States and the United Kingdom between 1821 and 1875 attributed the success of His ministry to the power and outpouring of the Holy Spirit. Finney is considered the father of modern revivalism and was the leader of the Second Great Awakening in America. Finney, in his memoirs wrote:

> When Christ commissioned his apostles to go and preach, he told them to abide in Jerusalem till they were endued with power from on high. This power, as everyone knows, was the baptism of the Holy Ghost poured out upon them on the day of Pentecost. This was an indispensible qualification for success in their ministry. I did not suppose then, nor do I now, that this baptism was simply the power to work miracles. The power to work miracles and the gift of tongues were given as signs to attest the reality of their divine commission. But the baptism itself was a divine purifying, a filling them with the Holy Ghost, bestowing on them a vast divine illumination, filling them with faith and love, with peace and power, so that their words were made sharp in the hearts of God's enemies, and were quick and powerful like a two-edged sword.[12]

It is certainly in the devil's best interests to convince people that they no longer need the power of the Holy Spirit in which to successfully spread the Gospel of Jesus Christ so that a culture can be spiritually enabled to resist his lies and temptations. The fact that Satan has been able to deceive some of the most learned and well-meaning individuals within Christendom shows that everyone, no matter how enlightened someone may think he or she is, is susceptible to buying into the subtle lies of the wicked one.

The great Christian apologist, Dr. Walter Martin, who did not accept Dispensational teaching in this area used to say that it was a direct contradiction of Romans 11:29 that reads: *"For the gifts and the calling of God are irrevocable."* In other words, once God gives something to the Church of Jesus Christ, He doesn't take it back unless He has put conditions on it such as taking away His protection for not obeying Him. But no such conditions have been put on the gifts and power of the Holy Spirit and the biggest problem with Dispensational teaching in regards to

Spiritual gifts is that it does away with the extremely essential need to seek the full power and function of the Holy Spirit.

Indeed, Dispensational teaching is one of the primary reasons why the Church of Jesus Christ lacks power and authority today––because so many Christians have been taught not to seek the Holy Spirit, the one person within the Triune God who can equip them with such power and authority.

But I do not believe that God gives power casually to His people; He only gives it to those who earnestly seek Him, like on the day of Pentecost. And today, with the vast majority of Christians or pastors not crying out to God for the baptism of the Holy Spirit—God, for the most part, isn't giving it. This is also the reason why America has not experienced another Great Awakening such as occurred under Jonathan Edwards and Charles Finney. God only gives His power to those who fervently seek it in order to change a lost world or nation and to win souls for Christ. But the American Church, for the most part, hasn't been asking let alone fervently seeking God for such an outpouring. Nor does it, in my estimation, corporately even see a need for it. The American Church is rich and comfortable in its prosperity and like the Church of Laodicea, thinks it has need of nothing. It doesn't perceive that it is really wretched and poor in Spirit—just as its counterpart was two thousand years ago.

How America would be transformed if God's people—those who profess the Biblical Jesus Christ as their Lord and Savior, sought the filling and power of the Holy Ghost. What a change would come over America if true Christians were endued with the power of the Holy Spirit, preached the plain truth of the Gospel with boldness, and went about healing the sick, restoring the physically handicapped, and delivering people from the clutches of the powers of darkness.

In some ways, the teaching of Dispensationalism or Cessationism is the most insidious false teaching of all because it prevents the Church from seeking the one thing that can make and keep it vibrant and at the same time guard against the kind of immoral, anti-God society in which we now live.

Eternal Security

The teachings on Eternal Security within the Christian Church have to do with whether someone who believes in Jesus Christ as his or her Savior from sin is forever secure in that salvation or can lose it as a result of deliberately and willfully committing habitual sin.[13] The two main positions of thought on this subject are outlined in Calvinism and Arminianism. The debate over these two views on the subject of salvation has been going on in Christendom at least since the sixteenth century when they were first articulated by John Calvin and Jacobus Arminius.

I have never become intimately familiar with the fine points of these two opposing doctrines because I decided, based on my own personal study of the Scriptures, to adopt the safest position. That position is—Only God knows whether an individual who professes Jesus Christ as his or her Lord and Savior is truly saved for time and eternity. While I believe that once a person is truly "born again," as Jesus teaches in John 3:1-8, and cannot lose his or her salvation (because—how can one be unborn once they are born?), I also believe that one can be deceived into thinking he or she is truly saved when one is not.

Both Calvin and Arminius agreed that the heart of man, in its natural state and without the influence of God and His Holy Spirit is, as the Bible in Jeremiah 17:9 says: *"... deceitful above all things, and desperately wicked, Who can know it?"* Because of this, I believe that a person can be self-deluded into thinking they are a true follower of Jesus Christ when they may not be. This can happen several ways: By not knowing or understanding the Bible correctly and instead accepting a false Jesus, one pedaled by a false teacher, or, By believing in a false Christ that a person has made up in their own mind. Being or becoming self-deceived can also happen when someone hears the Gospel of Jesus Christ and intellectually assents to it but does not really believe with their heart. Still another way someone can be self-deceived is by following Christ for a time and then when hard choices come, quietly takes the wrong side against God and Christ or makes decisions that actually deny both.

Jesus explains all the above in Matthew chapter 13 when He gives the parable of the sower. Jesus often spoke in parables or allegories to explain important spiritual truths. He often did this so His listeners could better relate to and understand what He was teaching, but also so that many of the wicked religious leaders who were always trying to trip Him up and catch Him in some wrong-doing or erroneous teaching wouldn't be able to understand what He was saying. But before you read the passage below, understand that the seed of the sower represents God's word, the Gospel message. In Matthew 13:3-8 Jesus gives the parable, then in verses 18 through 23, He gives the explanation of what it means.

Christ's parable:
Then he told them many things in parables, saying: "A farmer went out to sow his seed. As he was scattering the seed, some fell along the path, and the birds came and ate it up. Some fell on rocky places, where it did not have much soil. It sprang up quickly, because the soil was shallow. But when the sun came up, the plants were scorched, and they withered because they had no root. Other seed fell among thorns, which grew up and choked the plants. Still other seed fell on good soil, where it produced a crop—a hundred, sixty or thirty times what was sown."

Christ's explanation:
"Listen then to what the parable of the sower means: When anyone hears the message about the kingdom and does not understand it, the evil one comes and snatches away what was sown in their heart. This is the seed sown along the path. The seed falling on rocky ground refers to someone who hears the word and at once receives it with joy. But since they have no root, they last only a short time. When trouble or persecution comes because of the word, they quickly fall away. The seed falling among the thorns refers to someone who hears the word, but the worries of this life and the deceitfulness of wealth choke the word, making it unfruitful. But the seed falling on good soil refers to someone who hears the word and understands it. This is

the one who produces a crop, yielding a hundred, sixty or thirty times what was sown."

These verses give a good explanation of how one can think they are a true follower of Jesus Christ and secure in Him, when in fact, he or she may not be. So while I believe that a true follower of Jesus Christ can never lose their salvation, I also believe that only God knows whether or not that person's name is indeed written in the Lamb's (Jesus') book of life.

This is why we are told in the Scriptures to abide in Christ. Jesus tells his followers in John 15:1-8 to always abide in Him so they will have peace of mind and to ensure that they are indeed, truly His disciples: Verses 5 and 6 in particular read:

"I am the vine, you are the branches. He who abides in Me, and I in him, bears much fruit: for without Me you can do nothing. If anyone does not abide in Me, he is cast out as a branch and is withered; and they gather them and throw them into the fire, and they are burned."

So we see that abiding in Jesus is the mark of a true Christian. And to be a true follower of Christ means that one is to stay so close to Him in his or her thoughts and know His words and God's word as a whole so well that he or she cannot deceive themselves into thinking they are trusting in Him when they are not or are really believing in a different Jesus that is not taught in the Bible.

The above teaching is a safe and sound way of thinking about Eternal Destiny. Nevertheless, it is not practiced by everyone who professes to be a follower of Jesus Christ in America today.

A dangerous slant that has been introduced to this subject is that no matter what a professed believer in Christ does after being saved from their sins, that person can *never* lose his or her salvation. The problem is that many people who think they are Christians are really like the person who received the Gospel message among the thorns where the cares of the world have crept into their lives causing them to no longer be a vibrant witness for Christ or any kind of faithful witness at all. What is even more frightening is that person may have never been truly saved from their sins or born-again to begin with.

Without a doubt, in today's America, it is often difficult to tell a professing believer in Jesus Christ from an unbeliever; the two are often so similar and difficult to tell apart: in speech, in what they do, in what they participate in. The teaching of "once saved always saved," has comprised the Church and has led to sins that have destroyed the witness and effectiveness of Christians in America. It is this abuse of God's grace that has led many Christians, even pastors and other leaders, to lead double lives. Many outwardly appear pious and spiritual, but inwardly they are addicted to one or a number of sins such as: pride, covetousness, self-sufficiency, deceitfulness, love of money or security, pornography, adultery, homosexuality, and/or others. For example, a recent study reveals that as many as fifty percent of Christian pastors view pornography.[13] The article in which the results of the study are given goes on to say that because of guilt, these same pastors say they rarely preach on the subject. One can only imagine how prevalent this sin alone is among men within church congregations if it is this prevalent in church leadership and rarely if ever talked about or condemned from the pulpit.

Pornography is just one sin among many that has infected the modern Church. George Barna and David Barton report in their book, *U-Turn*, that nearly 40% of Christians overall in America want to see abortion protected and continued. They report even higher percentages among specific groups within the Church.[14] They also reveal that only 10% of Christians, who say they have had a "born-again" experience, possess a Biblical worldview. This can only mean that the vast majority of Christians living in America today do not read their Bibles often enough for its teachings to affect how they view the world in which they live. Barna's and Barton's book is a real eye-opener concerning the abysmal state of the Christian Church in America today.

It is anybody's guess whether or not so-called Christians involved in such habits and beliefs feel secure in their individually perceived eternal destinies, but the prevalence of these kinds of practices tells me that many within the Church must feel they are somehow tolerable and excused by God. This is dangerous thinking and has led to the kind of permissible, anything goes, Church culture that has infected American culture as a whole and now threatens us all.

The damage done by false teachings

I think it is safe to say that the average person identifying with Christ in America today thinks that no matter what he does, he cannot lose his salvation, and that God wants him to be prosperous and healthy and that he need not seek the filling of the Holy Spirit in order to change a lost world and if the culture that he has ignored goes rogue, God will take him out of the world so that nothing bad happens to him. This false sense of security that is so prevalent within the modern American Church has not only minimized the effectiveness of the average Christian called to be the "salt" and "light" within the culture, but has reduced its collective testimony in the eyes of the "unsaved" to the equivalent of used car salesmen.

In summation, the infiltration and acceptance of feel-good heretical teachings within the Church of Jesus Christ in America is why it is lukewarm and has retracted within the culture, thereby allowing evil to increase unchecked.

Becoming too much like the world

The Bible teaches that although Christians are in the world, they are not to be of the world. In other words, even though Christians become saved while in the world, they are warned by Scripture to no longer conform to the ungodly ways of the Satanic world system (Romans 12:1-2). This means that Christians are not to accept or practice things that are clearly against the Bible's teachings such as lying, cheating, adultery, sexual promiscuity and perversions, and other sins, even in the face of intense pressure by the un-Godly to be tolerant of everything. And contrary to the devil's lie, Christians are taught in the Bible to *judge*—to judge what is right and what is wrong and then to hold fast to what is good and shun or even run from what is evil. What Christians should not judge is the sinner and his or her eternal destiny, for only God is able to judge people's souls in that way. Instead, Christians are taught to love the sinner, but hate the sin, and share Christ's message of salvation to all and warn the person involved in sin of the consequences of it when they see it practiced by those within and without the Church of Jesus Christ.

Conclusion

While in this world, it is never too late to turn to God, or in the case of a prodigal follower of Jesus Christ, to turn *back* to God. And it is never too late, no matter how bad things are, or how far along evil has gotten, in any nation, for the sinner and saint to repent of the things they have wrongly done or believed that has contributed to his or her nation's downfall and ask God's forgiveness and pray that He might heal that nation.
II Chronicles 7:14 God says:

"if my people, who are called by my name, will humble themselves and pray and seek my face and turn from their wicked ways, then I will hear from heaven, and I will forgive their sin and will heal their land."

We desperately need another revival of the kinds that occurred under Jonathan Edwards and Charles Finney. The time has come for Christians in America to put everything on the line for their faith and stand up against the evil of the day no matter what the cost. Jesus talked about His people not loving their lives to the point that they were unwilling to sacrifice them for Him and the righteous cause of His Gospel. With so much heresy and false doctrine coming from so many claiming to speak for Christ, it can be difficult to tell sound doctrine from false. The only sure way to guard against becoming deceived or lukewarm is to humble yourself before the cross of Jesus Christ and be very familiar with the Bible and the God who gave it.

Chapter 10
Seeds of America's Destruction

The Bible tells the story in the Old Testament about the prophet Jonah who went to Nineveh, the capital city of the Assyrian empire, to warn the people living there of God's impending judgment for their wickedness. The Scripture candidly reveals that much to Jonah's surprise *and* dismay that when he gave God's warning to the people of the city, they repented of their sins.

The Bible tells that Nineveh was such *"an exceedingly great city"* that it was a three-day journey to walk across it and that it was home to over twenty thousand persons.

When Jonah arrived there, after his stubborn refusal to obey God and his ensuing three days and nights in the belly of a fish, he began walking through the city crying out to the people declaring, *"Yet forty days, and Nineveh shall be overthrown"* (From Jonah 3:4).

In Jonah 3:6-9, the Bible tells that the people of Nineveh *"Believed God, proclaimed a fast, and put on sackcloth, from the greatest to the least of them."*[1] This happened even *before* Jonah's word came to the king of Nineveh, but when it did, the Bible says that the king joined the people and *"arose from his throne and laid aside his robe, covered himself in sackcloth and sat in ashes."* The Scripture then says that the king and his nobles *"caused it to be proclaimed and published throughout Nineveh"* that *"neither man nor beast, herd nor flock, taste anything; do not let them eat, or drink water. But let man and beast be covered with sackcloth, and cry mightily to God; yes, let everyone turn from his evil way and from the violence that is in his hands* [because] *Who can tell if God will turn and relent, and turn away from His fierce anger, so that we may not perish."*

This was truly amazing because Nineveh was the capital of a Gentile nation that did not have the laws of Moses. In fact, the Ninevites, as were all the nations of the day, except Israel, pagan nations that worshipped many false gods, yet the Ninevites somehow knew that they had offended the God of Israel. This may have been because they knew about the mighty works the God of Israel had done for the Hebrew people during the time of the Exodus when He miraculously freed them from Egyptian bondage and was again with them when they later conquered the nation-cities of Canaan. Although this is certainly a possibility, I think it is unlikely because, even if the Ninevites knew these things, it was by this time hundreds of years later and old news.[2] I believe there is a more probable explanation.

Evidence of the Holy Spirit

In Jonah 4:11, God implies that the people of Nineveh were so ignorant of His ways that they could not *"discern between their right hand and their left."* To me, this means that for some reason, the Ninevites were not able to properly discern between right and wrong. Perhaps they had been sinning for so long as a culture and had so seared their national conscience that they no longer had any sense of morality. So the question is—How were they able to "believe" Jonah's exhortation?

I am convinced that the answer lies with the Holy Spirit of God. I believe that in His mercy, God poured out His Spirit upon the Ninevites in order for them to be able to understand that they had been transgressing against Him with their wicked practices and lifestyles so they would be able to repent of what they had been doing when given the opportunity that came when Jonah arrived.

After Nineveh repented and God *"saw their works, that they turned from their evil way,"* the Bible says that He *"relented from the disaster that He had said he would bring upon them, and He did not do it"* (Jonah 3:10). The next verse says that this displeased Jonah *"exceedingly"* and he became angry.

History tells us that the Assyrians were a brutal race of people and it is reasonable to assume that Jonah had probably wanted them to finally "get theirs."[3] When they didn't because they repented and God spared them, Jonah got angry. Then the narrative says that God questioned Jonah's attitude and even asked him if it was right for him to be angry.

The Bible tells that after Nineveh was spared, that Jonah sat stewing in his anger with his head exposed to the sun and that God prepared a plant to give him shade to help deliver him from his misery. The passage goes on to say that Jonah was very grateful for the plant. But then, before the next day, God caused the plant to wither so that when the sun came up again, it no longer provided any shade for Jonah causing him to feel miserable again. Then the Lord questions Jonah once more about his anger and makes a philosophical connection between the plant and the people of Nineveh and says to him: *"You have had pity on the plant for which you have not labored, nor made it grow, which came up in a night and perished in a night. And should I not pity Nineveh, that great city, in which are more than twenty thousand persons who cannot discern between their right hand and their left…?"* (Jonah 4:10-11)

The implication here is that the Lord *had labored* among the Ninevites. This could mean that possibly for years God's Holy Spirit had labored on the hearts and minds of the Ninevites trying to convict them of their sins and all that was needed by the time of Jonah, when God called him to go there, was for someone with boots on the ground to physically tell them plainly that they needed to repent of their sins.

The differences between Nineveh and modern America

The story of Nineveh proves that God cares for and is interested in all nations and peoples, even Gentile ones, and not only Israel, even in the Old Testament. The Ninevites had existed for centuries with no physical emissary from God telling them how they should conduct themselves, like God did with the Israelites. But such is not the case with America. America has had a long history of Christian witness and Godly heritage so many Americans know what the truth is and how they are supposed to behave and what they are to do. And now, millions of Americans are knowingly and defiantly turning their backs on God and His commandments and are in open rebellion against Him.

Although there are differences in circumstances and knowledge between ancient Nineveh and modern America, the warning is the same: *Repent or face national and personal disaster!*

The seeds of America's destruction

At the time of this writing, it appears as though God is lining up many disasters that could be brought to pass against America at any point for its growing wickedness. These are all warning signs directly given or allowed by God, but few appear to be heeding them, especially those inside government who are often doing all they can, either willfully or ignorantly, to make the country vulnerable to sudden destruction.

Electro-magnetic pulse

There is the danger of an electro-magnetic pulse (EMP) that could in a moment put America back technologically hundreds of years. An EMP event would instantly destroy all unprotected modern electronics that are in automobiles, farm equipment, factories, computers, electric power stations, communications, and more, rendering them instantly unworkable. An EMP could come as a natural occurrence as a result of a solar flare from the sun or from a manmade source such as one or more nuclear bombs detonated high into the atmosphere over North America. This could come from an enemy nation such as China, Russia, North Korea, Iran, or even from terrorists operating within or just outside the United States. An EMP event could result in as much as 90% of America's population dying off in just a matter of a few months.

Nuclear holocaust

Of course, America is also in danger of being attacked by any of the above nations or others using conventional nuclear weapons or devices. I shouldn't have to illustrate what a catastrophe it would be if America was hit by one or many nuclear bombs that targeted major U.S. cities and military installations. With the way the current presidential administration is handling world affairs, this is a real if not imminent threat. And with so many nations that now possess nuclear weapons, and many of them not friendly to America, we are actually in much more danger of nuclear annihilation today than we were during the cold war when we were at odds with only one "evil empire" that possessed nuclear weapons and delivery systems that could reach the U.S.—the Soviet Union. Some say today, and rightly so, that America is now the evil empire because of the many grievous sins it condones and promotes worldwide. On a side note, it is also interesting that a missile defense system that could have protected America against nuclear attack, although proposed under the Reagan administration in the 1980s, has foolishly never been implemented.

Cyber attack

A cyber attack is another on-going potentially debilitating threat currently facing America. Wikipedia informs us that a cyber attack "is any type of offensive maneuver employed by individuals or whole organizations that targets computer information systems, infrastructures, computer networks, and/or personal computer devices by various means of malicious acts usually originating from an anonymous source that either steals, alters, or destroys a specified target by hacking into a susceptible system." A successful widespread cyber attack from another country or a terrorist group upon America's computerized infrastructure could have devastating and life-threatening consequences to the nation as a whole, instantly plunging us into all-encompassing chaos.

Financial collapse

With America's national debt now exceeding its yearly Gross Domestic Product (GDP) and still growing, the nation is in imminent danger of total financial collapse. The nation is also reportedly leveraged against future generations to the tune of some two hundred and ten trillion dollars. So, the question isn't *If* America's economy collapses, but *When*. Why America is in its current financial straits is an extremely complex issue. But there is no doubt that the main culprit is thoroughly corrupt leadership emanating from within the Federal Government. Suffice to say that America's economy can explode at anytime and with the potential to make the Great Depression of the 1930s look like a cakewalk by comparison. And there is no one on the political or any other scene that has the courage or wherewithal to do what has to be done to reverse this continually burgeoning fiasco. And the problem is not just an American one, but worldwide, meaning that there is really nowhere to go to get away from the domino effect that will be created around the world when America's financial breakdown finally comes.

Domestic terrorism

The abject folly of the American people allowing its leaders to let into the country thousands of foreign nationals from outside our borders is tantamount to committing national suicide. The vast majority of this invasion is made up of people who are either re-introducing diseases that have been all but eradicated in the U.S. or are violent criminals from Muslim countries, drug cartels, and others bent upon doing evil in America. Of course the reasons for allowing this on the part of our lawless government is purely political and a way for America to ultimately lose its national identity and sovereignty and push us closer toward a one-world government that is being orchestrated by Satan and his anti-God proxies in the physical realm that control most of the money and power in the United States and the world. At some point, unless God intervenes, this influx of evil is going to adversely affect every American in a disastrous way.

Pandemic

As mentioned above, diseases that have been all but stamped out in America such as tuberculosis, leprosy, and malaria, to name just a few, are being re-injected into America through the flood of illegal "immigrants" coming in by the tens of thousands across our borders from underdeveloped countries. Add to this the reported increasing ineffectiveness of many drugs such as penicillin and antibiotics, and a pandemic is in the making similar to the flu virus that killed an estimated 20 to 100 million people worldwide in 1918 or the Black Death of the fourteenth century that killed as many as 20 million people in Europe alone over a period of only two years.

Famine

At the time of this writing, the bird flu virus has been raging in the American Midwest for several months killing tens of millions of domestic chickens and turkeys. The west coast has been experiencing the type of severe drought such as has not occurred in twelve hundred years and, according to a number of climatologists, could last up to a century in duration. With California alone being such a major food contributor to the nation, this, along with the continued spread of the bird flu virus, the stage is being set for a major food shortage in America. On top of this, many scientists are predicting that the world is in the beginning years of a new mini ice age or cooling period that could last decades and will lead to even less food produced across the U.S. and the world.

Another cause for less food production is the honeybee populations that have been steadily declining across the United States. This phenomenon was first noticed in 2006 when beekeepers began reporting the disappearance of thousands of honeybees within their respective colonies. This phenomenon has since been labeled: Colony Collapse Disorder (CCD) and reportedly accounts for at least a 30% decline in honeybees each year since it was first reported.[4] The primary culprit is thought to be the use of pesticides and insecticides although nothing has been done regarding their curtailment. With honeybees being the world's leading pollinators of plants and food crops, their continued decimation will mean another cause for the steady reduction of food production in America. The inaction on the part of America's leaders or the public to do anything about this other crisis in the making is another example of the delusion that has come over the people of America.

In the Old Testament, God would sometimes warn nations through their Godly leaders of coming droughts and famines, but since the vast majority of America's leaders lack wisdom and are at enmity with their Creator, virtually no one is listening for God, let alone doing anything about any of these potential disasters, any one of which could reduce America to less than a third-world country in a very short time.

Anarchy

As difficult as it is to believe, America's current presidential administration appears to be deliberately creating an atmosphere that is conducive to a total collapse of traditional America. Below is a sampling of its many policies that point to such an outcome:

• The government's printing and spending of money at a reckless rate. This will eventually lead to the further devaluation of the U.S. dollar until it is all but worthless and will be accompanied by a total collapse of America's financial system. This appears to be a deliberate attempt to force America into a "world" currency to be ultimately produced under a Satanically inspired New World Order that will be embraced by all nations that have been forced into similar financial straits by its respective utopian-driven leaders.

• The fomentation by the government of racial tension and riots in places such as Ferguson, Missouri and Baltimore, Maryland. This promotion of anarchy is most likely designed to bring America closer to martial law and the full implementation of the administration's diabolical schemes for the country.

• The government fraudulently allowing different ethnic groups into America that aren't interested in melting into society and becoming Americans like former, legal immigrants, but are more interested in practicing their own cultures within American society along with being sustained by government handouts. This will force America into even more multicultural factions and create the potential for more social unrest. The proof of this is the deliberate busing and flying into the country of known violent criminals such as Islamic jihadists and members of drug cartels.

The federal government under the current administration is also releasing into society tens of thousands of felons from prisons across the U.S. The negative effects of this nefarious tactic to destroy America is already bearing rotten fruit as career criminals are now preying upon law-abiding citizens in ever greater numbers.

• The importation of foreign troops onto American soil. As of 2014, nearly five hundred thousand United Nations troops are known to be in America. It is also known that the current administration has been purging the U.S. military of officers and other higher-ups in rank who will not obey the un-Constitutional decrees of the president that will likely include firing upon American citizens who do not go along with the administration or its evil policies. It is thought by some that these U.N. troops have been brought into the country to ensure that these unlawful edicts are carried out.

• The push to accept homosexuality and other deviant, sexual lifestyles through legal means is really an attempt to destroy the foundations of what traditionally made America a great and Godly nation. The 2015 Supreme Court decision redefining marriage is ultimately designed to that end. So, instead of America being a country from which good emanates as de Tocqueville witnessed, it is now being transformed into a modern-day Nazi Germany or Soviet Union where only evil reigns and is spread to the rest of the world.

• The making of treaties and deals with violent, Islamic jihadist states such as Iran is equal to inviting either national destruction or national extortion. Since Iran is America's mortal enemy, the current administration knows full well that Iran having a nuclear weapon will not only threaten our country, but our traditional ally, Israel, as well whose enemy is also Iran.

• Taking American support away from Israel and siding with its enemies like Iran is one of the most foolish and ill-conceived policies currently being promoted by the current administration and leaves America open to God's judgment for going against His chosen people as told in the Bible (Genesis 12:1-3 and Isaiah 60:12).

• At the time of this writing, the current administration has reduced America's nuclear arsenal by almost half during its tenure. It has also been said that our military has been reduced to pre-World War II levels. All this leaves America more vulnerable than ever before to single or simultaneous attacks by foreign enemies.

National judgment

Any one or combination of the above disasters has the potential to turn our nation quickly into a living hell. But do not doubt for a moment that all this is happening by accident; it is occurring because America has largely abandoned God. Because of this, God has allowed wicked men and women to rise to prominence as leaders of our nation, people who are wittingly or unwittingly led by Satan and bent on America's demise, not only as a world power but as an autonomous, sovereign country. Shockingly, many of these wicked people have been voted into office by either a rebellious or a willfully ignorant populace while the Church of Jesus Christ has mostly, except for a few lone voices crying in the wilderness, sat on the sidelines and done next to nothing.

When America as a nation honored God, the Almighty would protect us from disasters such as these. But now with so many

Americans, including our mainly foolish politicians, being in open rebellion against Him, God is slowly removing His divine protection from America.

A national delusion

A great many people in post-Christian America are under a grand delusion. And just like most deluded people, they don't even realize it. Despite evidence to the contrary, people for the most part:

- Don't believe in a personal, holy God.

- Do not believe in absolute laws and morals that come only from God.

- Don't believe that the Bible is from God or they believe that it is corrupted to the point of being unreliable or irrelevant.

- Have believed the lie of evolution even though there is virtually no evidence for it while all the evidence instead points to intelligent design and special creation.

- Believe that all roads lead to God and heaven even though all religions represent vastly different deities.

- Don't believe that there is a real devil named Satan who has, at his disposal, legions of demons whose only goal, night and day, 24/7, is to deceive people so that they will reject the Bible, its God, and their only means of rescue, Jesus Christ.

- Do not believe America was founded as a Christian nation, even though the evidence proving it is everywhere to be found by the person with the courage and sense enough to look for it.

- Don't believe that there is a hell with a lake of fire for all those who reject Jesus Christ even though the teaching comes from Christ Himself, the greatest person who ever lived.

- Don't think they are bad enough to need being saved from eternal damnation for their sins against God.

- Don't believe America is in imminent danger of God's judgment, in fact, they think that by rebelling against His commands in the Bible they are somehow enlightened and set free from debilitating moral shackles—Such is the depth of the delusion of most people living in America.

Are you one of these people?

Have you fallen for Satan's lies?

Will you gamble with your own soul and your eternal destiny?

Will you gamble that Jesus Christ is not the Way, the Truth, and the Life as John 14:6 says and that no person gets to Father God and heaven except through Him, as the verse also says?

Will you gamble that Jesus was just a prophet of some ethereal god whose words are irrelevant?

Will you gamble that all the things that Jesus said while on earth are untrue or are the ramblings of a madman?

It has been said that if you believe and trust in Jesus Christ and in the end, you are wrong, you will have lost nothing. However, if you reject Jesus Christ and He was *right* all along, you have lost everything—*forever*!

So what have you really got to lose by believing in God's only Savior from sin, Jesus Christ?

Hell and the lake of fire
The concept of a personal hell has lost all its meaning and reality in modern-day America. Although evil is recognized, emulated, and even celebrated everywhere in our society today, most people don't believe there is an actual hell, a place of

punishment, where all evildoers, called sinners in the Bible, those who are without Christ, will go when they die. Certainly many people have tried to live what they define as "good" lives, and have tried not to do anything bad enough to warrant winding up in a bad place. But even so-called good people do bad things. And even if their good deeds outweigh the bad, it's not enough to save them from the negative affects of sin in the eyes of God. It's only by people believing that Christ shed His blood on the cross for the forgiveness of their sins—the things they have done wrong, even the seeming little things—that they can make peace with God, cease their war against Him, and go to heaven when they die. But sadly, most people who have rejected Jesus Christ are relying on their own goodness and almost universally believe they will go to a good place or heaven when their earthly lives run out.

Satan and his legions have done their work well to cause the majority of mankind not to think about their ultimate end for rejecting the God of the Bible and Jesus Christ. He has successfully caused most unsaved people to buy into his pack of lies—hook, line, and sinker—by either causing them to believe in Godless evolution where they think they will cease to exist when they die, or by causing them to erroneously believe they will go to heaven in spite of not accepting Jesus Christ into their hearts.

Jesus made a startling statement regarding heaven and salvation that was recorded partially in the Gospel of Luke and more fully in the Gospel of Matthew.

In Luke 13:23-24, when the apostles asked Jesus if few would be saved, He replied: *"Strive to enter through the narrow gate, for many, I say to you, will seek to enter and not be able."* Matthew 7:13-14 gives more of Jesus' response to the apostles' question:

"Enter by the narrow gate; for wide is the gate and broad is the way that leads to destruction, and there are many who go in by it. Because narrow is the gate and difficult is the way which leads to life, and there are few who find it."

In the above passages, Jesus is the narrow gate and the difficult way, and hell is the place of destruction for those who take the wide, broad and easy path in their earthly lives, the kind that requires little self-control or diligence to find out the truth about Christ and the eternal life that He offers to all, but which only a relative few accept.

Are you one of those who are walking the easy path of little resistance on your own, without Christ, hoping that in the end it will somehow work out all right and lead to eternal life? Have you gone in through the wide gate that leads to the broad way to hell and destruction so you can be accepted by an unbelieving world of people who are in rebellion against the God of the Bible and Jesus Christ? If you are reading this, it is not too late to get off the wrong path you are on and choose the narrow gate that is Christ, the one that leads to eternal life.

It was the subject of hell and the rejecters of Jesus Christ ending up there that made Jonathon Edwards sermon, *Sinners in the hands of an angry God,* so effective in eighteenth century America. But Americans today think they are too enlightened or sophisticated to believe in a literal hell. In fact, jokes are made about it such as: Hell won't be that bad, especially since all my friends will be there. It is this kind of dismissive attitude that many have regarding this last destination of eternal torment for all those who reject Jesus Christ.

But the reality is far different. The closest idea we have of what hell is like for people who die without God and Christ is Jesus' story about the rich man and Lazarus as noted in an earlier chapter and recorded in Luke 16:19-31:

"There was a rich man who was dressed in purple and fine linen and lived in luxury every day. At his gate was laid a beggar named Lazarus, covered with sores and longing to eat what fell from the rich man's table. Even the dogs came and licked his sores. The time came when the beggar died and the angels carried him to Abraham's side. The rich man also died and was buried. In Hades, where he was in torment, he looked up and saw

Abraham far away, with Lazarus by his side. So he called to him, 'Father Abraham, have pity on me and send Lazarus to dip the tip of his finger in water and cool my tongue, because I am in agony in this fire.' But Abraham replied, 'Son, remember that in your lifetime you received your good things, while Lazarus received bad things, but now he is comforted here and you are in agony. And besides all this, between us and you a great chasm has been set in place, so that those who want to go from here to you cannot, nor can anyone cross over from there to us.' He answered, 'Then I beg you, father, send Lazarus to my family, for I have five brothers. Let him warn them, so that they will not also come to this place of torment.' Abraham replied, 'They have Moses and the Prophets; let them listen to them.' 'No, father Abraham,' he said, 'but if someone from the dead goes to them, they will repent.' He said to him, 'If they do not listen to Moses and the Prophets, they will not be convinced even if someone rises from the dead.'" (NIV)

And so it is today.

Even though Jesus Christ has risen from the dead to prove that what He said while on earth is true, most people reject Him anyway, sealing their own fates to eternal damnation in hell, just like the rich man.

The purpose of hell

Many people wonder how a good God could make a place of eternal torment and pain such as hell. But the Bible says that hell and the lake of fire weren't created for mankind at all. It was originally created by God for the devil and his angels as a place of punishment for their rebellion against Him (Matthew 25:41). Now, much of mankind has joined Satan and his minions in this rebellion so it is also the last abode for all those who have not submitted to God or accepted His son for the remission of their sins.

Dr. Walter Martin used to say that hell is to be avoided at all costs. Hell is so bad, in fact, that even the demons are terrified of it and will do anything to keep from going there. Matthew 8:28-

32 tells of two demon-possessed men who Jesus delivered that is very revealing. The Bible says that when the demons, while still inside the men, saw Jesus coming, that they suddenly cried out saying, *"What have we to do with You, Jesus, You Son of God? Have you come to torment us before the time?"* The Bible then relates that the demons literally begged Jesus, before He had cast them out of the men, to let them go into a herd of swine that were grazing nearby. Although Jesus let them do as they asked,[5] as soon as the demons entered the pigs, the pigs ran headlong into a lake and were drowned. The demons had to have known this would happen, but obviously hell (or the "abyss" as stated in this passage) is so bad that it was better to inhabit another earthly creature for a few moments longer than to immediately have to go back there.[6]

And this is the place that so many people without Christ ignore, hoping that their willful ignorance about it will somehow make it not real.

I believe that God made hell such a terrible place to be a deterrent to keep people from entertaining thoughts of rebelling against Him, and also as a compelling reason for them to consider and accept His way of deliverance from it by obeying His Son. But this has largely not happened because tragically, the vast majority of people either ignore Jesus Christ and His words or are in open rebellion against Him. And unfortunately, the truth is— most will discover the reality of hell only after it is too late.

Imagine for a moment

If you are reading this and are not a Christian, imagine for a moment that you have died not believing in Christ. After your last breath and heartbeat on this earth you are suddenly transported to a dark, foreboding place. Perhaps there are nauseating smells and sounds or shrieks of torment coming from all around you. You look into the gloom that is highlighted by flashes of flickering flame and see people you recognize. Some were famous in life and some were just ordinary people, but all look traumatized and terrified beyond what words are capable of expressing. You suddenly *realize* where you are, and you know immediately that it sure isn't heaven. Perhaps you even see your mother or your father. Maybe he or she looks at you and although for a moment you notice a glimmer of recognition in their staring, terrified eyes, they quickly turn away and back into their own nightmare because they know and now you know too that your individual fates have been sealed for all time and eternity and *absolutely nothing else matters!* There is no one to help you or them. There is no one for you to call out for. There is no one to come to your rescue. There is no one anymore for you to even pray to because you know full well you wanted nothing much to do with God and rejected Jesus Christ in life and now you are totally and forevermore without hope. You have only been in hell for a few moments but already your earthly life is barely a dim memory and your new horrible abode already seems like an eternity. It doesn't matter anymore that the person whose gaze you just met was your father or mother or sibling or other relation, or even your own spouse—Because now all of your fates are sealed forever and even though you are all together, you are all completely alone—without hope, forever and forever, for beyond even the time when the last star of the last galaxy runs down and burns out. And you haven't even been cast into the lake of fire yet.

Making a decision

If you are not a believer in Jesus Christ, I do not give the above scenario lightly or for the sake of sensationalism, I give it to you in love to scare you straight and into seriously considering Jesus Christ, your only hope to avoid hell—before it is too late! Believe in Christ for salvation and heaven *now*, while you still can, and don't put it off till another time after which death finds you unprepared and the decision you have been delaying is suddenly and unexpectedly, too late to make!

Life is *not* a game that you can live recklessly and without giving thought to your eternal destiny like so many do. It is a choosing ground to find Christ, to accept Him or reject Him. Your choice will determine where you will spend eternity, in heaven with God, or in hell without Him.

Time is running out

There is every reason to believe that time is running out for America and that we may be approaching the end of the age when Christ returns to gather up His true followers to Himself, then pour out His wrath against all those who oppose God. Jesus said in Matthew 24:37-39:

"But as the days of Noah were, so also will the coming of the Son of Man be. For as in the days before the flood, they were eating and drinking, marrying and giving in marriage, until the day that Noah entered the ark, and did not know until the flood came and took them all away, so also will the [second] *coming of the Son of Man be."*

The Bible also says in II Timothy 3:2-4 that in the last days men would be:

...lovers of their own selves, covetous, boasters, proud, blasphemers, disobedient to parents, unthankful, unholy, without natural affection, trucebreakers, false accusers, incontinent, fierce, despisers of those that are good, traitors, heady, highminded, lovers of pleasures more than lovers of God.

I Timothy 4:1-2 reads:

Now the Spirit speaketh expressly, that in the latter times some shall depart from the faith, giving heed to seducing spirits, and doctrines of devils; Speaking lies in hypocrisy; having their conscience seared with a hot iron.

And II Timothy 4:3-4 warns:

For the time will come when they will not endure sound doctrine; but after their own lusts shall they heap to themselves teachers, having itching ears; And they shall turn away their ears from the truth, and shall be turned unto fables.

It is not difficult to see from the above passages that America has all the earmarks of a nation ripe for God's judgment and that we may indeed be living near the end of time when Christ returns to earth. But one thing is certain—we are most definitely in the last days of America unless its people humbly repent before God and accept Jesus Christ as the only Savior for their sins.

Summary

The narrative of the Bible is admittedly a fantastic one—God creating a good and perfect Satan, then Satan sinning by wanting to be like God thereby injecting sin into God's creation, then getting kicked out of heaven and down to the earth where he can tempt mankind. Then God also creating man good and perfect, and man listening to Satan who is already in a beautiful paradise to tempt him into disobeying God, which man does. God then determining to rescue man from his sin by becoming the perfect sacrifice for sin by coming to earth as a man and dying for sinners. Then God allowing into heaven all those who entrust their souls to this God-man so they can spend eternity in heaven with God and the angels who remained loyal to Him. With God knowing everything that would happen before He created anything, but choosing to do it anyway as the best way to get a race of people who freely choose Him, and not from compulsion or fear or for some other kind of gain, but because they recognize God's love and goodness that caused Him to sacrifice Himself so that they and others among mankind can be reconciled to Him forever.

This is all certainly incredible, but no more fantastic than the universe and the world we live in with all its mind-boggling complexity and design. The thought of the universe and life itself existing and what we humans are capable of such as: thinking, crying, laughing, experiencing sorrow, joy, anger, being self-aware—the list can go on and on, is beyond belief, yet it is reality. Like Gerald Schroeder essentially wondered—How can all this possibly be?

Conclusion

This is for sure a mystery. All of it is—I'm not going to pretend it isn't. But it is no more mysterious than the universe and life coming out of nothing—an idea most people don't seem to have a big problem with.

The biggest misunderstanding that people in America have about God is that when they die, they think that as long as they haven't done anything really bad in their lives, that God will accept them with all their supposedly less egregious faults. Well––No, He won't! Because according to the Bible, sin is sin whether it's lying or cheating or murdering! And the truth is, and as mysterious as it is—A sinner with his sin intact can't survive in the presence of a holy God! And for reasons only known to God—it's only if somebody truly believes in Jesus Christ and His sacrifice on the cross, that a person can go to heaven and stand in the presence of that same God and live. The Bible makes it clear that there is no other way under heaven by which people can be saved from the negative results of their sins!

The people of America need to believe in Jesus Christ in order to turn our country around. But time is running out! Many in America have been waging war against God for a very long time. And in the last few years, especially under our current political leadership, the war has increased in intensity where now all manner of what used to be considered egregious sin is being accepted—in government, on TV, in the movies, in public debate, even in many of our so-called churches, which is why I believe God's judgment is not far away, evidenced by our very means of destruction that is even now forming all around us as a nation.

All this is happening because America has turned away from the God of the Bible. And like Jonathon Edwards warned in his famous sermon over 250 years ago—The only thing that keeps America from going over the cliff to destruction is God's seemingly infinite patience. But it won't last forever and the next second could bring total chaos and calamity. Edwards even said that a person's own personal end will come when they least expect it and at any moment, they could find themselves in eternity before they even know what happened.

Scary stuff! And yet people gamble with America's future and their own eternal destiny every second of every day, betting that destruction will never come and that their earthly life will somehow last forever. They continue to ignore the Bible and God's warnings in it, laid out for all to see. They gamble that America will somehow be okay, despite the prevalent rot of corruption across the land and the persistent rebellion against God's laws everywhere! They gamble that Jesus Christ is irrelevant—that His Gospel message of hope and salvation is somehow just religious mumbo-jumbo. Even our Christian churches are neither hot nor cold for Christ, but lukewarm like the Church of Laodicea that Jesus sternly warned in the book of Revelations to turn back to Him so they could receive the crown of life.

And that's what I say to America—to the non-believer in Christ or the lukewarm Christian who is reading this book— Wake up and turn to Jesus Christ!

Repent of the part you have played in this war against the God of the Bible.

If you will not accept and follow Christ as your Savior, then, as the Bible says: He will be your judge!

Time is running out, and the choice will not be yours much longer!

Epilogue

God has made it very easy to avoid hell and gain eternal life in heaven. The Bible says:

... that if you confess with your mouth the Lord Jesus and believe in your heart that God has raised Him from the dead, you will be saved. For with the heart one believes to righteousness, and with the mouth confession is made to salvation.
Romans 10:9-10

Notes

Introduction

1. John Winthrop, *Life and Letters of John Winthrop* edited by Robert C. Winthrop, Boston: Little & Brown, 1869.
2. What de Tocqueville said was that the American colonists "brought with them into the New World a form of Christianity which I cannot better describe than by styling it a democratic and republican religion. This contributed powerfully to the establishment of a republic and a democracy in public affairs; and from the beginning, politics and religion contracted an alliance which has never been dissolved." (*Democracy in America Vol. 2* by Alexis de Tocqueville, pg. 311)

Chapter 1

1. On average, women give at least 3 reasons for choosing abortion. 75% say that having a baby would interfere with work, school or other responsibilities; about 75% say they cannot afford a child; and 50% say they do not want to be a single parent or are having problems with their husband or partner (Guttmacher Institute). Only 12% of women included a physical problem with their health among reasons for having an abortion (National Abortion Federation (NAF). One per cent (of aborting women) reported that they were the survivors of rape (NAF).
2. From abortionfacts.com
3. Some may still insist that having an abortion is not equal to making war against God. There are several definitions of "war." One of them, according to the Oxford dictionary is, "a sustained effort to deal with or end a particular unpleasant or undesirable situation or condition." I contend that many would say that the "unpleasant or undesirable situation" in America today is the presence and knowledge of the Christian God in our society.
4. Israel is made up of 12 tribes stemming from the 12 sons born to Jacob whose name was later changed to Israel after the Bible says that he literally wrestled with God. In fact, the name Israel means, "Wrestler with God."
5. *Slouching Towards Gomorrah: Modern Liberalism and American Decline* by Robert H. Bork, HarperCollins, 1996, pg. 35.
6. *The Politically Incorrect Guide to Islam (And the Crusades)* by Robert Spencer, Regnery Publishing, 2005, pg. 77.
7. Darwin never speculated on how life came to be in *On The Origin Of Species*. In the chapter titled: Instinct, he states: "I must premise, that I

have nothing to do with the origin of the primary mental powers, any more than I have with that of life itself."

8. It is interesting to note that according to *Foxe's Book of Martyrs*, that chronicles persecuted Christians in the Old World from the time of Christ to the late 1800s, that it was with the Christian princes living in Germany where persecuted believers from the other European countries could find asylum.

9. In one instance, it was a passage from the New Testament that saved the Jamestown Colony from extinction. When the Jamestown colonists first arrived on the shores of what is now the state of Virginia, a socialistic form of government had been chosen that allowed everyone to partake equally from a common food storehouse. The problem was, not everyone contributed to the storehouse equally, with many refusing to work or work hard enough to help provide the food that would keep the settlement from starvation. It was only when Captain John Smith did away with the common-store system and adopted the New Testament principle taken from II Thessalonians 3:10 that states, "that if there were any, which would not work, that he should not eat" that the colony was saved from disaster. Source: *Forged in Faith* by Rod Gragg, Howard Books, 2012, pgs. 18, 19.

Chapter 2

1. *An Expository Dictionary of Biblical Words* by W.E. Vine, Merrill F. Unger & William White, Thomas Nelson, 1984, pg. ix.
2. At least the ones God wanted passed down to subsequent generations.
3. *In Defense of the Bible* Edited by Steven B. Cowan and Terry L. Wilder, B&H Academic, 2013, pg. 133.
4. Ibid., pg. 148.
5. Ibid., pgs. 150, 151.
6. *Evidence That Demands a Verdict* by Josh McDowell, Here's Life Publishers, 1979, Pg. 15. Primary source: *All About the Bible* by Sidney Collet, Old Tappan: Revell, no date of publication, pgs. 314, 314.
7. Ibid, pg 17. Primary source: Pg. 88, *The Books and the Parchments by F. F. Bruce*, revised edition, Westwood: Fleming H. Revell Company, 1963.
8. *Biblical Demonology* by Merrill F. Unger, Kregel Publications, 1994, pg. 21.
9. *In Defense of the Bible*, pg. 55.
10. Ibid., pg. 55 (in footnote). Primary source: *The Popular Encyclopedia of Apologetics* by Norman Geisler and Larry Wilson, Harvest House, 2008, pg. 103.
11. Ibid., pg. 91.
12. Ibid., pg. 152.
13. Ibid., pg. 156.

14. Ibid., pg. 161. Primary source: Appendix, *Misquoting Jesus* by Bart Ehrman, HarperOne, 2007.
15. Ibid., pg. 161.
16. Ibid., pg. 148.
17. According to Joseph M. Holden and Norman Geisler, the Dead Sea Scrolls contained a scroll of the Old Testament book of Isaiah in its entirety that dates back to the second century BC. Source: *The Popular Handbook of Archaeology and the Bible*, by Joseph M. Holden and Norman Geisler, Harvest House Publishers, 2013, pg. 37.
18. *In Defense of the Bible*, pg. 151.
19. Ibid., pg. 133.
20. Ibid., pg. 143.
21. Ibid., pg. 73.
22. Ibid., pg. 74.
23. Ibid.
24. Ibid., pg. 75.
25. Ibid., pg. 413.
26. Ibid., pg. 403.
27. Ibid.
28. Ibid., pg. 428.
29. Ibid.
30. *The Popular Handbook of Archaeology and the Bible*, pgs. 214 to 220. The event is told about in the Old Testament in the book of Genesis 18:20-33 and 19:1-29.
31. Ibid., pgs. 213. The event is told about in the Old Testament in the book of Genesis 11:1-9.
32. Ibid., pgs. 222-224. The event is told about in the Old Testament book of Exodus.
33. *In Defense of the Bible*, pg. 220.
34. *The Popular Handbook of Archaeology and the Bible*, pg. 181.
35. Ibid., pg. 186.
36. Ibid., pg. 233.
37. *The Bible as History* by Werner Keller, Bantam Books, 1981, pgs. xxii-xxiv.
38. For a more complete exposition and compelling scientific evidence for a worldwide flood, see pgs. 196-214 of *Reasons Skeptics Should Consider Christianity* by Josh McDowell and Don Stewart, Here's Life Publishers, 1981.
39. See the Appendix for Chapter 2 for more on this subject.
40. *Evidence That Demands a Verdict*, pg. 22. Primary source: *The Incomparable Book* by Wilbur M. Smith, Beacon Publications, 1961, pgs. 9, 10.
41. *Things to Come* by J. Dwight Pentecost, Zondervan, 1964, Preface.

42. "The Bible contains over 2000 prophecies that have been fulfilled, many with very specific details." http://www.bibleevidences.com/prophecy.htm

43. *The Evidence of Prophesy: Fulfilled Prediction as a Testimony to the Truth of Christianity* by Robert C. Newman, 1988, pg. 182.

44. According to topsecretwriters.com (http://www.topsecretwriters.com/2011/03/the-many-failed-edgar-cayce-prophecies/) "Out of the thousands upon thousands of Edgar Cayce's prophecies, only 40% can be considered remotely correct, and even that percentage is open to debate. The other 60% were either too vague to interpret, multiple-intent, or just plain wrong."

45. According to clairvoyantencounters.com, "her correct predictions were fewer than those that didn't come true" http://www.clairvoyantencounters.com/jeane-dixon-predictions-and-misfires/

46. Article ID: DN088 by Steve Bright (http://www.equip.org/article/nostradamus/#christian-books-2)

47. *Miracles* by C. S. Lewis, HarperCollins, 2001, pg. 5.

48. *In Defense of the Bible*, pg. 430.

49. C. S. Lewis said, "You are probably quite right in thinking that you will never see a miracle done... They come on great occasions: they are found at the great ganglions of history—not of political or social history, but of that spiritual history which cannot be fully known by men." *The Quotable Lewis* edited by Wayne Martindale and Jerry Root, Tyndale House Publishers, pg. 434. Primary source: *Miracles* by C.S. Lewis, HarperCollins, 2001, pg. 273.

50. *In Defense of the Bible*, pg. 80.

51. Physicist and Hebrew scholar, Gerald Schroeder, in his book, *God According to God*, states: "The lack of repetition has not stopped scientists from speculating on the causes of the two most fundamental phenomena crucial to our existence: the big-bang creation of the universe and the origin of life from nonliving matter. Were these miracles? Afterall, they were both onetime events." HarperOne, 2009, pg. 16.

52. *An Expository Dictionary of Biblical Words* by W.E. Vine, Merrill F. Unger & William White, pg. vii.

53. The four Gospels have never been seriously questioned as to authenticity.

54. *In Defense of the Bible*, pg. 270.

55. Ibid., pg. 273.

56. *Alleged Discrepancies of the Bible* by John W. Haley, Baker Book House, 1983, pg. 2.

57. Ibid., Preface.

58. *Lost Christianities: The Battles for Scripture and the Faiths We Never Knew* by Bart Ehrman, Oxford University Press, 2005.

59. *In Defense of the Bible*, pg. 181.

60. http://www.geocities.ws/gary_bee_za/bible/dss.htm

Chapter 3

1. *Reason in the Balance: The Case Against Naturalism in Science, Law & Education* by Phillip E. Johnson, InterVarsity Press, 1995, pgs. 78, 79.
2. Darwin said of his theory, "The preservation of favourable variations and the rejection of injurious variations, I call Natural Selection." *The Origin of Species* by Charles Darwin, Bantam edition, 2008, pg. 82.
3. An interesting observation has been made by Phillip Johnson where he postulates why evolutionists so desperately want to believe in evolution: "Modernist naturalism is liberating, especially in the area of gender roles and sexual behavior, because it frees people from the illusion that outdated cultural norms have permanent validity as commands of God. Persons who attack scientific naturalism or the theory of evolution probably do so as part of a disguised agenda to reestablish a stifling patriarchal code of sexual behavior. I have found that any discussion with modernists about the weakness of the theory of evolution quickly turns into a discussion of politics, particularly sexual politics. Modernists typically fear that any discrediting of naturalistic evolution will end in women being sent to the kitchen, gays to the closet and abortionists to jail. That kind of consideration explains why any perceived attempt to undermine the teaching of evolution as fact in the schools is met with such fierce opposition; much more than a scientific theory is deemed to be at stake." *Reason in the Balance*, pgs. 46, 47.
4. Ibid., pg. 107.
5. Ibid., pg. 86.
6. See chapter two under the section titled: History and Archaeology
7. *Reasons Skeptics Should Consider Christianity*, pg. 167.
8. *Reason in the Balance.* Johnson quotes well-known biochemist and evolutionist, Francis Crick: "The Astonishing Hypothesis is that 'You,' your joys and your sorrows, your memories and your ambitions, your sense of personal identity and free will, are in fact no more than the behavior of a vast assembly of nerve cells and their associated molecules." Pg. 63. Primary source: *The Astonishing Hypothesis: The Scientific Search for the Soul*, Scribner's, 1994, pg. 3.
9. *God According to God*, pg. 49, Schroeder quotes *Scientific American* article: "Life: Origin and Evolution" by Clair Folsome, Pg. 79.
10. *Reasons Skeptics Should Consider Christianity*, pgs. 135.
11. *God According to God*, pgs. 32, 33.
12. http://www.npr.org/templates/story/story.php?storyId=1295624
13. http://www.smithsonianmag.com/science-nature/a-fossilized-blood-engorged-mosquito-is-found-for-the-first-time-ever-1749788/?no-ist See also: http://www.nwcreation.net/fossilsliving.html
14. *Decision* magazine in an article titled: Dismantling Darwinism, pg. 17.

15. *God According to God*, pg. 220.
16. Ibid., pg. 21. Primary source: *The Mysterious Universe* by James Jeans, Cambridge University Press, 1931.
17. Ibid., pg. 2.
18. Ibid., pg. 220.
19. Ibid., pg. 21.
20. *Decision* magazine: Dismantling Darwinism, pg. 16.

Chapter 4

1. Having no religion but believing in some higher power is the most hip of all because it means you're too enlightened to be bogged down by anyone's religious dogma.
2. Universalism in the 18th and 19th centuries was a heretical sect of Christianity that did not teach eternal punishment in hell for those who reject Jesus Christ and also taught that mankind was incapable of good or responding to God in a repentant way and that because of this, Universalism falsely teaches that all people universally go to heaven when they die because of Jesus Christ's payment for the sins of mankind on the cross. Source: *The Original Memoirs of Charles G. Finney*, edited by Garth M. Rosell & Richard A. G. Dupuis, Zondervan, 1989, pgs. 38, 39. NOTE: More on sin and Jesus Christ in the following chapters.
3. https://www.psychologytoday.com/conditions/dissociative-identity-disorder-multiple-personality-disorder
4. In knowing good and evil.
5. The source material for Mormonism is taken from *The Kingdom of the Cults* by Walter R. Martin, Bethany House Publishers, 1977.
6. www.equip.org/article/philosophical-problems-with-the-mormon-concept-of-god/#christian-books-4
7. The source material for Jehovah's Witnesses and the Watch Tower Bible and Tract Society is taken from *The Kingdom of the Cults*.
8. Much of the source material for this section on Islam is taken from *The Politically Incorrect Guide to Islam (and the Crusades)* by Robert Spencer, Regnery Publishing, Inc. 2005.
9. Or Abū al-Qāsim Muḥammad ibn ʿAbd Allāh ibn ʿAbd al-Muṭṭalib ibn Hāshim, depending upon where one looks.
10. There is strong credible evidence to suggest that Allah represents the moon-god named Sin worshipped by ancient Mesopotamians (Middle East) (Source: http://www.biblebelievers.org.au/moongod.htm). It is interesting to note that the Sin deity was represented by the crescent moon that, along with a star, is the internationally recognized symbol of Islam.
11. There are some exceptions to Jehovah's prophets in the Bible. Elijah for instance killed the false prophets of Baal in First Kings 18:40. But instances such as this are rare in Scripture and not the normal deeds of

Biblical prophets who were primarily used by God to communicate His will to His people.

12. Canaan, now considered Palestine, was made up of several cities that were also considered individual nations by the Israelites. Some of these nation-cities that inhabited the region called Canaan are named in the Old Testament: The Hittites, Hivites, Perizzites, Girgashites, Amorites, and the Jebusites.

13. *Archaeology and the Old Testament* by Merrill F. Unger, Zondervan, 1968.

14. One rare exception to this is told in I Kings 18:40 when Elijah personally, it seems, executed the false prophets of the pagan god Baal at the Brook of Kishon.

15. *The Life of Muhammad* by A. Guillaume. Published by Oxford University Press.

16. From: http://www.aboutbuddhism.org/buddhism-beliefs.php/

17. Hebrews 9:28: "And it is appointed for men to die once, but after this the judgment."

18. http://www.buddhanet.net/e-learning/qanda03.htm

19. *Time Magazine* May 06, 1991, By Richard Behar Monday

20. http://www.equip.org/article/scientology/

21. Ibid.

22. Ibid.

Chapter 5

1. All these verses except otherwise noted are from the NIV Bible.

2. http://www.bibleheadquarters.org/THE613LAWSoftheOLDTESTAMENT.html

3. Technically, the New Testament teaches that how the Mosaic Law applied universally to mankind changed with the start of the ministry of John the Baptist (see Luke 16:16), primarily because it was John who ushered in the new age of the Messiah and the time of the Gentiles.

4. http://www.equip.org/article/cherry-picking-the-commandments/

5. Although the Hebrew people are God's chosen people and God still has a plan for them, many of them continue to be in rebellion against Him because they have not kept the Mosaic law nor accepted their Messiah. This is in contrast to many others from every nation who have recognized Jesus Christ as not only the Jewish Messiah, but also as the only hope for mankind's salvation from sin.

6. http://www.equip.org/bible_answers/does-homosexuality-demonstrate-that-the-bible-is-antiquated-and-irrelevant-2/

7. See: Numbers 35:16, 31, Exodus 21:12, 23, Leviticus 24:17.

8. http://www.dailymail.co.uk/news/article-1348624/Children-broken-homes-likely-suicidal-thoughts.html

9. http://cnsnews.com/news/article/fewer-half-american-children-growing-intact-families-survey-finds

10. Although the term fornication is not used in regards to individuals in the Old Testament, it is used often to warn individual perpetrators in the New.
11. See also Exodus 22:16-17.
12. http://www.patheos.com/blogs/christianpiatt/2012/07/billy-graham-punish-america-or-apologize-to-sodom-gomorrah/
13. See http://www.equip.org/article/is-there-a-gay-gene/ for a more in-depth explanation.
14. *What Demons Can Do To Saints* by Merrill F. Unger, Moody Publishers, 1991, pg. 163.
15. http://www.equip.org/bible_answers/does-homosexuality-demonstrate-that-the-bible-is-antiquated-and-irrelevant-2/

Chapter 6

1. *The Invisible War* by Chip Ingram, Baker Books, 2006, pg. 37.
2. When the Bible refers to the world in texts like: John 14:30 and James 4:4, it is referring to a world system that is at enmity with God and unified under Satan and his minions in and out of the spiritual realm.
3. Michael in verse 7 is an archangel (Jude 9) or "chief prince" and leader (Daniel 10:13) of others from God's angelic order. Although Michael is a high-ranking angel, he is probably not as innately powerful as Satan.
4. See also Leviticus 17:7 and Psalm 106:37.
5. Chafer's book *Satan* has been recently released as an ebook titled: *The Biblical Doctrine of Satan (Annotated)*.
6. *Satan*, by Lewis Sperry Chafer, www.bookjungle.com, pg. 14.
7. See Note 1 in Appendix for Chapter 6.
8. *Biblical Demonology* by Merrill F. Unger, Kregel Publications, 1994, pg. 15.
9. *Satan*, pgs. 41, 42.
10. Ibid., pg. 35.
11. http://www.nbcnews.com/news/us-news/jillian-mccabe-heard-voices-killing-autistic-son-family-says-n241986
12. http://www.telegraph.co.uk/news/uknews/crime/7740805/Man-murdered-pregnant-woman-after-hearing-voices.html
13. http://news.sky.com/story/972491/jersey-murder-trial-killer-hearing-voices
14. http://townhall.com/tipsheet/danieldoherty/2013/09/17/report-navy-yard-shooter-was-hearing-voices-n1702443
15. *Biblical Demonology*, pgs. 35, 36.
16. *Satan*, pg. 49.
17. *Biblical Demonology*, pgs. 181, 182.
18. Adam is representative of the whole of mankind.
19. *Biblical Demonology*, pgs. 72, 73.
20. *Paradise Lost*, by C.S. Lewis, pg. 102. Also page 528. *The Quotable Lewis* by Wayne Martindale and Jerry Root.

21. Occultism is one of the ways Satan and his demons draw people to them and disseminate their anti-God doctrines.
22. *Biblical Demonology*, pg. 27.
23. *Satan*, pg. 34.
24. Ibid., pgs. 49, 50.
25. *Biblical Demonology*, Page 26.
26. Christ, the second Adam, according to scripture, defeated and condemned Satan by shedding His perfect blood for all mankind on the cross and by His subsequent resurrection. The first Adam introduced sin into the world by believing Satan's lie and the second Adam, Christ, takes away the spiritual death caused by sin, for all those who believe in Him.
27. *Satan*, pgs. 17, 18.
28. *Biblical Demonology*, pgs. 1 and 25.

Chapter 7

1. *The 5000 Year Leap* by W. Cleon Skousen, National Center for Constitutional Studies, 2005, pg. 84. Primary Source: *Democracy in America* by Alexis de Tocqueville.
2. According to Gragg, of the major world powers at the time, the Reformation Movement really only took hold in England.
3. *Forged in Faith* by Rod Gragg, Howard Books, 2012, pg. 50. Primary source: *Travels and Works of Captain John Smith* by John Smith, pgs. 391, 392.
4. See the Appendix for this chapter for the entire *Mayflower Compact*.
5. The Quakers were a sect of Christianity. Rod Gragg recounts how they got their name: "Quakerism was a spin-off Puritan sect. It began in England in the early seventeenth century, and was founded by a shoemaker-turned-preacher named George Fox. The sect's theology was largely defined by Fox, and its unusual name also originated with him—indirectly. Sentenced to jail for his beliefs in 1650 [in England], Fox warned the presiding judge that he should tremble in fear of God for engaging in persecution. 'You folk are the tremblers,' the judge retorted, 'you are the quakers.' The name 'Quaker' stuck."
6. See the Appendix for William Penn's entire letter to the Native Americans.
7. *Forged In Faith*, pgs. 92, 93. Primary source: *Federal and State Constitutions, Colonial Charters and Organic Laws and Colonial Laws of New York From the Year 1664 to the Revolution.*
8. *Forged in Faith*, pgs. 97, 98.
9. Ibid., pgs. 99, 100. Primary source: *Thoughts on the Revival of Religion in New England* by Jonathon Edwards, 1740.
10. Ibid., pg. 103.
11. Ibid.
12. Ibid., pg. 109.

13. Ibid.. pg. 114. Gragg explains that, "Spiritual revival supporters became known as 'New Lights' and opponents to revival were called 'Old Lights.'"
14. Dissenter denominations were those that did not agree with the state-sanctioned Anglican Church of England.
15. Ibid., pgs. 116-118.
16. See the Appendix for this chapter for a list of the colleges and universities that were founded by people of Christian faith.
17. *Forged in Faith*, pg. 185.
18. Ibid., pg. 186.
19. Ibid.
20. *His Excellency George Washington* by Joseph J. Ellis, Knopf, 2003, pg. 151.
21. *By the Hand of Providence* by Rod Gragg, Howard Books, 2011, pg. 1. Primary source: *George Washington Papers*, 1741-99.
22. Ibid., pg. 8.
23. Ibid., pg. 18.
24. Ibid., pgs. 19, 20.
25. *Forged in Faith*, pg. 183.
26. Webster's 1913 dictionary states that Unitarianism is a Christian doctrine that stresses individual freedom of belief and rejects the Trinity. Dictionary.reference.com says Unitarianism is a system of Christian belief that maintains the unipersonality of God, rejects the Trinity and the divinity of Christ, and takes reason, conscience, and character as the criteria of belief and practice.
27. *Forged in Faith*, pgs. 183, 184.
28. Ibid., pg. 184.
29. Ibid., pgs. 150, 151.
30. Ibid., pg. 150.
31. Ibid., pg. 125.
32. Ibid., pg. 129.
33. Ibid., pg. 130.
34. Ibid., pg. 120.
35. Ibid., pg. 139.
36. Ibid., pg. 150.
37. Ibid., pg. 141.
38. Ibid., pg. 126.
39. Ibid., pg. 128.
40. Ibid., pg. 126.
41. Ibid., pg. 127.
42. Ibid., pg. 128.
43. Ibid., pgs. 128, 129.
44. Ibid., pg. 129.
45. Ibid., pg. 157.

46. Ibid.
47. From an article by Joel McDurmon titled: "'Bring Your Pieces to Church' Sunday" http://americanvision.org/2342/bring-your-guns-to-church-sunday/
48. Ibid.
49. *Forged in Faith*, pg. 132.
50. Ibid., pg. 173.
51. Virginia's pre-Continental Congress, House of Burgesses, was the equivalent to a modern-day state legislature.
52. *Forged in Faith*, pg. 145.

Chapter 8

1. *In Defense of the Bible*, edited by Steven B. Cowan and Terry L. Wilder, B&H Publishing group, 2013, pg. 183.
2. Because mythical figures cannot be substantiated by other writings or geographic or archaeological evidence that attest that they actually existed and the detailed facts surrounding Jesus Christ can, similarities do not exist.
3. *In Defense of the Bible*, pg. 186.
4. Ibid., pg. 189.
5. *Evidence That Demands a Verdict* by Josh McDowell Here's Life Publishers, 1979, pg. 81.
6. *In Defense of the Bible*, pg. 242.
7. The Town of Galilee sat next to the Sea of Galilee. Both are in Israel and within walking distance of Jerusalem.
8. *Who Is Jesus* by Darrell L. Bock, Howard Books, 2012, pg. 18.
9. *The Popular Handbook of Archaeology and the Bible* by Joseph M. Holden and Norman Geisler, Harvest house Publishers, 2013, pgs. 295, 296.
10. Josephus is probably referring here to the Jewish religious leaders called Pharisees who were pressuring Pilate to crucify Jesus, and since Josephus was himself a Pharisee, although he became one later than in this time frame, he writes: "the principle men among us."
11. The Antiquities of the Jews, Chapter 18.3.1ff, *The Works of Josephus*, Hendrickson Publishers, 1987, pg. 480.
12. *Evidence That Demands a Verdict*, pg. 82.
13. Ibid., pg. 83.
14. Ibid., pg. 84.
15. Ibid.
16. *The Popular Handbook of Archaeology and the Bible*, pgs. 300, 301.
17. Ibid., pg. 307.
18. All references about the James Ossuary are taken from pages 310-315 of *The Popular Handbook of Archaeology and the Bible* and pages 203-204

of *Biblical Archaeology: An Introduction with Recent Discoveries that Support the Reliability of the Bible* by David E. Graves, 2014.

19. *Unger's Bible Dictionary.*
20. The first prophecy of Jesus's to be fulfilled concerned His own impending death, His three days of being dead, and His subsequent resurrection (Matthew 12:39, 40, 16:21, 26:32, Mark 9:9, John 2:19). One might say that Jesus was able to predict His own death because He caused it to happen. However, when one reads the prophesies made hundreds of years before concerning the details of everything surrounding His death, it will be realized that Jesus couldn't possibly have controlled these details and events as a mere man.
21. *Who Is Jesus*, pgs. 21, 22.
22. *The Bible as History* by Werner Keller, Bantam 1988, pg. 383.
23. *The Popular Handbook of Archaeology and the Bible*, pg. 310. See also *The Bible as History* by Werner Keller, Bantam, 1988, pg. 393.
24. *The Case For Easter* by Lee Stroble, Zondervan 2003, pgs. 15-22.
25. Luke 23:39-40 and John 19:31-34 tell of the criminals who were crucified with Christ.
26. It is also vital to note here that Jesus Christ went through all of the above excruciating tortures willingly, even though He was completely innocent of the charges made against Him. He did this so He could pay for the sins of mankind so those who believe on Him can be reconciled to God.
27. *Who Moved the Stone* by Frank Morrison, Zondervan, 2002, pg. 116.
28. Luke tells in his Gospel in Luke 23:50 that, "Joseph, a council member, a good and just man… had not consented to their council and deed." The "council" was made up of the Jewish religious leaders including Pharisees. It is reasonable to assume that, since Nicodemus was also a follower of Jesus, that he too must not have consented to the council's plot to kill Him.
29. Merrill F. Unger contends that Mary the mother of Joses (Mark 15:47), Mary the mother of James and Joses, and the mother of Zebedee's sons (Matthew 27:56) are the same person as Mary the mother of James and Salome (Mark 16:1) as is Mary the wife of Clopas (John 19:25). This Mary, according to Unger, is also Jesus' mother, Mary's sister. Although the apostles refer to this "other Mary" differently in the Gospels, in actuality, according to Unger, their exact names given at birth may have been Mariam and Maria. *Unger's Bible Dictionary.*
30. The guards are only mentioned by Matthew (Matthew 27:62-66 and 28:11-15).
31. Matthew 28:11-15. Although it is probable that the soldiers had been awake and witnessed the stone being rolled away and Jesus exiting the tomb alive, nowhere are we told in the New Testament that any or all of these soldiers became followers of Christ as a result of what they saw. This may possibly be because, although Matthew doesn't allude to any such thing, the soldiers ran away out of fear or superstition when they saw the

stone suddenly being moved of its own accord and never stayed long enough to actually see Jesus exit the tomb. At any rate, the soldiers did not appear to be around by the time the two women arrived back at the tomb that resurrection morning.

32. *Who Moved the Stone*, pgs. 95, 96.
33. Ibid., pg. 176.
34. Ibid., pgs. 116, 117.
35. *The Case for Easter*, pg. 87.
36. *In Defense of the Bible*, pg. 250.
37. *The Search For The Twelve Apostles* by William Steuart McBirnie, Tyndale House Publishers, 1978, pg. 66.
38. Ibid., pg. 65. The prison of the Mamertine was also called Gemonium or the Tullian Keep.
39. *Who Moved the Stone*, pg. 168.
40. *The Case for Easter*, pg. 69.
41. *In Defense of the Bible* from Charles L. Quarles, pg. 86.
42. When a person died under the old covenant that was in effect before the coming of the Messiah, the New Testament teaches that their soul went to the pleasant or good side of Hades called Paradise (the bad side, a place of punishment and torment, was called Gehenna) where all awaited the coming of the Messiah to gather them and bring them to heaven. The New Testament shows that this is exactly what happened after Christ died on the cross and was dead for three days—He was in Paradise, also referred to as Abraham's bosom (Luke 16:19-31), showing Himself to the souls there. He then brought them with Him when He ascended to heaven (Ephesians 4:8, 9). The souls of those who reject Christ still go to Gehenna today.
43. *The Language of God* by Francis S. Collins, Free Press, pgs. 221-223. The C.S Lewis quote is from *Mere Christianity* by C.S Lewis.

Chapter 9

1. The phrase "separation of church and state" comes from a letter by Thomas Jefferson who wrote to a group of Baptists assuring them that the United States government, because of the First Amendment, could not sanction a particular Christian denomination as the state church as Britain had done when it declared the Anglican Church as the official church of Great Britain. Jefferson's actual words were: "the First Amendment has erected a wall of separation between church and state." For a full explanation see: http://www.myfathershouse.com/pdf/Separation_of_Church_and_State-not-separation-of-God-from-state.pdf
2. From 501(c)3 Facts, http://hushmoney.org/501c3-facts.htm
3. http://www.irs.gov/Charities-&-Non-Profits/Charitable-Organizations/Exemption-Requirements-Section-501(c)(3)-Organizations

4. The Catholic Church as a monolithic group has reportedly set up different types of tax exemptions with the IRS. For more information see: http://www.catholicworldreport.com/Item/1891/the_church_nonprofits_an d_taxes.aspx

5. *Christianity in Crisis* by Hank Hanegraaff, Harvest House Publishers, 1997, pgs. 11, 12 and 13.

6. From Matthew 24:21 and Revelation 7:14.

7. Some of the many prophecies concerning Israel becoming a nation once again are quite compelling. For instance, the prophet Jeremiah, who wrote the Old Testament book of his name approximately 700 years before Jerusalem was destroyed by the Romans in 70 AD prophesied: *"However, the days are coming," declares the Lord, "when it will no longer be said, 'As surely as the Lord lives, who brought the Israelites up out of Egypt,' but it will be said, 'As surely as the Lord lives, who brought the Israelites up out of the land of the north and out of all the countries where he had banished them.' For I will restore them to the land I gave their ancestors."* (Jeremiah 16:14-15 (NIV)). Also, the prophet Ezekiel who prophesied over 600 years before Israel was dispersed in 70 AD wrote: *"Hold before their eyes the sticks you have written on and say to them, 'This is what the Sovereign Lord says: I will take the Israelites out of the nations where they have gone. I will gather them from all around and bring them back into their own land. I will make them one nation in the land, on the mountains of Israel. There will be one king over all of them and they will never again be two nations or be divided into two kingdoms. They will no longer defile themselves with their idols and vile images or with any of their offenses, for I will save them from all their sinful backsliding, and I will cleanse them. They will be my people, and I will be their God."* (Ezekiel 37:20-23 (NIV)).

8. Jesus refers to the fig tree in Matthew 24:32, Mark 13:28, and Luke 21:29. The fig tree is believed by Biblical scholars to be a metaphor for the nation of Israel.

9. Some other verses that are thought to refer to a rapture are: I Corinthians 15:50-56, and Luke 17:34-35.

10. God ceased to reveal Himself solely through the Jewish people because they have largely and traditionally rejected Him for the false gods of the nations around them. Because of this, God sent His Son, Jesus, who would not only be the Savior and promised Messiah of the Jewish people but His Gospel would also bring spiritual enlightenment to the Gentile nations as well, thereby directly giving them the opportunity to choose Him and God's way of salvation.

11. Instead of "Comforter," some English Bible translations use the names: "Helper," "Advocate," or "Counselor."

12. *The Original Memoirs of Charles G. Finney*, edited by Garth M. Rosell & Richard A. G. Dupuis, Zondervan, 1989, pg. 43.

13. Taken from: http://www.sermoncentral.com/pastors-preaching-articles/paul-kendall-pastors-and-pornography-721.asp
Non-premeditated sinning vs. the deliberate practicing of sin are two different things in the Bible. The Scripture teaches that we are all sinners, even after one becomes a Christian, and in need of Jesus Christ (I John 1:8), but it distinguishes between those who sin inadvertently as a result of their sinful nature and those who practice sin as a habit, perhaps even the same re-occurring sin. This is a much involved topic, but I will suffice and say that a person who willfully and habitually practices sin as a lifestyle is in danger of God's judgment and although he or she may even be a professing Christian, that individual should question whose gospel they have accepted and whether or not they are a true disciple of the Jesus Christ as revealed in the Bible. The safest course for a follower of Christ who is practicing sin is to ask God's forgiveness, then, as Jesus said to the woman caught in adultery, "Go and sin no more." The safest course for an unbeliever is to repent of the sins, abandon them, then accept and follow Christ.

14. *U-Turn: Restoring America to the strength of its Roots* by George Barna and David Barton. Frontline, 2014, pg. 109.

Chapter 10

1. People wore sackcloth, a rough fabric, and sat in ashes as a way of showing God their repentance and deep sorrow for things they had done that displeased Him.
2. Jonah most likely lived in Israel during the 8th century BC. God delivered Israel from Egyptian slavery around 1500 to 1400 BC and also gave the Law to Moses during that same time period.
3. This is probably why Jonah resisted obeying God in the first place which led to him being thrown overboard from the ship he was on and being swallowed by the "great fish."
4. For a fuller explanation of this potential crisis go to: http://www.nature.com/scitable/blog/green-science/global_crisis_honeybee_population_on
5. Some say that Jesus allowed this because pig or pork was not allowed to be eaten by the Hebrew people under Mosaic law, so by allowing the demons to inhabit the pigs for a few moments, knowing that the pigs would go crazy and kill themselves, Jesus got rid of the unlawful pigs.
6. The current abode of Satan and his demons is probably not literally hell, since, in this present age, the Bible says they inhabit the spiritual dimension around earth. However, it appears as if their current habitation that Matthew and Luke both refer to as the "abyss" may be almost as bad as hell and the lake of fire they will eventually find themselves in at the

end of this age. At any rate, it seems that inhabiting a mortal creature allows them to stay out of whatever it is, if only for a relatively short time.

Appendix

Chapter One

1. The following is the prayer that was read to America via national radio by President Roosevelt on the evening of D-Day, June 6, 1944 although there is no mention of it in his memorial or the WWII Memorial:

"My Fellow Americans. Last night, when I spoke with you about the fall of Rome, I knew at that moment that troops of the United States and our Allies were crossing the Channel in another and greater operation. It has come to pass with success thus far. And so, in this poignant hour, I ask you to join with me in prayer: Almighty God: Our sons, pride of our nation, this day have set upon a mighty endeavor, a struggle to preserve our Republic, our religion, and our civilization, and to set free a suffering humanity.

Lead them straight and true; give strength to their arms, stoutness to their hearts, steadfastness in their faith. They will need Thy blessings. Their road will be long and hard. For the enemy is strong. He may hurl back our forces. Success may not come with rushing speed, but we shall return again and again; and we know that by Thy grace, and by the righteousness of our cause, our sons will triumph.

They will be sore tried, by night and by day, without rest -- until the victory is won. The darkness will be rent by noise and flame. Men's souls will be shaken with the violences of war. For these men are lately drawn from the ways of peace. They fight not for the lust of conquest. They fight to end conquest. They fight to liberate. They fight to let justice arise, and tolerance and goodwill among all Thy people. They yearn but for the end of battle, for their return to the haven of home. Some will never return. Embrace these, Father, and receive them, Thy heroic servants, into Thy kingdom. And for us at home -- fathers, mothers, children, wives, sisters, and brothers of brave men overseas, whose thoughts and prayers are ever with them -- help us, Almighty God, to rededicate ourselves in renewed faith in Thee in this hour of great sacrifice. Many people have urged that I call the nation into a single day of special prayer. But because the road is long and the desire is great, I ask that our people devote themselves in a continuance of prayer. As we rise to each new day, and again when each day is spent, let words of prayer be on our lips, invoking Thy help to our efforts. Give us strength, too -- strength in our daily tasks, to redouble the contributions we make in the physical and the material support of our armed forces. And let our hearts be stout, to wait out the long travail, to bear sorrows that may come, to impart our courage unto our sons wheresoever they may be. And, O Lord, give us faith. Give us faith in Thee; faith in our sons; faith in each other; faith in our united crusade. Let not the keeness of our spirit ever be dulled. Let not the impacts of temporary events, of temporal matters of but fleeting moment -- let not these deter us in our unconquerable purpose. With Thy blessing, we shall prevail over the unholy forces of our enemy. Help us to conquer the apostles of greed and racial arrogances. Lead us to the saving of our country, and with our sister nations into a world unity that will spell a sure peace -- a peace invulnerable to the schemings of unworthy men. And a peace that will let all of men live in freedom, reaping the just rewards of their honest toil. Thy will be done, Almighty God. Amen."

2. The following is General Eisenhower's D-Day statement to soldiers, sailors, and airmen of the Allied Expeditionary Force before the invasion. The words in bold are what appear on the memorial:

"Soldiers, Sailors and Airmen of the Allied Expeditionary Forces:
You are about to embark upon the Great Crusade, toward which we have striven these many months. The eyes of the world are upon you. The hopes and prayers of liberty-loving people everywhere march with you. In company with our brave Allies and brothers-in-arms on other Fronts you will bring about the destruction of the German war machine, the elimination of Nazi tyranny over oppressed peoples of Europe, and security for ourselves in a free world.
Your task will not be an easy one. Your enemy is well trained, well equipped and battle-hardened. He will fight savagely.
But this is the year 1944. Much has happened since the Nazi triumphs of 1940-41. The United Nations have inflicted upon the Germans great defeats, in open battle, man-to-man. Our air offensive has seriously reduced their strength in the air and their capacity to wage war on the

ground. Our Home Fronts have given us an overwhelming superiority in weapons and munitions of war, and placed at our disposal great reserves of trained fighting men. The tide has turned. The free men of the world are marching together to victory.

I have full confidence in your courage, devotion to duty, and skill in battle. We will accept nothing less than full victory.

Good Luck! And let us all beseech the blessing of Almighty God upon this great and noble undertaking."

Chapter 2

There are some who postulate that before the flood of Noah, a green-house type affect existed around the earth where a canopy of water vapor created a tropical climate over all the globe that allowed plants and animals to grow much larger than plant and animal life generally grow today. They assert that this is why tropical rain forests have been discovered to have once existed at the Antarctic.[1] At the time of the flood, this water vapor came down as rain and combined with the water that the Bible says came up from the deep (Genesis 7:11). This made it possible to cover the globe to a depth sufficient enough to cover the highest hills or mountains that existed at the time by approximately 22.5 ft. (or 15 cubits by the Biblical measurement). McDowell and Stewart hypothesize that this water, along with the silt and sediment it contained, and the almost year's length of time that the Bible says it took for the waters to recede enough for Noah and his passengers to leave the ark for dry land (Genesis 7:11, 8:13, 14), would have created the layers of sediment and conditions for both fossils and coal to have formed into what we see today.

The formation of coal is another element that appears to be generally misunderstood. We have been told that coal is formed in swampy areas over millions of years and involve mostly swamp-related plants that have died and compressed year after year after year, eventually creating coal. But upon closer examination, most coal is not made up of only localized compressed plant life, but, according to McDowell and Stewart, is actually comprised of vegetation from many different areas and climates. They hypothesize that this could only happen if many different types of plant and other organic life were mixed together in the kind of watery soup caused by a worldwide flood.[2]

Also, in the last few years, partially fossilized dinosaur bones have been found where soft tissue such as veins and DNA information have been preserved. One researcher said of a T-Rex femur that was found and examined in 2013, "Not only is the tissue intact, it's still transparent and pliable. Tiny interior structures resembling blood vessels, and even cells, are still present in the tissue."[3] How can this possibly be for an animal that supposedly died off 65 million years ago? It defies credulity. Some scientists have contrived convoluted explanations for how soft tissue can remain for all this time, but they still don't explain the phenomenon sufficiently unless these tissues aren't really 65 million years old. But this scenario is rarely postulated because it goes against the sacred evolutionary hypothesis and can cost a scientist his or her job like it did for Mark Armitage. In 2014, Armitage, "a widely published scientist of more than 30 years"[4] examined a partially fossilized Triceratops' horn and found it contained, "Soft fibrillar bone tissues."[5] After publishing his findings in a peer-reviewed journal, he was fired by California State University of Northridge, allegedly because his findings did not hold to the "long-standing dogma of the evolution industry."[6]

1. http://newsfeed.time.com/2012/08/03/from-leafy-to-lifeless-tropical-rainforest-once-covered-antarctica/ and
2. http://www.bbc.com/news/science-environment-12378934
3. For a more complete exposition and compelling scientific evidence for a worldwide flood, see *Reasons Skeptics Should Consider Christianity* by Josh McDowell and Don Stewart, 1981, pgs. 196-214.
4. http://news.discovery.com/animals/t-rex-fossil-soft-tissue-found.htm
5. http://www.darwinthenandnow.com/2014/08/scientist-fired-dinosaur-discoveryort/
6. www.sciencedirect.com/science/article/pii/S0065128113000020

Chapter 6

1. On a side note, it is interesting that Satan is referred to in the scriptures as *"the prince and the power of the air."* This explains a lot about ET and UFO sightings in America and around the world. Many Christians believe these sightings and their accompanying reports of alien abductions are nothing more or less than Satan and his demons masquerading as Extra-Terrestrials. According to creation.org: "Alleged alien abductions rarely if ever occur with real Christians. People who claim to have had abduction experiences are

frequently those who are involved in some occult activities, or who may have family members involved in those activities that have drawn the attention of demons into their homes. Some invite the abduction problem into their lives by actively seeking out opportunities to have contact with what they mistakenly believe are aliens... The common thread among.... these demon/human interactions is that the guidance the demons offer, whether it be through direct contacts or through cult materials, is always a distraction away from saving knowledge of Jesus Christ, and to attempt to destroy the credibility of the Bible." One thing is for certain, although so-called alien sightings and abductions have been around for decades in America, there is still no concrete evidence of their existence. On the other hand, we do know from the Bible that Satan and his demons inhabit the atmosphere around earth and are very powerful, even to the point of being able to create believable apparitions that are visible to the human eye.

Paul Christopher in his book *Alien Intervention* written in 1998 says this about the perpetrators for the belief in UFOs and extraterrestrials: "It is difficult to imagine the extent of the conditioning process that is at work within the UFO phenomenon. It pervades every level of our society as we know it. And, particularly as we approach the twenty-first century, the human population is being conditioned to accept the deluded notion that an extraterrestrial race exists and that these extraterrestrials are now making contact with earth. One wonders why it has not become evident to more people that a *sinister* intelligence does exist and is cleverly and cunningly at work behind an "alien" smoke screen, concealing its actual intentions. In order to achieve the primary goal, this insidious intelligence is manipulating key people on earth, either directly or indirectly. Through an ingenious process, these key individuals are accepting an entirely new belief system and, in turn, influencing our established religious, political, and social structures. Through the "channels" of our technological advancements (i.e., television, radio, motion pictures, computers, the Internet, etc.), these new beliefs are becoming accepted instantly as fact by thousands of people the world over. How long will it be before this crafty intelligence accomplishes its overall secret agenda, before everyone believes in UFOs and accepts these "aliens" as our extraterrestrial saviors? It is plausible that UFO sightings, UFO contacts with alien beings, and telepathic communications with so-called outer space entities are all part and parcel of a deceptive masterminded plan. The driving, motivating force behind this plan… is to condition and deceive the entire population into thinking we are now being visited by a superior extraterrestrial civilization. The conditioning process is, therefore, brainwashing humanity which, in turn, is promoting the universal acceptance of "extraterrestrial" intervention here on earth. As this conditioning process continues, a very dangerous and malicious force is presently and continually at work fulfilling its desired mission… It has become apparent that a unique stratagem is at work on this planet, targeting the human *mind*. This mission is being undertaken by skilled, masked invaders who do not really reside on the planet Mars or Venus or any other planet. These invaders are, in fact… [demonic] initiators of this ingenious, yet deceptive *supernatural* operation."[1]

David Ruffino and Joseph Jordan in their book *Unholy Communion* add: "It is pretty well known in the UFO realm, and this is backed up by our research, that all [so-called alien] abductees have had some sort of direct involvement with the occult, either through direct involvement or through the involvement of a close blood relative."[2] They also cite the well-known and highly credentialed, secular UFO researcher, Dr. Jacques Vallée. They say that after years of studying and doing extensive research into the UFO/alien abduction phenomenon, Vallée came to the conclusion in his book, *Confrontations*, that alleged "extra-terrestrials" or "aliens" aren't coming from outer space but right from here on earth or around the earth. They quote Vallée: "The 'medical examination' to which abductees are said to be subjected, often accompanied by sadistic sexual manipulation, is reminiscent of the medieval tales of encounters with demons" and that essentially, according to Ruffino and Jordan, Vallée believes that the demons of old and the alien abductors of today are the same beings.[3]

1. *Alien Intervention* by Paul Christopher, Huntington House Publishers, 1998, pgs. 116-118.
2. *Unholy Communion: The Alien Abduction Phenomenon, Where It Originates And How It Stops* by David Ruffino and Joseph Jordan, Defender, 2010, pg. 23.
3. Ibid., pgs. 63-65. Primary source: *Confrontations—A Scientists search for Alien Contact* by Vallée, pgs. 13, 160-161.

Chapter 7

The Mayflower Compact

In the name of God, Amen. We, whose names are underwritten, the loyal subjects of our dread Sovereign Lord King James, by the Grace of God, of Great Britain, France, and Ireland, King, defender of the Faith, etc.

Having undertaken, for the Glory of God, and advancements of the Christian faith and honor of our King and Country, a voyage to plant the first colony in the Northern parts of Virginia, do by these presents, solemnly and mutually, in the presence of God, and one another, covenant and combine ourselves together into a civil body politic; for our better ordering, and preservation and furtherance of the ends aforesaid; and by virtue hereof to enact, constitute, and frame, such just and equal laws, ordinances, acts, constitutions, and offices, from time to time, as shall be thought most meet and convenient for the general good of the colony; unto which we promise all due submission and obedience.

In witness whereof we have hereunto subscribed our names at Cape Cod the 11th of November, in the year of the reign of our Sovereign Lord King James, of England, France, and Ireland, the eighteenth, and of Scotland the fifty-fourth, 1620.

William Penn's Letter to the Indians

My friends—There is one great God and power that hath made the world and all things therein, to whom you and I, and all people owe their being and well-being, and to whom you and I must one day give an account for all that we do in the world; this great God hath written his law in our hearts, by which we are taught and commanded to love and help, and do good to one another, and not to do harm and mischief one to another. Now this great God hath been pleased to make me concerned in your parts of the world, and the king of the country where I live hath given unto me a great province, but I desire to enjoy it with your love and consent, that we may always live together as neighbours and friends, else what would the great God say to us, who hath made us not to devour and destroy one another, but live soberly and kindly together in the world? Now I would have you well observe, that I am very sensible of the unkindness and injustice that hath been too much exercised towards you by the people of these parts of the world, who sought themselves, and to make great advantages by you, rather than be examples of justice and goodness unto you, which I hear hath been matter of trouble to you, and caused great grudgings and animosities, sometimes to the shedding of blood, which hath made the great God angry; but I am not such a man, as is well known in my own country; I have great love and regard towards you, and I desire to win and gain your love and friendship, by a kind, just, and peaceable life, and the people I send are of the same mind, and shall in all things behave themselves accordingly; and if in any thing any shall offend you or your people, you shall have a full and speedy satisfaction for the same, by an equal number of just men on both sides, that by no means you may have just occasion of being offended against them. I shall shortly come to you myself, at what time we may more largely and freely confer and discourse of these matters. In the mean time, I have sent my commissioners to treat with you about land, and a firm league of peace. Let me desire you to be kind to them and the people, and receive these presents and tokens which I have sent to you, as a testimony of my good will to you, and my resolution to live justly, peaceably, and friendly with you.

I am your loving friend,
WILLIAM PENN

American Colleges founded before the American Revolution:

Brown University – Founded in 1764 by The Baptist Church.

College of William & Mary – Founded in 1693 by the Anglican Church.

Columbia University – Founded in 1754 by the Episcopalian Church.

Dartmouth College – Founded in 1769 by the Congregational Church.

Harvard University – Founded in 1636 by Puritans of the Massachusetts Bay colony.

> Harvard's initial admissions requirements contained the words: "Let every Student be plainly instructed and earnestly pressed to consider well, the main end of his life and studies is to know God and Jesus Christ Life (John 17:13 and… the only foundation of all sound knowledge and learning."[1]

University of Pennsylvania – Founded in 1740 by Ben Franklin.

Princeton University – Founded in 1746 by New Light Presbyterians for the purpose of training ministers of the Gospel of Jesus Christ.

Rutgers (formerly Queens College) – Founded in 1766 by the Dutch Reformed Church to train ministers.

Yale University - Founded in 1701 by the Presbyterian Church to train ministers.

1. Forged in Faith, pg. 154.

Dear Reader,

Thanks so much for reading my book.

If you have enjoyed it, I humbly ask that you leave a review on the site on which you purchased it. As an indie writer, reviews can greatly impact my career.

Also, if you would like to keep in touch with me or see all of my books, go to my web site at https://lornedey.com and signup for email updates regarding interviews, promotions or give-ways as well as alerts to new fiction and non-fiction books as they become available.

I enjoy hearing from my readers and welcome you to email me at: lorne@lornedey.com if you have a comment or question.

All the best in all your endeavors,

Lorne Dey

Other Non-fiction by Lorne Dey

We live in a violent world filled with evil and people who appear to be driven by evil intents. **The Great Delusion** *demonstrates that there are invisible, malevolent forces at work that continually prey upon people and attempt to manipulate them for the purpose of destroying them, both physically and spiritually.* **The Great Delusion** *explores how this has been done down through the ages and how to avoid being one of the manipulated in the modern world.*

You can purchase a paperback or Kindle version of
The Great Delusion on Amazon

Animals and the Afterlife is designed to provide hope for people who love animals and have lost a beloved animal through death. Any real hope for whether or not the bereaved will ever again see in the afterlife their animal companion who has died comes from the only source from which any real hope on spiritual matters can come—The Holy Bible. The Bible has much to say about animals. In this book, Lorne Dey delves into all the verses and passages in the Old and New Testaments that have anything to say about animals, even examining words in the original Hebrew and Greek to help get an idea of exactly what God has to say about the innocent, sinless creatures He has created.

You can purchase a paperback or Kindle version of
Animals and the Afterlife on Amazon

Still other books by Lorne Dey are also available on Amazon.